ASIA-PACIFIC TRADE AND INVESTMENT REPORT 2016

Recent Trends and Developments

UNITED NATIONS
ESCAP
Economic and Social Commission for Asia and the Pacific

ASIA-PACIFIC
TRADE AND INVESTMENT REPORT 2016

Recent Trends and Developments

Shamshad Akhtar
Executive Secretary

Hongjoo Hahm
Deputy Executive Secretary

Susan F. Stone
Director, Trade, Investment and Innovation Division

United Nations publication
Sales No. E.16.II.F.23

ISBN: 978-92-1-120732-3
e-ISBN: 978-92-1-058673-3
ISSN: 2221-500X
ST/ESCAP/2760

Reference to dollars ($) are to United States dollars unless otherwise stated.

A space is used to distinguish thousands and millions.

FOREWORD

The 2030 Agenda for Sustainable Development recognizes international trade as a generator of inclusive economic growth. It adds value to economies, provides foreign exchange earnings to help finance development and enables job creation, all of which contribute to poverty reduction. Taking advantage of its dynamism, diversity and labor markets has enabled Asia and the Pacific to be competitive in international markets. This is evidenced by the rise in the region's share of global trade and participation in associated value chains.

Like elsewhere, however, the Asia and Pacific region has faced protracted global headwinds since 2007, which has impacted the trade sector and its prospects. This latest *Asia-Pacific Trade and Investment Report 2016* highlights that the region's trade flows are wavering amid continued sluggish global economic and trade growth, downward movement of world commodity prices and an uncertain policy environment. These outcomes come at a time when the need for trade growth to support the 2030 Agenda for Sustainable Development is critical.

Even though regional trade did gain some momentum during 2010-2014, the nominal value of Asia and Pacific exports and imports in 2015 experienced a major slump of 9.7 per cent and 15 per cent, respectively. Sluggish growth in trade is expected to continue through to the end of 2016. Forecasts, presented in this Report, do offer hope for a rebound in trade, more so in value, but growth in exports and imports in volume terms will be around 2.2 per cent and 3.8 per cent, respectively.

To its credit, most of Asia's exporting economies have decoupled from the economic cycles in traditional exports markets, like the United States and the European Union, by not only diversifying their export markets but also through boosting domestic consumption and the services sector. Notwithstanding, the region has the potential to lead by example and revitalize its trade momentum, which will be critical to ensuring our future is sustainable and that our societies are more equal.

Concurrent to trade, foreign direct investment (FDI) flows to developing countries have also slowed. FDI flows and regional integration policies have been adversely affected by populist sentiments which have been growing globally. In Asia and the Pacific, growing discontentment with liberalization has to a certain extent been influenced by the inequitable distribution of the benefits of liberalization and rising inequalities. In this context, it is of little surprise that a number of new restrictive trade measures, particularly in G20 countries, were implemented in 2016.

This year's edition of the *Asia-Pacific Trade and Investment Report* (APTIR) does, however, reveal positive news. With a share of 40%, the Asia-Pacific region is still the largest goods exporting region globally. The region's share in commercial services trade continues to strengthen and restrictiveness of services trade has not increased in the region's economies. Furthermore, the region's active actions towards international investment liberalization helped greenfield FDI inflows grow much faster than the global average. Significant progress was also witnessed in the region's efforts to decrease trade costs, illustrated by *the Framework Agreement on Facilitation of Cross-border Paperless Trade in Asia and the Pacific*. A significant number of economies in our region have also already ratified the WTO Trade Facilitation Agreement, with the 12 remaining Asia-Pacific economies on track to ratify the Agreement soon.

In addition to these developments, Asia and the Pacific also witnessed the first signs of some consolidation among the preferential trade activities in the region. Nevertheless, after the results of the recent United States election, it appears that at least one of the mega-regional agreements signed in 2016, has an uncertain future. This is disappointing, and represents a considerable loss in terms of time and costs for the countries that were involved in negotiating this agreement. Moving forward, these developments may, however, allow the region's economies to focus more on South-South integration and enable them to promote trade and investment linkages suited to their development aspirations.

I recommend the *Asia-Pacific Trade and Investment Report 2016: Recent Trends and Developments* to all Governments, development partners and other stakeholders. Together with 5 subregional and almost 30 country trade briefs, this Report offers comprehensive evidence that will help in the introduction of well-informed trade and investment trends and policies across the region. Given that the short-term prospects for international trade are not promising, the changing patterns and prospects outlined in this Report highlight that achieving the 2030 Agenda will require the continued and dedicated efforts of our region's economies to create a strong, vibrant and enabling environment for international trade and investment.

Shamshad Akhtar
Under-Secretary-General of the United Nations and
Executive Secretary, United Nations Economic and
Social Commission for Asia and the Pacific

November 2016

EXECUTIVE SUMMARY

The stakes on international trade have been raised considerably by the adoption of the 2030 Agenda for Sustainable Development, which identifies trade as one of its key means of implementation. The expansion of global trade and the adoption of trade-led development strategies by countries such as China (Asia-Pacific Trade and Investment Report 2013) was one of the key factors contributing to reducing absolute poverty prior to the adoption of the 2030 Agenda. Can we continue to rely on trade to drive economic growth and lift the remaining 600 million poor in our region out of poverty? Recent trends and short-term prospects discussed in this Report do not give a reassuring message. Merchandise and services export growth weakened further in 2015 despite relatively robust economic performance in many Asia-Pacific economies. By now, most of Asian exporter economies have at least partially decoupled from the economic cycles in the traditional export markets of North America and the European Union. However, as they have been reorienting to export-demand from the region, and especially China, they now face the need to further adjust to the transition of the Chinese economy to domestic consumption and services-sector driven growth. The Asia-Pacific region is expected to exhibit a 5.2% and 4.9% decline in nominal export and import values, respectively, in 2016. The volume of trade in the region is expected to grow in 2016, although only feebly, by 0.7% and 0.1% for exports and imports, respectively; this is far from the heights of around 7% seen globally in the early 2000s. The main causes for trade faltering in 2015 and previous years range from cyclical to structural – sluggish global economic growth, a downward movement of commodity prices, adverse movements of exchange rates, capital flow volatility, maturation of global value chains and a decline in productivity growth. Most of these factors will have also been at work in 2016, although later in the year some economic indicators signaled more robust performance and return of stability, at least in emerging markets in Asia. Thus, expectations are that nominal exports and imports will bounce back in 2017 with a 4.5% growth in exports and 6.1% growth in imports. The 2017 expansion of trade will be due to a mixture of expected increased prices and expected real growth; export and import price indices are expected to grow by 3% and 2.3%, respectively, while export and import volumes are projected to increase by 1.5% and 3.8%, respectively. Nevertheless, deceleration of merchandise and services trade in 2015 and so far in 2016 has had an impact on greenfield foreign direct investment (FDI) flows as well, with upward changes mostly seen in mergers and acquisitions (M&A) flows. The Asia-Pacific region recorded only a 5.6% increase in FDI inflows in 2015, resulting in a 10 percentage point decline in the region's share of global FDI inflows from its 2014 share of 42%. This overall reversal was not felt equally in the region and it is mainly attributed to a sharp decline in FDI in the North and Central Asia as well as the Pacific subregions and somewhat to a slowing of FDI activity in South-East Asia. Amid these disconcerting trends, a positive aspect is that the share of intraregional greenfield FDI inflows in total flows reached 52% in 2015. ASEAN, including its least developed economies, and India have been attracting an increasing portion of FDI inflows, both from outside and inside the region. Further deepening and broadening of regional cooperation and integration through initiatives such as the One Belt-One Road are expected to create growth in demand for FDI across the region. A similar effect is expected from infrastructural investment in support of improved trade facilitation and implementation of the WTO Trade Facilitation Agreement, which is moving steadily towards ratification in WTO. While economies in Asia and the Pacific continue to make improvements in trade facilitation, large gaps among subregional economies remain; there is much more to be done to reduce trade costs of those economies that are greatly in need of more intense trade with the rest of the region and the world. Regrettably, the efforts undertaken to reduce trade costs by improving trade facilitation have been partially offset by the imposition of a large number of new trade distortive measures globally and regionally. The rhetoric of protectionism that is gaining popularity among G20 economies, together with events such as "Brexit" and uncertainty arising from the presidential election results in the United States, does not raise much hope for a reversal of these practices soon. Economies of Asia-Pacific alone have introduced, on average, 6.6 restrictive measures per month since 2014. Most of these new measures belong to the non-tariff category, often decreasing transparency in trade policy of countries and thus contributing even more to trade costs. This appliese specially to measures affecting agricultural and food trade but also trade in services, which supply an increasing proportion of industrial exports and are thus one of the key enablers of economic diversification and sustainable development. In addition, it appears that the increasing number of preferential trade agreements (PTAs) have not shown a strong potency in dealing with such non-tariff barriers to trade. Almost 170 PTAs are being implemented in 2016 by the regional economies, and they are steadily encompassing new areas such as investment, government procurement or competition. Nevertheless, not much information is available on their utilization by businesses and the jury is still out on determining if the multiple PTAs among the same members (the so-called "noodle bowl"phenomenon) is also adding to trade costs, thus working against the primary aim of PTAs to enable trade. More and more of these PTAs include provisions of e-commerce. In general, there is an expectation that further digitalization of trade and the growth of e-commerce will have a positive effect not only on the volume of trade but also on making the benefits from trade more broadly felt; in fact,e-commerce is hailed as a great "equalizer" by many of its advocates in the region. However, much work on collecting evidence on the extent and distributional effects of e-commerce is needed before suggesting specific policy reforms. It would be very useful to have these sooner rather than later to complement policy responses to challenges in mainstream trade and associated investment to strengthen their effectiveness in shielding the region against the headwinds in its path to trade-led sustainable development.

Merchandise trade in trouble

Trade in the Asia-Pacific region experienced a major slump in 2015, with the United States dollar value of exports and imports declining significantly by 9.7% and 15%, respectively. Little improvement, if any, is expected in 2016 as trade is estimated to contract by around 5% in nominal terms. Despite these bleak numbers, the region is still being hailed as the best performer in the global environment in which trade recorded a fall of around 13% in nominal terms in 2015. Therefore, despite contractionary trends, the Asia-Pacific region has consolidated its share of global exports at 40% mark and thus retained its position as the largest exporter in the world. However, the share in global imports still declined. Altogether, 2015-2016 capped a five-year period in which the Asia-Pacific region's trade grew below the pre-crisis average. Such a long and uninterrupted trade slowdown is unprecedented, and is a cause for concern that the world is now reaching a new normal of weaker trade growth.

The relative success of the Asia-Pacific region is again largely due to the contribution by China, whose exports declined by only 2.9%. China accounts for 34% of the region's merchandise exports, so when it is excluded the developing Asia-Pacific region performs similarly to the global economy, with a 13% decline in exports.

Falling prices were mainly responsible for the fall in trade values in 2015. While the quantity (volume) of exports in fact still grew at 3% in 2015, there was a sharp fall in export and import prices by 10% and 12%, respectively. The plunge in prices was due to a number of factors, both from the demand and the supply side. Slower growth in emerging markets, particularly in China, has led to sharp drops in commodity prices across the board. These, in turn, lower the cost of production which is then passed onto the price of manufacturing products. Furthermore, the appreciation of the United States dollar in 2015 added significant weight to other factors in import demand by developing economies, and affected the value of trade transactions, which are customarily expressed in United States dollars.

For the second year in a row, Asia-Pacific region has seen a decreasing importance of intraregional demand from developing regional economies. The share of exports to the developing Asia-Pacific region fell from a peak of 48.2% in 2013 to 47.6% in 2015.

A major factor in the slowing intraregional demand is related to the ongoing economic rebalancing of China towards consumption and services, which is the largest individual trading partner for the rest of the region, taking nearly 20% of exports. China's economic slowdown is especially affecting commodity exporting countries whose exports to China are substantial, e.g., more than 80% in the case of Mongolia. Also, the country's economic rebalancing is affecting manufacture exporting countries tied to China through global value chains, as the region has seen a gradual decline in China's import dependence, especially in intermediate products.

Looking ahead, there are headwinds to trade in the Asia-Pacific region and worldwide. Countries that export primary commodities – largely low income economies – are still exposed to the risks of declining commodity prices, due to declining global demand for energy and non-energy commodities, especially in China. The expected decline in growth rates within the region and in key world importing economies in 2016, together with falling price indices, means that a regional trade recovery is not expected in the near future.

The Asia-Pacific region as a whole is expected to exhibit a 5.2% and 4.9% decline in nominal export and import values in 2016, before bouncing back in 2017 with 4.5% growth in nominal exports and 6.1% growth in nominal imports. In real terms, the trade volume of the Asia-Pacific region in 2016 is still growing but only slightly, with the estimated growth rates of 0.7% and 0.3% for exports and imports, respectively. A slow recovery of export demand is anticipated for 2017 when the growth may return to 1.5%. The growth of import volume will be higher than export volume, reflecting an import recovery from the low-base level and a side effect of the shifting of growth strategy from export-driven to consumption-driven models in major Asia-Pacific economies.

Trade in commercial services sliding downhill

The performance of the Asia-Pacific region's commercial services sector, following the global trend, dropped dramatically in 2015 compared with the previous year, due to the global economic slowdown and prevailing economic uncertainty. Export growth declined from 5.1% in 2014 to -4.5% in 2015, while import growth fell from 6.1% to -4.9% during the same period. However, the Asia-Pacific region maintained its share of global exports and imports of services (29.2% and 31.8%, respectively).

Intraregional demand for services in 2015 has severely declined, reflecting the regional trade contraction and economic slowdown. Trade in Asia and the Pacific commercial services was dominated by a small number of countries, especially China, India, Japan and Singapore, which represented more than half of the region's trade. Specifically, business and travel services together accounted for about 53.4% of total commercial services exports. However, the continuation of China's economic slowdown, together with global trade stagnation, is creating gloomy prospects for services exports in 2016 and beyond, especially in the tourism sector.

The share of services trade in total trade of least developed countries continues to be negligible yet concentrated in only few service sectors, mainly tourism. Overall, in 2015, least developed countries in the Asia-Pacific region exported commercial services worth $13 billion and contributing 36% of the exports by the whole group of least developed countries. Myanmar was the largest services exporter in the Asia-Pacific group with a share of 32%, followed by Cambodia at 30%. These two Asian least developed countries recorded an extraordinary growth in tourism in more recent years which has been largely driving the overall services export growth of the Asia-Pacific group of least developed countries. Furthermore, Bangladesh has become an emerging exporter of information and communications services and a hub for freelance IT services, including simple data entry to more complex IT services, via online sites.

Foreign direct trade investment makes a modest comeback

Global foreign direct investment (FDI) inflows, at $1.76 trillion in 2015, reached their highest level since the financial crisis of 2008-2009. However, the increase was attributable to cross-border mergers and acquisitions (M&A) used for corporate reconfiguration, including tax inversions.

The Asia-Pacific region continued to receive a significant amount of FDI inflows, totalling $559 billion in 2015. However, the region experienced weaker growth in FDI inflows, mainly resulting from a sharp decline in North and Central Asia, due to low commodity prices, economic contraction, and the direct and indirect impacts of geopolitical tensions. Asia and the Pacific also experienced a reduced level of FDI outflows, with $435 billion in 2015, a 22% decrease compared with the previous year. Still, the outflows in 2015 were close to the region's average recorded since the recovery after the global financial crisis.

Contrary to the overall FDI flows, greenfield FDI inflows to the region increased sharply by 26% in 2015, to $352 billion in total. Greenfield FDI outflows from the Asia-Pacific region in 2015 also increased by 15% to $263 billion. In addition, intraregional greenfield FDI inflows have continuously increased recent years – replacing FDI from the traditional big investors such as the United States and countries in Europe – as the economic relevance and dynamism of the Asia-Pacific region increases.

In recent years, the Association of Southeast Asian Nations (ASEAN) has become a popular destination for intraregional FDI. In 2015, $83 billion was received from countries in the Asia-Pacific region, amounting to 46% of total greenfield intraregional inflows. As production costs are rising in labour-intensive industries in China, these industries in the smaller and less developed countries in ASEAN are benefiting from a shift of FDI despite the overall poor investment climate of those economies.

There were no universal tendencies observed in the composition of industries and sectors with regard to FDI inflows in the region. Instead, with some mixed experiences of individual economies in different industry sectors, many economies in the region are paying more attention to attracting FDI to technologically more advanced industries, in order to move away for reliance on labour-intensive manufacturing. It is believed that such FDI inflows will bring about desired spillover effects to the economy alongside capital inflows, and thus contribute to sustainable development.

Asian and Pacific countries are in the lead in investment liberalization and promotion policies. In 2015, the region adopted 46 investment policies affecting foreign investment; of these measures, 43 were related to liberalization, promotion and facilitation of investment, while only three introduced new restrictions or regulations on investment. In particular, two of the largest emerging economies in Asia, China and India, were the most active in opening up various industries to foreign investors in 2015. Special Economic Zones (SEZs) were used in many economies as one of the modalities to attract FDI.

Increasingly, economies in Asia and the Pacific have assumed a crucial role in shaping the global international investment agreements (IIAs) universe. In 2015 alone, the Asia-Pacific region witnessed the signing of 18 IIAs and an additional 13 IIAs entering into force, including movement towards the formation of so-called "mega-regional" agreements such as the Trans-Pacific Partnership (TPP), the ASEAN Economic Community (AEC) and the Eurasian Economic Union (EAEU). The region is also leading the shift in the paradigm of IIAs, moving to a more balanced investment regime that serves the interests of foreign investors and host countries.

Trade facilitation in the region helps to reduce trade costs

Trade facilitation and the reduction of international trade transaction costs remain an important priority for many countries of the Asian and Pacific region. Two-thirds of the Asia-Pacific members of WTO have now ratified the WTO Trade Facilitation Agreement and are well on their way towards implementation. In addition, ESCAP member States, after several years of deliberations and negotiations on how to facilitate the electronic exchange of trade-related data across borders, in May 2016 finalized a regional treaty on cross-border paperless trade facilitation. Open for signature at the United Nations Headquarters in New York until 30 September 2017 to all member countries of ESCAP, this innovative United Nations treaty is expected to greatly support the region in maintaining its trade competitiveness and reaping the benefits from the fast-growing digital economy.

While no economy in the Asia-Pacific region has fully realized cross-border paperless trade, strides are being made at the national, regional and global levels in that direction as well as towards more comprehensive trade facilitation reform. Overall, steady improvements are being made in reducing trade costs and facilitating trade, although great diversity remains across countries and subregions. Key indicators measuring the ease of trading across borders and logistics performance show that some of the best performers in the region (and the world) are continuing to make progress in this regard. However, other economies in the region, such as landlocked countries or Small Island Developing States (SIDS), still face multiple challenges and thus have achieved more mixed results.

In order to reduce this regional trade cost and facilitation gap, countries will need to implement more comprehensive trade facilitation reforms that address both "hard" and "soft" infrastructure bottlenecks, including by: (a) establishing effective institutional arrangements to enhance cooperation between relevant trade agencies as well as with the private sector to facilitate trade; (b) ensuring greater transparency and predictability of trade regulatory procedures; (c) increasing efforts to harmonize and automate trade procedures across borders; and (d) effectively monitoring implementation of trade facilitation measures and their impact.

Regional trends in trade policies: Building taller fences?

Trade policies reflected the general trends in terms of increased sentiment towards globalization. During the reporting period (mid-October 2014 to mid-May 2016), there has been an increase in restrictiveness of trade policies within the region. In fact, the region introduced more restrictive then liberalizing trade policy measures overall, while the opposite was true globally. Furthermore, both in the region and globally, policymakers got busier on a monthly basis as there was a noticeable surge in the number of trade restrictive measures adopted per month from mid-Oct 2015 to mid-May 2016. In 2015, trade-restrictive State measures (that extend beyond WTO disciplines) outnumbered trade-liberalizing ones by three-to-one; the region was responsible for 60% of these measures. Analyses of trade policies of the G20 economies have revealed that the major G20 economies of the region also showed strong protectionist tendencies, nudging Christine Lagarde, the head of the International Monetary Fund, to state that such policies restricting trade were a form of "economic malpractice" that would choke growth, hit jobs and reduce wages. In addition to exposing the role of Asia-Pacific countries in the most recent rising tide of protectionism, this Report delves deeper into the escalation of trade policy tensions in the global steel industry and contends that the rise in tensions can be partly attributed to the long-term impacts of trade distorting measures of the past as well as excess capacity in many industries.

In 2015, the region also registered a record increase in number of certain key non-tariff measures (NTMs); such NTMs are increasingly becoming a bigger impediment to international trade when compared to tariffs.

The services sector is gaining importance in international trade in its own right as well as through its role in facilitating global value chains, especially in the manufacturing sector. Analysis of the trade policies in the services sector, although plagued by severe data limitations, shows there was no substantial increase in protectionism in the sector.

Role of preferential trade agreements still strong

The negotiation of preferential trade agreements (PTAS) all around the world continues to grow amid the current global economic slowdown (and the consequent lower growth of trade) and the stagnation of multilateral trade negotiations. The Asia-Pacific region is now the major contributor to the build-up in the number of PTAs. More and more economies are becoming involved in agreements that not only allow liberalization in trade in goods, but also commitments in trade in services as well as harmonization of rules in many other areas, whether they are covered by WTO Agreements or not. The region lacks efforts to fulfil the obligations of transparency in WTO that are related to preferential trade agreements. There are several PTAs that should have been notified to WTO; however, this has not yet happened. Similarly, some agreements have been nullified and have become inoperative, yet have not been notified as such to WTO, and thus continue to create doubt about their operations.

An important message to policymakers involved in PTAs negotiations is that the analysis here finds no strong links between the number of PTAs, trade intensity among the partners in those agreements and the actual utilization of preferences. While some economies have rationally chosen the partners with which to conclude trade agreements, with much of their trade being covered under such agreements, it is still not certain how much trade utilizes negotiated preferences. Data on preferential utilization rates is very scarce (typically available for trade by developed countries). By using the examples of Turkey, Thailand and Sri Lanka, it is argued that more efforts are needed to fully use existent PTAs. A strong argument is made for better statistics on utilization of preferences. This will not only help policymakers to better evaluate the benefits of each PTA; it will also help them to learn how to negotiate new PTAs that are more easily used by the private sector. Furthermore, an audit of PTAs by using the extent of utilization of preferences would indicate which agreements could be terminated without any loss of trade. Finally, information will also be useful for the private sector in seeking redress through trade defence mechanisms under PTAs.

Globally, but particularly in the Asia-Pacific region, there has been a lack of effort by economies to abolish or annul bilateral agreements between economies that have moved on and signed regional or plurilateral agreements among the same set of economies (ESCAP, 2015). The proliferation and overlapping of PTAs, a phenomenon called the "noodle-bowl", continues to impose challenges for, and additional burdens on firms; this is particularly the case when data show that there is no correlation between the number of PTAs and the share of trade and its expansion under PTAs. In order to reduce that impact, several economies are involved in mega-regional initiatives aimed at consolidating their multiple and overlapping network of PTAs. The most important efforts in the Asia-Pacific region that are underway are the TPP, RCEP and EAEU. While each initiative has its own characteristics and challenges, all have the potential to reduce the complexity of PTA networks in the region. Once a larger PTA with additional countries is signed, it is necessary that the bilateral PTAs and partial scope plurilaterals should be nullified. Such a phenomenon was seen in the past in the process of consolidation by the European Union, but only recently and somewhat recently in the Asia-Pacific region.

Looking forward towards digitalization of trade

Despite world-wide recognition of its importance, there are no official statistics on e-commerce or digital trade. Existing studies, mainly based on unofficial data, are difficult to generalize. As a consequence, key questions for proper policy design and regulation remain unanswered.

Using available official statistics, chapter 7 aims, to some extent, to fill the knowledge gap by highlighting major trends and policy implications within cross-border digital trade. This chapter also focuses on a factual exploration of digital trade at the global and Asia-Pacific levels. Although major policy implications are mentioned, suggesting comprehensive policy actions is beyond the scope of the chapter.

Growing digital intensity has caused fundamental changes in trade, and thus there is the need for the improvement of trade statistics to catch up with this process. The study shows that data requirements for analyses on digital trade issues need a combination of data on trade in services, input-output linkages and merchandise statistics at the most detailed level that are comparable across countries.

Through a careful selection of the proxy for digital trade, exporters in the Asia-Pacific region are rapidly increasing the use of digital technology to support their export activities, both directly and indirectly. The growth of digital intensity in exports by the Asia-Pacific region increased faster than that of the world, with the growth rate ranging between 11% and 15% annually, depending on the proxy used.

The growth of digital trade has a relatively stronger impact on service trade than merchandise trade. The digital-intensive industries are relatively high-tech or high value-added. The digital-intensive services sectors include financial services (for example, Internet banking), telecommunication services, R&D and business services, and renting of machinery and equipment (car rental services etc.). For manufacturing, the publishing industry, chemical products, computer equipment, and electrical machinery and transport machinery are among the sectors with high digital intensity.

The availability of digital infrastructure is important for the development of digital trade. Imports of telecommunication and computer equipment play an important role in digital trade, especially for Asia and the Pacific. This has opened intraregional trade opportunities as intraregional sourcing for those digital infrastructure products has been growing. However, the export opportunities are mainly clustered in large economies, especially China, India, Japan and the Republic of Korea.

The digitalization of international trade brings about a greater need for an open environment and international cooperation. Non-discriminatory principles and international harmonization of rules and regulation are essential. The concept of open environment is not new, but what is added by the digital trade is that "openness" not only means free flows of goods or services, but also the need for the free flow of data across national borders. In addition, the growing importance of digital trade brings to the fore a greater need for international cooperation, as a supportive environment for digital trade is more dependent on multilaterally-agreed policies than on unilateral ones.

ACKNOWLEDGEMENTS

The Asia-Pacific Trade and Investment Report (APTIR) 2016 was prepared under the overall guidance of Hongjoo Hahm, Deputy Executive Secretary of the United Nations Economic and Social Commission for Asia and the Pacific (ESCAP), and Susan F. Stone, Director, Trade, Investment and Innovation Division (TIID) of ESCAP. Under the substantive direction and inputs of Mia Mikic, Chief, Trade Policy and Analysis Section, TIID the core team of authors comprised TIID staff (in alphabetical order) Maame Agyeben (chapter 4), Witada Anukoonwattaka (chapters 1, 2 and 7), Yann Duval (chapter 4), Arun Jacob (chapter 5), Soo Hyun Kim and Marc Proksch (chapter 3), and Rajan Sudesh Ratna (chapter 6). The consultants and research assistants who contributed to drafting or data compilation and analysis included Chorthip Utoktham (chapter 4), Pascale Bouquin and Anders Kirstein Moeller (chapter 5), Louis Graham (chapter 1), Chanipun Chatrungrueangchai (chapter 2), Diago Llasa (chapter 6) and Pakkaporn Visetsilpanon (chapter 7). Several research assistants from the Asia-Pacific Research and Training Network on Trade (ARTNeT) together with ESCAP interns contributed to the report through the compilation and tabulation of statistical data, the preparation of country and subregional trade briefs as well as undertaking background research and referencing. They include (in alphabetical order) Chen-Wen Cheng, Lars Engen, Chiti Mbizule, Beier Pan, Tian Yi and Chen Yu.

Eric Hermouet, Krisana Boonpriroje and Panpaka Supakalin of the ESCAP Statistics Division and Pakkaporn Visetsilpanon of TIID collaborated in the preparation of the trade performance indicator tables available on the ESCAP online statistical database. Pakkaporn Visetsilpanon and Chelsea Ngoc Minh Nguyen, guided by Witada Anukoonwattaka and Arun Jacob, produced the country trade briefs.

Several collaborators and researchers from ARTNeT institutional members as well as interns assisted in translating the country briefs into various languages for more effective dissemination. We are grateful to all those in the ARTNeT community who contributed to this endeavour as well as to Haniff Ahamat, UKM, and Saman Kelegama, IPS, for contributions, respectively, to the boxes in chapters 5 and 6.

Special acknowledgement and appreciation is extended to the following peer reviewers from ESCAP and other institutions for their efforts to ensure the quality and relevance of APTIR and the trade briefs: Jose Antonio Pedrosa Garcia, Joseph George, Steve Loris Gui-Dilby, Daniel Lee, Hamza Ali Malik, Iosefa Maiava, Hiroaki Ogawa, Kilaparti Ramakrishna and Vatcharin Sirimaneetham (all from ESCAP); Jo-Ann Crawford (WTO); Simon Evenett, (St. Gallen University); Martina F. Farricane (ECIPE); Adam Heal (UNDPA); Bernard Hoekman (European Union Institute); Jan Hoffman (UNCTAD); Marko Javorsek (ECLAC); Laura Paéz (UNECA); Martin Wermelinger (OECD); and Ben Shepherd (Developing Trade Consultants).

Robert Oliver provided copy editing of this Report, while Charuwan Chongsathien of TIID assisted in final checks. The graphic concept, design and layout were carried out by Clung Wicha Press Co., Ltd. Chen-Wen Cheng produced infographic material. The Strategic Partnerships, Communications and Advocacy Section of ESCAP provided support in disseminating and communicating the APTIR findings through media outlets, while Martin Dressart helped with arrangements for timely online publication and ensuring that APTIR 2016 is accessible by readers worldwide.

CONTENTS

CONTENTS *(continued)*

BOXES

FIGURES

CONTENTS *(continued)*

CONTENTS *(continued)*

TABLES

CONTENTS *(continued)*

ABBREVIATIONS

AD	anti-dumping
ADB	Asian Development Bank
AEC	ASEAN Economic Community
AIFC	Astana International Financial Centre
APEC	Asia-Pacific Economic Cooperation
APTIAD	Asia-Pacific Trade and Investment Agreements Database
APTIR	Asia-Pacific Trade and Investment Report
ARI	assessment of regulatory impact
ASEAN	Association of Southeast Asian Nations
ATIGA	ASEAN Trade in Goods Agreement
AVE	ad valorem (tariff) equivalents
B2B	business-to-business
B2C	business-to-consumer
BITs	bilateral investment treaties
BKR	Belarus, Kazakhstan and the Russian Federation
BPM6	IMF Balance of Payments and International Investment Position Manual, sixth edition
BRI	Belt and Road Initiative
BRICS	Brazil, Russian Federation, India, China and South Africa
CIS	Commonwealth of Independent States
Comtrade	United Nations Commodity Trade Statistics Database
CSN	countries with special needs
CU	custom union
CVD	countervailing duties
DFQF	duty-free quota-free
EAEC	Eurasian Economic Community
EAEU	Eurasian Economic Union
EEC	Eurasian Economic Commission
EFTA	European Free Trade Association
EGA	Environmental Goods Agreement
EIA	economic integration agreement
EGS	environmental goods and services
EPA	economic partnership agreement
EU	European Union
FDI	foreign direct investment
FTA	free trade agreement
FTZ	free trade zone
GATS	General Agreement on Trade in Services

GCC	Gulf Cooperation Council
GDP	gross domestic product
GTA	Global Trade Alert
GVCs	global value chains
HS	Harmonized Commodity Description and Coding System
ICT	information and communications technology
IIAs	international investment agreements
IMF	International Monetary Fund
IPR	intellectual property right
IT	information technology
ITA	Information Technology Agreement
ITC	International Trade Centre
ITU	International Telecommunications Union
LPI	Logistics Performance Index
LSCI	Liner Shipping Connectivity Index
M&As	mergers and acquisitions
MFN	most-favoured-nation
MOFCOM	Ministry of Commerce, China
NTMs	non-tariff measures
OECD	Organisation for Economic Co-operation and Development
PIDEs	Pacific island developing economies
PPP	purchasing power parity
PSA	partial scope agreement
PTA	preferential trade agreement
R&D	research and development
RCEP	Regional Comprehensive Economic Partnership
RTA	regional trade agreement
SAARC	South Asian Association for Regional Cooperation
SAFTA	South Asian Free Trade Area
SDGs	Sustainable Development Goals
SES	single economic space
SEZ	special economic zone
SIDS	small island developing States
SOEs	state-owned enterprises
SPS	sanitary and phytosanitary
STRI	Service Trade Restrictive Index
TAB	trading across borders
TBT	technical barriers to trade
TFA	Trade Facilitation Agreement
TiVa	trade in value added
TNCs	transnational corporations

TPP	Trans-Pacific Partnership
UNCTAD	United Nations Conference on Trade and Development
UNNExT	United Nations Network of Experts on Paperless Trade and Transport for Asia and the Pacific
UNWTO	United Nations World Tourism Organization
USITC	United States International Trade Commission
WHO	World Health Organization
WITS	World Integrated Trade Solution
WSA	World Steel Association
WTO	World Trade Organization

CHAPTER 1

MERCHANDISE TRADE STILL IN TROUBLE[1]

While the dollar values traded at the global level as well as by the Asia-Pacific region continued to be higher than in the years preceding the global financial crisis, the growth of trade not only slowed down from a historical perspective and relative to economic growth, but turned negative in 2015. World exports recorded a fall of 13.2% in nominal terms, after a meagre increase of 0.6% in 2014. Exports and imports in 2015 by the Asia-Pacific region, which amounted to $6,601.9 billion and $5,966.2 billion, respectively, reflect a fall on the export side of 9.7% and on the import side of 15% over values in 2014. The global and regional deceleration in trade, predominantly driven by a large fall in the prices of traded merchandise, significantly threatens the economic stability of developing countries in the region.

Despite moving in the same downward direction as the global trend, the Asia-Pacific region has consolidated its share of global exports at the 40% mark and thus retained its position as the largest trading region in the world. However, that coincided with a "normalization" of the average levels of trade openness (expressed as the share of exports or imports in gross domestic product, (GDP) as these returned to the level of the early 2000s after a decade of continuous increase. Several factors create further risks to global and regional trade prospects – i.e. the continued economic slowdown and structural change in China, prolonged economic stagnation in many of the world's larger economies, and the recent uptick in protectionism globally (as discussed in chapter 5) – without much correction through preferential liberalization and in the absence of major multilateral agreements (as noted in chapter 6). A slower than expected recovery in the United States of America and European Union countries, despite continued strong (but less trade-intensive) growth in India (7.3% in real terms in 2015), is unlikely to bring back the high levels of Asia-Pacific trade growth witnessed in the years prior to the global financial crisis. Altogether, 2015-2016 has been a worrying period for trade in the Asia-Pacific region and worldwide, and there are few signs that the current economic and trade slowdown is simply a temporary phenomenon. Instead, this pattern may be the result of a change in the fundamental structure of world trade, which may lead to persistent trade stagnation, increasingly labelled as "great normalization".

This chapter presents and explains regional trade patterns in recent years. It then explores overall regional performance, and details how subregions trade with each other and with the world. This is followed by a breakdown of trends in trade statistics by types of goods traded. The chapter then turns to examining a structural change in regional and global trade. Finally, forecasts for the near-future are presented, followed by the conclusion.

As a spoiler, readers should be warned that the messages are far from positive. According to the merchandise trade data, global and regional trade has flattened out and there are no expectations for a rebound in a near future. After decades of double or higher growth than the global economy, global trade will be barely inching up by half of that rate in 2016. As argued below, factors contributing to this flattening of merchandise trade (as well as commercial services and foreign direct investment) are of a structural nature reflecting the "new normal" in the global economy with a lesser role for cross-border flows. However, not all agree with this gloomy picture. The plateau in international trade is found to coincide with a surge in cross-border data flows, pointing to a different type of a structural shift – the rise of digital economy.

According to a McKinsey Global Institute report (2016), the flow of digital information around the world more than doubled to an estimated 290 TB per second in only two years, between 2013 and 2015. Not all of those cross-border flows generate economic value, but an increasing portion is doing so. The spread of digital economy is just substituting for the "old" ways in which the world produced and traded, goes the argument. Thus, when reversal in trade growth is recorded, it does not mean that firms and consumers are trading less; it only means that they are doing it differently and not by sending container ships across oceans. While this is certainly true, Asia-Pacific Trade and Investment Report 2016 discusses the "old" dimensions of globalization – movements of goods, services and foreign direct investment across borders as well as policies that affect such movements. Even for these century-or-more old aspects of globalization, data and statistical issues still persist for a number of countries in the Asia-Pacific region that prevent a comprehensive analysis, not to mention the statistical requirements for studying these new cross-border data flows.

A. FIFTH YEAR OF WEAK GROWTH IN REGIONAL TRADE

For five consecutive years the Asia-Pacific region's trade growth has performed below the pre-financial crisis levels. Such a long and uninterrupted trade slowdown is unprecedented, and is a cause for concern that a "new normal" of weaker trade growth is being reached. Trade by the Asia-Pacific region contracted noticeably in 2015. The contraction occurred despite an increase in GDP growth among countries in the European Union, and continued but lower than expected growth in the United States, suggesting that this growth in Asian traditional export markets did not transfer to increased demand for the regional good.[2] Furthermore, weak demand by developing countries within and outside the Asia-Pacific region set the path for regional exports to fall by 9.7% in 2015. In turn, regional imports contracted by 15%. The European Union strengthened its economic growth to 2% in 2015 from 1.4% in 2014, while the United States remained stable at 2.4%. According to the International Monetary Fund (IMF) data, the three economies classified as "developed countries" in the Asia-Pacific region grew at different speeds – Japan at 0.6%, Australia at 2.5%, and New Zealand at 3% (IMF, 2016a).[3] Developed markets in general were traditionally the main sources of demand for exports from Asia and the Pacific, although in more recent years (the turning point being the global financial crisis in 2008-2009, demand has increasingly depended on South-South (especially intraregional) links.

It comes as no surprise that declining growth among regional and world developing countries in 2015 adversely affected the Asia-Pacific region's trade. In particular, China's continued transition to a "new economic growth normal" was associated with GDP growth slowdown to 6.9% in 2015, from 7.3% in 2014 and 7.7% in 2013. In addition, the Russian Federation suffered another weak year with its GDP contracting by 3.7%, which was the result of falling oil prices and trade sanctions. Brazil, a large exporter of commodities and whose largest export partner is China, recorded a similar GDP contraction of 2.9%. These impacts, combined with continued sluggish growth in Japan and increasing recourse to protectionism globally,[4] have meant that levels of trade in Asia and the Pacific have dramatically decreased in 2015. Some economies in the region that rely largely on commodity exports have been particularly hit, both by China's continued slowdown and the persistent decreases in commodity prices through 2015.[5]

The continuing weak demand from outside and within the region has left developing Asia-Pacific economies with no choice but to rebalance their sources of demand from export to domestic consumption. However, the degree to which domestic demand can offset trade contraction differs across countries as it depends on factors including economic size and the level of trade dependency of each country. In addition, the fact that trade has been a channel for knowledge transfer and for improving resource allocation makes it challenging for small developing economies to maintain the development pace.

"Asia-Pacific merchandise exports fell in nominal terms by 9.7% and imports by 15% in 2015 – the single largest drop in the region's trade since the global financial crisis of 2008-2009."

The relative success in the Asia-Pacific region in "outperforming" the global economy in 2015, with an export reduction of only 9.7% compared with the global decline of 13.1%, is largely explained by the relatively good performance of China, whose exports declined by only 2.9%. Excluding China, which accounted for 34% of the region's merchandise exports, the Asia-Pacific region registered a 13% decline in exports, which was similar to the world average (figure 1.1). While the 2015 export value growth is highly disappointing, it must be noted that the quantity (volume) of exports still grew at 3% in 2015 (a similar annual rate to that recorded since 2012).[6] The fall in export value has thus been driven primarily by a sharp fall in prices in 2015, due in turn to slower demand growth by regional powers (in particular China) and elsewhere.[7]

As stated, Asia-Pacific imports contracted by much more than the region's exports in 2015. This amounted to a 15% fall overall, including a 14.2% decline for China (the largest drop since 1976), a 14.4% fall among other regional developing economies and a 19.1% decrease among regional developed economies. Consequently, the Asia-Pacific region experienced a substantial improvement in the regional surplus, which more than doubled from $291 billion in 2014 to $635 billion in 2015.

Figure 1.1 **Flattening of merchandise trade growth across Asian and Pacific economies, 2007-2015**

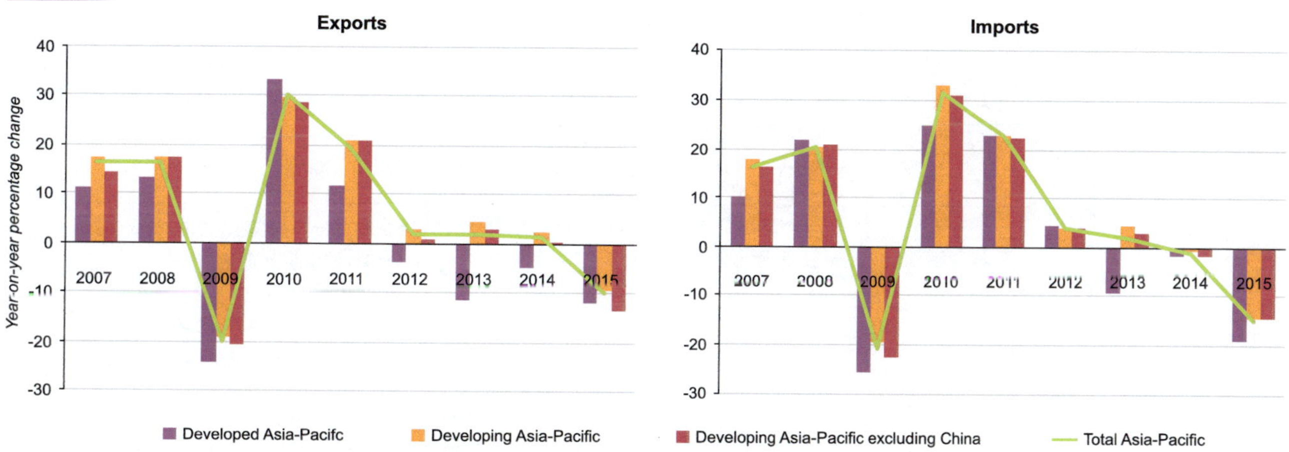

Sources: ESCAP calculation based on country data from WTO International Trade Statistics Database (accessed June 2016). Country data are available from the ESCAP website (ESCAP Statistical Database).

The deceleration of trade growth is worrying for the whole region given that the rapid growth of China and developing Asia-Pacific economies during the past 25 years is often considered to be the result of an export-led strategy.[8] In addition, a structural rebalance towards domestic demand-led growth in China will have knock-on effects for other developing countries in the region, for which exports and production have been highly integrated with China's economy through both forward and backward linkages in global value chains (GVCs). China has been the largest individual trading partner in the region; in 2015, the rest of the Asia-Pacific region exported 19.8% of their goods to China (compared with 11.3% to the United States). These linkages also mean that Asia-Pacific economies participating in GVCs will be adversely affected if China's internal rebalancing includes a shift to higher domestic content in its production and exports. This is particularly worrying given the fact that imports by China have fallen more than exports since early 2014.[9]

> *"The region's trade sector is facing a depressed immediate future."*

At the time of writing this report,[10] it was still uncertain if and by how much merchandise trade in the Asia-Pacific region could improve by the end of 2016. As depicted in figure 1.2, export and import values declined further in the first seven months of 2016 in eight major developing economies in the region. Year-on-year monthly changes continue to be negative or, if positive, they are very small with little indication

Figure 1.2 **Monthly trade growth in selected developing Asia-Pacific economies, 2011-2016**

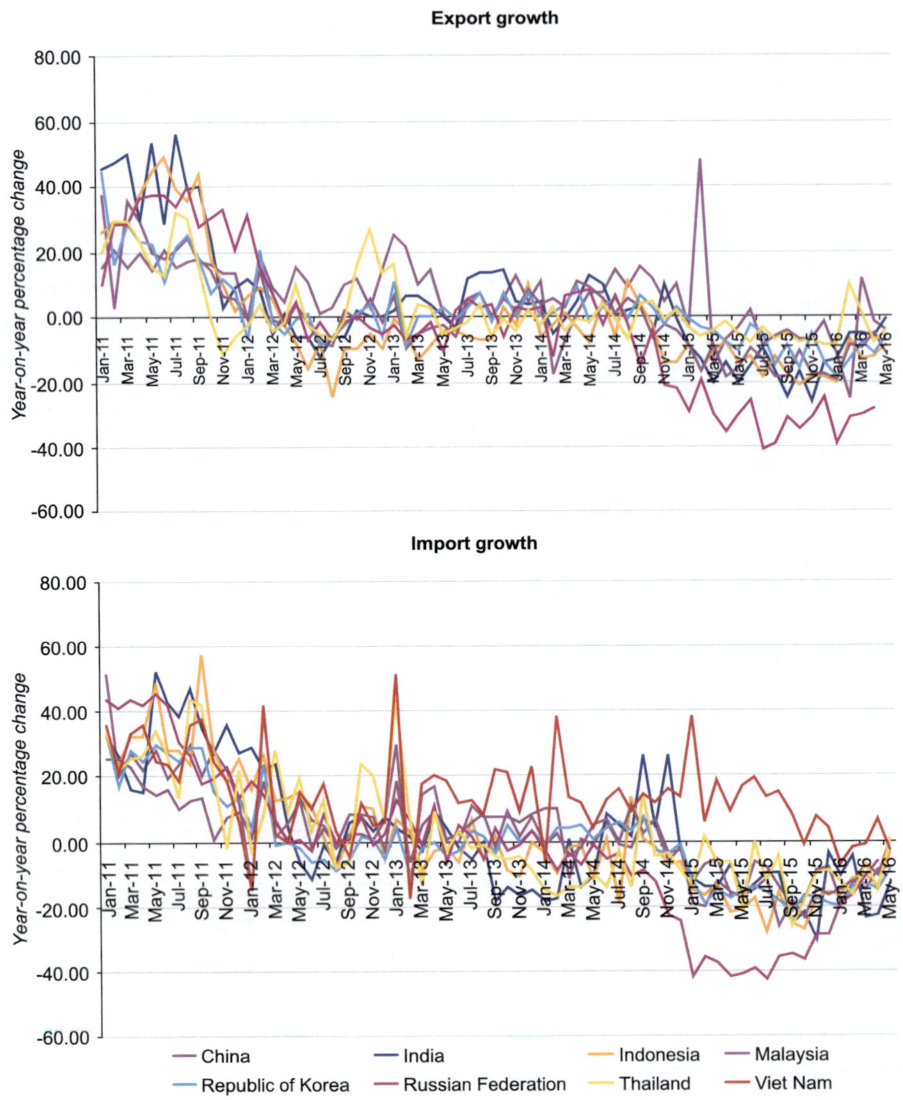

Sources: ESCAP calculation based on WTO online short-term statistics (accessed September 2016).

Notes: Change in United States dollar value year-on-year (i.e. 10-11 January), encapsulating volume and price changes.

of an upward movement in trade values. There has been no indication of any pick-up of intraregional and global demand. China is of particular interest due to its economic size, as that country's import and export values have again contracted so far in every month of 2016 except March. Adding to this somewhat gloomy picture are the IMF (2016a) and ESCAP (2016) projections for GDP growth in 2016.[11] China's economic slowdown is expected to continue in 2016, with the projected annual growth rate declining further to 6.6%.[12] In addition, the IMF (2016b) has forecast that the United States economy will grow only 1.6% in 2016, a significant decrease compared with 2015. The expected resulting reduction in demand for regional exports to China and the United States may be countered somewhat by a better picture emerging in the European Union. Despite uncertainties stemming from the United Kingdom's decision to leave the European Union, the growth in Euro-zone countries is expected to be resilient at 1.6% in 2016, which is only slightly less than in 2015.

Of all regional economies, only India is expected to experience dynamic growth performance in 2016, at 7.6%, and might have an increase of import demand. This may provide a boost to exports from countries in South and South-West Asia, which are linked to India through a network of preferential trade agreements.

B. SUBREGIONAL PERFORMANCE: EAST AND NORTH-EAST ASIA PERFORMS BETTER THAN OTHER SUBREGIONS

> *"Asia-Pacific increased its share of world exports in 2015 to 40% while its share of imports declined to 36%."*

The Asia-Pacific region retained its position as the world's largest trading region in 2015, despite the large trade contraction discussed above. Overall, due to an even greater global reduction in trade, the region increased its share of world exports to 40% in 2015 from 38.6% in 2014 while its share of global imports fell slightly to 35.6% from 36.9% in the previous year.[13] This dominance was again driven primarily by the trade performance of the economies of the East and North-East Asia subregion, which accounted for more than 64% of total Asia-Pacific trade with the world (table 1.1). In other words, exports by this subregion are considerably higher than those by other subregions – from more than tripple that of South-East Asia, to 18 times of the Pacific subregion.

In 2015, China was the main force behind the dominant position of East and North-East Asia in regional trade, with its world export and import share of 13.8% and 10%, respectively. East and North-East Asia increased its regional export share by 3.3 percentage points in 2015, a substantial change reflecting this subregion's disproportionately small export contraction of 4.8% (in turn, driven largely by the small export decline by China of only 2.9%, as stated above). This increased share came mainly at the expense of North and Central Asian economies, whose export share fell sharply from 8.8% to 6.6%. This was largely due to the massive fall in values of exports and imports by the Russian Federation in 2015 (31% and 37%, respectively), as the result of declining oil prices and political sanctions.[14] As the Russian Federation is the dominant economy in the subregion (accounting for 78% of North and Central Asia's exports and 71% of its imports), this translates into a large fall in the world trade share for this subregion.

South-East Asia's share of the region's total exports remained large and fairly stable. Compared with other subregions, trade is relatively well-distributed among subregion's economies, although still driven primarily by the performances of five members of the Association

Table 1.1 Shares in Asia-Pacific total trade, by subregion, 2013-2015

(Percentage)

Subregion	Exports			Imports		
	2013	2014	2015	2013	2014	2015
East and North-East Asia	60.2	60.8	64.1	59.4	59.8	60.1
South-East Asia	17.7	17.7	17.6	17.6	17.6	18.3
South and South-West Asia	8.6	8.7	8.2	12.5	12.6	12.7
North and Central Asia	9.4	8.8	6.6	6.3	5.8	4.6
Pacific	4.2	4.0	3.5	4.2	4.2	4.3

Source: ESCAP calculation based on country data from WTO International Trade Statistics Database (accessed July 2016).

Note: Calculations in United States dollar values. Import data are not available for Guam and Nauru. Although Taiwan Province of China is not a member of ESCAP, it is included in calculations for East and North-East Asia due to its share in the region's trade.

of Southeast Asian Nations (ASEAN), i.e. Indonesia, Malaysia, Singapore, Thailand and Viet Nam. The shares held by the South and South-West Asia as well as Pacific subregions declined by 0.5 percentage points from an already low base; trade performance is highly dependent on a few economies of those two subregions. Trade by South and South-West Asia remained dominated by India, which captured 50% of the areas exports and imports, while Turkey captured a further 27%. Hit by the commodity price plunge, those two countries experienced a 17% and 10% decline, respectively, in merchandise export value in 2015. Similarly, exports by the Pacific subregion, dominated by Australia and New Zealand, have also shown a stagnant, and even slightly declining, share of world exports and imports.

C. INTRAREGIONAL EXPORTS AND IMPORTS CONTINUE MOVING IN DIFFERENT DIRECTIONS

> *"For the second year in a row, the share of total Asia-Pacific exports going to countries within the region declined."*

While intraregional trade continues to dominate region's trade, trade with countries in the European Union and the United States remains important, as they accounted for 29% of regional exports and 21% of regional imports in 2015 (figures 1.3 and 1.4). Driven primarily by the slowdown of exports to advanced markets since the 2008-2009 global financial crisis, the share of exports to developing Asia-Pacific economies, especially to China, increased steadily from 43% in 2008 to a peak of 48.2% in 2013, before falling slightly to 47.6% in 2015.

Absolute values of exports in 2015 fell for each destination in figure 1.3, except the United States, although not symmetrically. Exports to the European Union saw the largest decline in absolute value; hence its share of region's exports declined by 1 percentage point in 2015, continuing a decline that started after 2008. Similarly, the share of exports to developed Asia-Pacific countries fell by 0.4 percentage points, continuing a trend that had been evident since 2002. Exports to China also fell substantially in value terms, although given the decline of exports to all main markets that fall translates into a small decline in the share of exports, from 12.8% in 2014 to 12.6% in 2015, thus reflecting the impact of China's economic new normal on the rest of the region in 2015. Since reaching its peak in 2010, the share of regional exports to China has consistently fallen, demonstrating China's slowdown in regional integration (see section D for more details). The share of exports going to other developing Asia-Pacific economies did not change much in 2015 following a long growth

Figure 1.3 Destinations of merchandise exports from Asia and the Pacific, 2002-2015

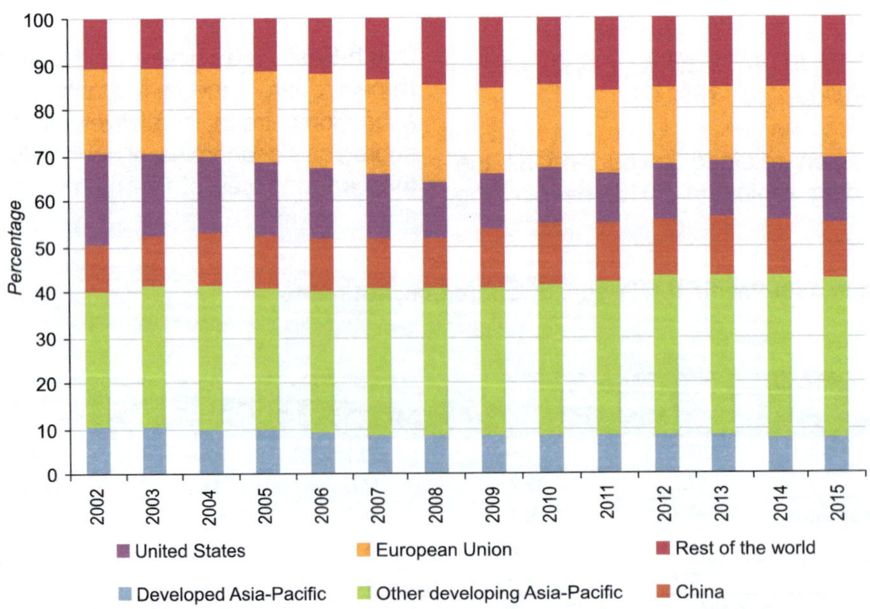

Source: ESCAP calculation based on IMF Direction of Trade Statistics (accessed August 2016). Country data are available from the ESCAP online statistics database.

Figure 1.4 Sources of Asia-Pacific merchandise imports, 2002-2015

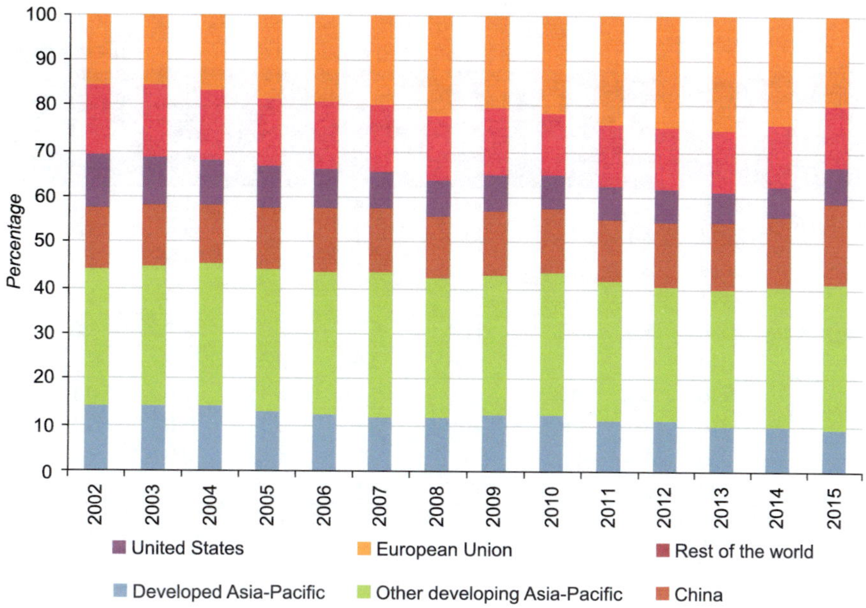

Source: ESCAP calculation based on IMF Direction of Trade Statistics (accessed August 2016). Country data are available from the ESCAP online statistics database.

period, with the difference being made up by an increase in the share of exports to the United States (12.3% in 2014 to 13.8% in 2015) and to the rest of the world (15.2% in 2014 to 15.4% in 2015).

> *"In 2015, interregional imports increased reaching almost 60% of total imports."*

The intraregional import share increased in 2015 to 59% of total imports in the Asia-Pacific region, a slightly higher level than that seen during 2002-2015. While the share of imports from developed Asia-Pacific countries declined slightly (continuing a long downward trend), China and other developing Asia-Pacific countries increased their share by 2.4 and 1.3 percentage points, respectively. This was mainly at the expense of the import share of the rest of the world, which shrank from 24.1% in 2014 to 20.1% in 2015 (figure 1.4).

As global economic growth remains more anaemic, intraregional South-South cooperation is in a better position and carries greater potential than cooperation with countries outside the region. The increase in the intraregional import share reflects the fact the while the absolute value of intraregional imports fell in 2015, it did so by less than the overall contraction in imports into the region. This is particularly the case for imports from China, which fell only slightly in 2015. Hence the severe contraction in world trade in 2015 and the reduced output among several extraregional developing countries has produced the opportunity for relatively more intraregional trade. However, the risk that China's demand for imports from the region will fall further (as stated above, Asia-Pacific exports to China have declined in relative terms since 2010) is looming with its move to a lower growth model that has an increased focus on services and domestic production, rather than manufacturing and product assembly for export.

> *"Exports by South and South-West Asia, and North and Central Asia are still shipped to countries outside the region, while exports by the rest of the region go mainly to East and North-East Asia."*

Intraregional trade remained dominated by East and North-East Asia in 2015 (table 1.2). Outside of South and South-West Asia, at least 50% of intraregional exports went to East and North-East Asia, reflecting a combination of the latter subregion's large demand for final goods and still strong (though weakening) role as a centre for assembling intermediate goods into final goods to be shipped globally. However, South and South-West Asia as well as North and Central Asia remain relatively disengaged from the region in terms of exports. More than 70% of exports from South and South-West Asia and 63% of exports from North and Central Asia went to countries outside of the Asia-Pacific region, highlighting the lack of integration of both subregions into regional production

Table 1.2 **Intraregional merchandise exports, by Asia-Pacific subregion, 2014-2015**

(Percentage of total exports)

Subregion	Year	ENEA excl. China	China	ENEA	SEA	SSWA	NCA	Pacific	Total Asia-Pacific	Rest of the world
		Destination of exports								
East and North-East Asia (ENEA)	2015	21.7	12.9	34.6	12.4	4.8	1.8	2.1	55.5	44.5
	2014	22.4	13.1	35.5	12.1	4.5	2.6	2.0	56.6	43.4
South-East Asia (SEA)	2015	22.1	12.6	34.7	24.4	5.3	0.5	3.8	68.6	31.4
	2014	22.7	12.4	35.2	25.4	5.2	0.5	4.3	70.5	29.5
South and South-West Asia (SSWA)	2015	5.9	5.5	11.4	5.5	9.0	2.7	1.0	29.5	70.5
	2014	6.6	7.1	13.6	5.5	9.5	3.2	0.7	32.6	67.4
North and Central Asia (NCA)	2015	8.1	10.2	18.4	1.9	8.1	7.9	0.1	36.5	63.5
	2014	7.6	9.4	17.0	2.6	7.1	5.8	0.1	32.5	67.5
Pacific	2015	24.5	28.8	53.3	9.9	4.5	0.3	7.4	75.4	24.6
	2014	26.3	30.5	56.7	10.5	3.8	0.3	7.4	78.7	21.3

Source: ESCAP calculation based on IMF Direction of Trade Statistics (accessed August 2016). Country data are available from the ESCAP online statistics database. Data given in percentages (rows show percentage of export to each destination from each source, e.g. 12.9% of East and North-East Asian exports go to China).

chains as well as their close ties with European Union countries (which received 25% and 47% of exports from South and South-West Asia and North and Central Asia, respectively). This is in contrast to South-East Asia and the Pacific subregions, which are highly integrated regionally in terms of exports. Of the total exports by South-East Asia and the Pacific subregions 75.4% and 68.6% were within the Asia-Pacific region, with the bulk going to East and North-East Asia.

As mentioned above, China has become a major destination for intraregional exports, accounting for nearly 20% of total exports by the rest of the region.[15] However, this number does not reveal the fact that 10 Asia-Pacific economies export to China more than 20% of their total exports (figure 1.5). Of those 10 economies, China is the destination of more than 50% of total exports by Mongolia, the Democratic People's Republic of Korea, Turkmenistan, Solomon Islands and Hong Kong, China. That strong reliance on exports to China makes those 10 economies highly vulnerable to further economic slowdown in China in the immediate future.

"East and North-East Asia is the largest destination for exports by all subregions in Asia and the Pacific."

In terms of imports, those from East and North-East Asia account for well over 60% of intraregional imports, and between 24% and 44% of total imports by every subregion in the Asia-Pacific region (table 1.3). In 2015, the share of imports by East and North-East Asia from every subregion increased (except North and Central Asia, for which a slight decline was recorded) as did the share of imports by China. Again, this should be seen in the light of a fall in trade everywhere and a disproportionately small decline in imports from China within the region (in contrast to the pattern of Chinese exports to the world). Further, there is scope for increased trade within subregions with imports accounting for less than 23% of total imports outside of East and North-East Asia, and less than 10% in South and South-West Asia and the Pacific. The share of imports from countries in the same subregion fell, both in South and South-West Asia and the Pacific, largely due to a disproportionate reduction in demand from key importers within those subregions (particularly India and Australia). Other subregions increased their within-subregion trade, although for North and Central Asia this reflects, in large part, a collapse in trade with other subregions.

Figure 1.5 **Share of exports from selected economies to China, 2015**

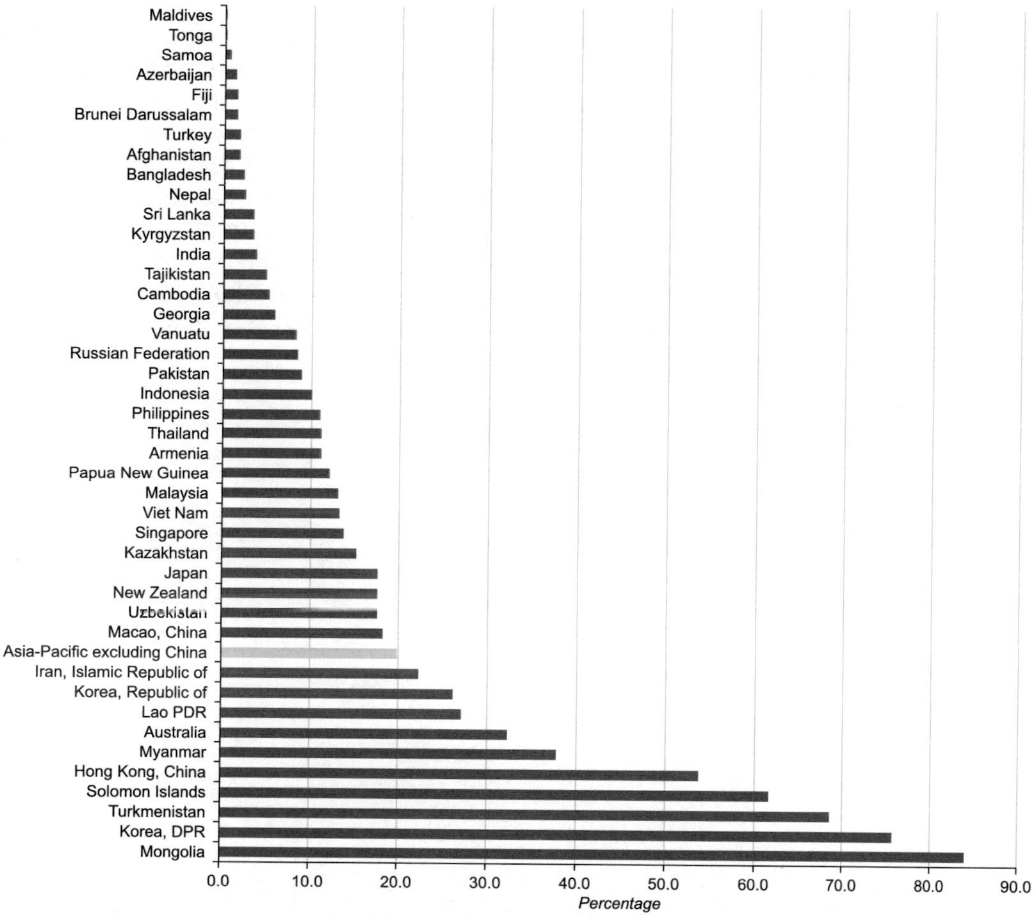

Source: ESCAP calculation, based on IMF Direction of Trade Statistics (accessed August 2016). Country data are available from the ESCAP online statistics database.

Table 1.3 **Intraregional merchandise imports, by Asia-Pacific subregion, 2014-2015**

(Percentage of total imports)

Subregion	Year	Source of imports								
		ENEA excl. China	China	ENEA	SEA	SSWA	NCA	Pacific	Total Asia-Pacific	Rest of the world
East and North-East Asia (ENEA)	2015	21.3	16.0	37.3	12.4	2.1	2.5	4.2	58.4	41.6
	2014	19.6	13.9	33.5	11.7	2.4	2.8	4.7	55.1	44.9
South-East Asia (SEA)	2015	22.6	21.3	44.0	23.0	2.4	1.1	2.2	72.6	27.4
	2014	21.8	17.6	39.5	23.0	2.3	1.7	2.4	68.8	31.2
South and South-West Asia (SSWA)	2015	7.4	16.7	24.1	7.7	6.8	4.1	1.5	44.3	55.7
	2014	6.7	14.8	21.5	7.6	7.2	4.4	1.5	42.2	57.8
North and Central Asia (NCA)	2015	6.1	20.2	26.3	3.0	6.3	13.1	0.3	48.9	51.1
	2014	7.5	19.3	26.8	2.7	5.8	7.3	0.3	42.9	57.1
Pacific	2015	14.6	22.2	36.8	16.5	2.4	0.3	6.3	62.2	37.8
	2014	13.6	19.6	33.2	18.8	1.8	0.6	7.0	61.4	38.6

Source: ESCAP calculation based on IMF Direction of Trade Statistics (accessed August 2016). Country data are available from the ESCAP online statistics database. Data in percentages (rows give percentage of imports from each source; e.g. East and North-East Asia sources 16% of the subregion's imports from China).

D. FACTORS AFFECTING TRADE PERFORMANCE

Since the 2008-2009 global financial crisis, the world has seen a decline in the growth rate of the ratio of global trade to GDP (figure 1.6), including Asia and the Pacific, which gives cause for concern that global trade has reached its peak, and that weak trade growth will be a new normal. This section explores whether changes in the composition of regional trade, dominated by China, have been important contributors to the new normal of global trade. Factors which might influence regional performance in future are also discussed.

1. Trade composition by the stage of processing and use[17]

Since 1988, the share of exports for each production stage (raw materials, intermediate goods, consumer goods and capital goods) has remained fairly constant, with a slight downward trend for capital goods (figure 1.7). The Asia-Pacific region as a whole is a manufacture exporting region, and is predominantly an exporter of capital and consumer goods. These two categories contributed 65%-75% of total regional exports from 1988 to 2002. Raw materials accounted for a share of between 5% and 15% of regional

Figure 1.6 Ratio of imports to GDP

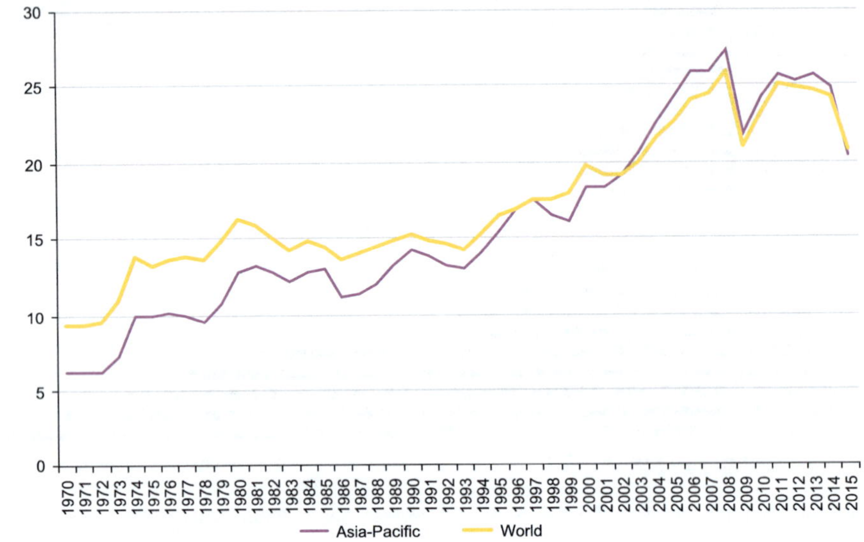

Source: ESCAP Statistics Online, accessed in November 2016.

Figure 1.7 Asia-Pacific exports and imports, by production stage, 1988-2014[a]

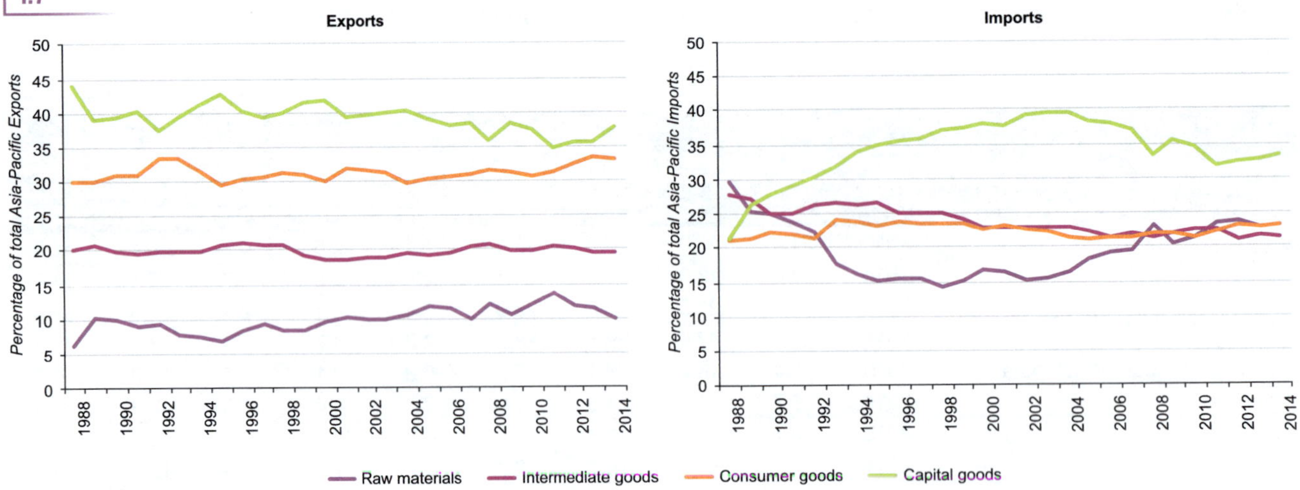

Source: ESCAP calculation based on United Nations COMTRADE data accessed through the World Bank World Integrated Trade Solutions (WITS) database (accessed July 2016).[b]
Note: Product classification follows the list of UNCTAD Stages of Processing provided in WITS.

a 2015 data on international trade by stages of processing and uses are not available for most of the large Asia-Pacific economies at the time of writing this report (September 2016).

b The World Bank's World Integrated Trade Solutions (WITS) database does not include trade data for Taiwan Province of China, which is not an ESCAP member, but is included in other figures and tables as explained in endnote 1.

exports, although there are commodity-based exporting countries that still have a relatively small share in total regional exports. The import composition shows a mirroring trend between raw materials and capital goods. After peaking at 39.4% of regional imports, the import shares of capital goods have fallen since 2003 in a reverse pattern to that of raw material imports.

2. The influence of China: increasing exports of capital goods

However, there is significant variation among countries within the Asia-Pacific region. In particular, the above patterns are heavily influenced by China, which accounted for 35% of total regional exports and 28% of imports. Since 1992, China has seen a significant increase in its ratio of capital goods exports to total exports, from 10% to a peak of 48% in 2010 and then a decline to 44% of Chinese exports in 2014 (figure 1.8).

The pattern is reversed when looking at exports by the rest of Asia and the Pacific. This may be a result of China's rising position as an export platform of capital goods for the rest of the region during those years. Further, despite the perception that China is simply a final assembly centre for parts and components from the rest of the world, China has seen a large drop in imports of intermediate goods as a percentage of total imports since 2000 (figure 1.9), compared with the stable (or even increasing) ratios for other countries in the region. Imports of intermediate goods have

Figure 1.8 Exports for the Asia-Pacific region (excluding China) and for China, by production stage, 1992-2014

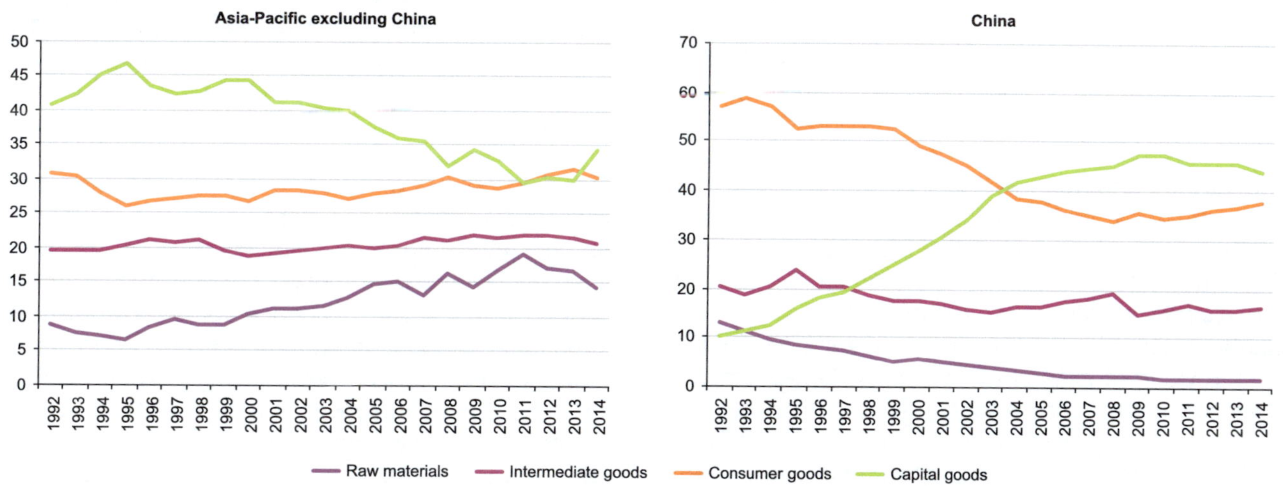

Source: ESCAP calculation based on United Nations COMTRADE data accessed through the World Bank World Integrated Trade Solutions (WITS) database (accessed July 2016).

Figure 1.9 Imports for the Asia-Pacific region (excluding China) and for China, by production stage, 1992-2014

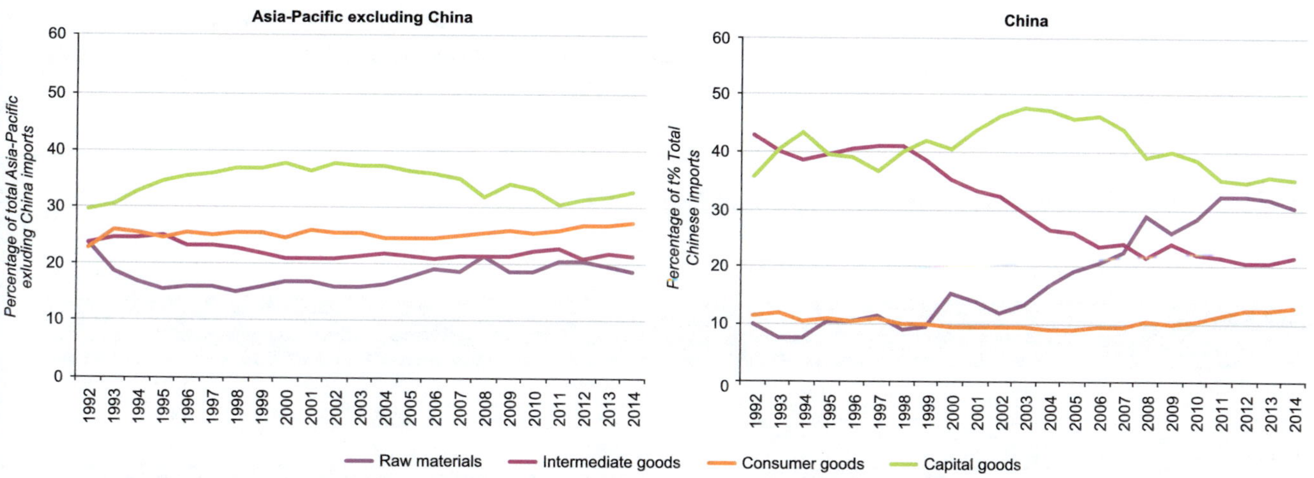

Source: ESCAP calculation based on United Nations COMTRADE data accessed through the World Bank World Integrated Trade Solutions (WITS) database (accessed July 2016).

largely been replaced by imports of raw materials. One possible reason for the faster growth of raw material imports than those of intermediate imports by China during those years is the rapid rise of commodity prices during those years. Another possible reason could be that China's need for raw materials was pushed up by the rapid growth of domestic consumption as well as production for exports while the country's need for intermediate imports was mainly for the latter purpose.

3. Sectoral contributions to export growth

Sectoral growth in the Asia-Pacific region has been highly heterogeneous, with various sectors contributing in different ways to overall trade growth. Overall, exports grew at a rapid rate of 14% from 1988 to 2008, before dropping to a 7.6% growth rate since 2009 (due, in part, to the large declines in export value levels in 2009). Capital goods contributed around 40% to total export growth until 2008,[18] the highest level of any category (table 1.4). The export growth of capital goods, consumer goods and intermediate goods was in the 12%-16% range until 2008. Thus, it is largely the relative size of the sectors that determine their contribution. While exports of raw materials grew faster (around 17.5%), the small share of overall exports (reaching a maximum of 12% of total exports in 2008) limited the contribution of that export sector. Since 2011, falling prices have meant that the value of exports of raw materials has shrunk, while consumer goods and capital goods accounted for most of the (limited) growth. Since the 2008-2009 global financial crisis, consumer goods have been the largest contributor to export growth, while the contribution of intermediate goods has fallen, perhaps suggesting a decline in the relative importance of GVCs to regional trade (see discussion below).

4. Structural changes affecting global and intraregional trade

There are several possible factors causing global trade slowdown, some of which are structural factors (box 1.1). Among them, GVC proliferation is one of the factors highlighted in the literature (e.g. Constantinescu, Mattoo and Ruta, 2015). GVCs, in which production stages for the manufacturing of a good are split across countries, spread rapidly from the 1980s onwards, according to a study by Gangnes, Ma and Van Assche (2015), particularly in East and South-East Asia. The same study indicated that as trade patterns are usually measured in gross, not value-added, terms, GVCs entail "double counting" for intermediate goods. Consequently, a rapid increase in GVCs is expected to temporarily increase the growth in trade and trade elasticity:[19] this is termed the "adoption effect" (Gangnes, Ma and Van Assche, 2015). Further, if GVCs are mainly focused on more elastic sectors, an increase in GVC trade as a proportion of total trade would increase trade elasticity permanently (the "composition effect"), a pattern exacerbated by an international "bullwhip effect". A slowdown or reversal in GVC expansion would then lower trade growth and elasticity correspondingly. Although limited data are available for assessing this effect, one measure (the share of foreign value-added in gross exports) shows limited evidence for a slowdown in international production-sharing for the world as a whole. However, it also shows stronger evidence that following a sharp increase in the late-1990s, China has reduced its reliance since the mid-2000s on foreign inputs for export production (figure 1.10). This complements the data in the previous section showing that China reduced its imports of intermediate goods as a percentage of total imports during the 2000s, suggesting that it has moved to produce intermediate goods previously produced abroad. Further, there is evidence of a slowdown of GVC proliferation in several specific industries, e.g. the electronics industry (Thorbecke, 2015).

Table 1.4 **Asia-Pacific export growth decomposition, 1988-2014**

(Percentage)

	Average annual contribution				
	Raw materials	Intermediate goods	Consumer goods	Capital goods	Total export growth
1988-2000	11.8	17.5	30.9	39.8	13.7
2001-2008	10.4	20.4	28.7	40.5	14.7
2009-2014	-14.3	13.3	55.3	45.7	7.6

Source: ESCAP calculation based on United Nations COMTRADE data accessed through the World Bank World Integrated Trade Solutions (WITS) database (accessed July 2016).

Box 1.1 Is the global trade slowdown cyclical or structural?

Since 2011, world trade has exhibited a pronounced slowdown, provoking a flurry of academic literature. While world trade volumes (i.e. real trade) grew at an average of 6.9% per year from 1990 to 2007, the average annual growth from 2008 to 2015 was only 3.1%. This slowdown can also be seen in terms of the elasticity of trade with regard to GDP, which refers to the percentage change in global trade, given a 1% change in global GDP. Calculated in five-year periods,[a] trade elasticity has fallen from a high of 2.5 (i.e., a 1% increase in GDP is linked to a 2.5% increase in global trade) in the mid-1990s to around 1 since 2009 (see figure below[b]). This therefore suggests that trade growth has become less responsive to global GDP growth in recent years. Further, using a more formal econometric technique (an error correction model[c]) to capture the long-term elasticity of trade with regard to GDP, Constantinescu, Mattoo and Ruta (2015) found that this elasticity fell in the early 2000s, from 2.2 during 1986-2000 to 1.3 in post-2000. Other authors have found that this pattern also holds for China and the ASEAN-5 countries (European Commission, 2015), which have exhibited declining trade elasticities in recent years (e.g. from 2 in 1999-2003 to 1 in 2009-2013 for China). While some authors question these findings,[d] this apparent fall in elasticity has led to a debate over its potential causes, and in particular whether it is the result of temporary fluctuations in the world economy ("cyclical" factors) or the result of changes to the macroeconomic structure underlying world trade ("structural" factors).

Figure. Global trade and GDP growth, and five-year elasticities of trade with regard to GDP

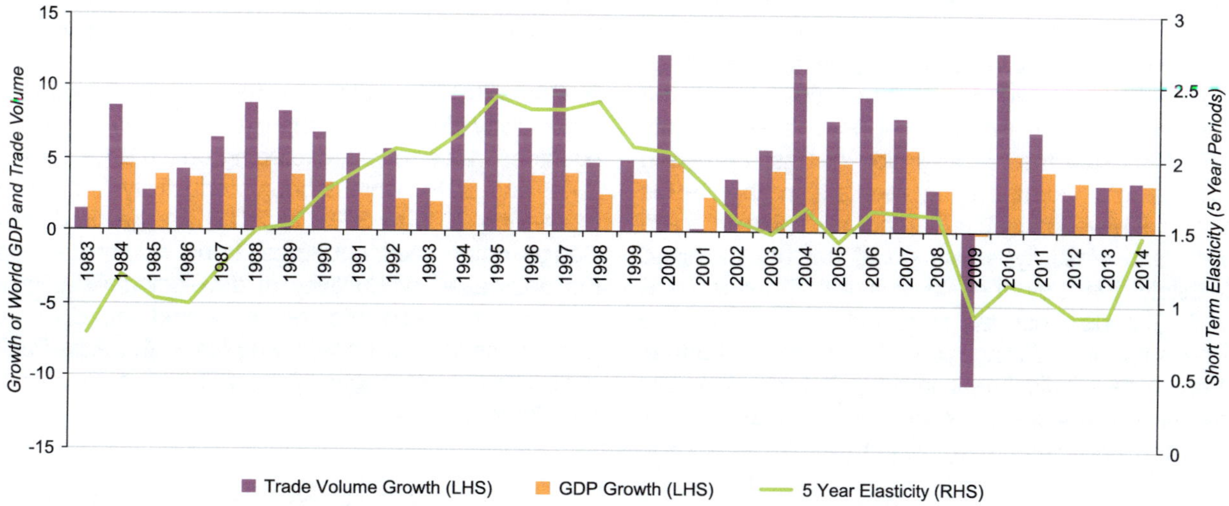

Source: ESCAP calculation based on IMF World Economic Outlook data (accessed August 2016).

A fall in trade growth is certainly an expected outcome of the prolonged (cyclical) financial crisis seen since 2008, particularly as the crisis has disproportionately affected major global trading powers. The European Union, in particular, saw GDP growth rates fall from an average of 2.6% in 2000-2007 to an average of 0.4% in 2008-2015 in a protracted slump. Consequently, this lowered the average annual growth of European Union exports from 11.3% during 2000-2007 to only 0.8% during 2009-2015 (with similar figures for regional import growth). As intraregional trade among European Union countries accounts for one third of world trade (Hoekman, ed., 2015, p. 8), this slowdown has dragged down the global rate of trade growth. Further, the global crisis has reduced demand disproportionately in trade-intensive areas of GDP: in particular, due to the 2008-2009 global financial crisis, GDP composition has shifted away from trade-heavy investment towards government consumption and private non-durables consumption, which have lower trade intensities (Ollivaud and Schwellnus, 2015). However, several authors have argued that in addition to these cyclical factors, the slowdown in trade and the related fall in the trade elasticity have occurred, at least in part, due to changes in the macroeconomic structure of global trade.[e] Key to this argument is the observation that global trade elasticity began falling in the early 2000s, prior to the global financial crisis in 2008-2009, thus suggesting that the subsequent cyclical downturn is not solely responsible for the trade slowdown. Constantinescu, Mattoo and Ruta (2015) found that while cyclical factors explained most of the trade patterns in 2009-2010, by 2013 at least 48% of the decline in import growth compared with the pre-crisis period could be explained by structural factors. Many structural changes to global trade may be rooted in the Asia-Pacific region, particularly in China, and the impact of a trade slowdown will be felt throughout the area.

Box 1.1 *(continued)*

a This figure gives the average annual trade growth over the five preceding years divided by the average global GDP growth over the five preceding years.

b This figure is an updated version of that presented in the European Commission's Winter 2015 Economic Forecast.

c An error-correction model is an econometric technique used for time series processes exhibiting co-integration. It gives estimates for the long-term relationship between variables, the short-term response function and the speed at which the relationship returns to equilibrium. Specifically, the model is:

$$\Delta lnTradeVol_t = \beta_0 + \beta_1 \Delta lnGDP_t + \beta_2 lnTradeVol_{t-1} + \beta_3 lnGDP_{t-1} + \varepsilon_t$$

where Δ refers to first differences. The long-term elasticity is then given by $-\frac{\beta_3}{\beta_2}$, the short-term response function by β_1, and the speed of adjustment by $-\beta_2$. Formal tests can be carried out to determine structural breaks in the long-term elasticity. The likelihood of reverse causality means that these coefficients cannot be taken to indicate a causal relationship between global income and trade, but rather they highlight the correlation between the two variables.

d Ollivaud and Schwellnus (2015) argued that the decline in elasticity after 2000 captured by Constantinescu, Mattoo and Ruta (2015) was mainly due to the latter's use of a PPP-based GDP measure rather than a market exchange rate measure. Using the latter, they found a reduction in the long-term elasticity of trade with regard to GDP only after the global financial crisis of 2008-2009. They thus argued that this could be explained by the cyclical effect of the global economic downturn.

e See Hoekman, ed. (2015) for a summary of several articles discussing the structural and cyclical causes of the recent trade slowdown.

Another potentially important factor in the structural change is the slowdown in China's integration into world trading markets following an initial rapid increase in the 1990s and following China's accession to the World Trade Organization in 2001 (Pei, Yang and Yao, 2015). Alongside the re-integration of East European countries into world trading markets in the 1990s this could have caused a temporary spike in trade growth and elasticity, which could not be sustained indefinitely. Similarly, the slowdown in Chinese GDP growth (the new normal) in recent years may have played a role in reducing global trade growth. Further, China's recent adjustment in its policy on domestic consumption led growth away from an export focus (Pei, Yang and Yao, 2015), which may lower supply-side incentives for exporting, while at the same time increasing Chinese imports of some final goods.

ESCAP (2016) indicates that the growth of total factor productivity declined by more than half in developing countries in the region, averaging only 0.96% between 2008 and 2014, while labour productivity declined by more than 30% to 3.9% in 2013. As the productivity wedge determines countries' trade competitiveness, the decreased productivity of developing Asia-Pacific adds another structural factor behind the economic and, consequently, trade slowdown in the Asia-Pacific region in the aftermath of the 2008-2009 economic and financial crises.

Figure 1.10 **Foreign-added share in gross exports, 1995, 2000, 2005 and 2008-2011**

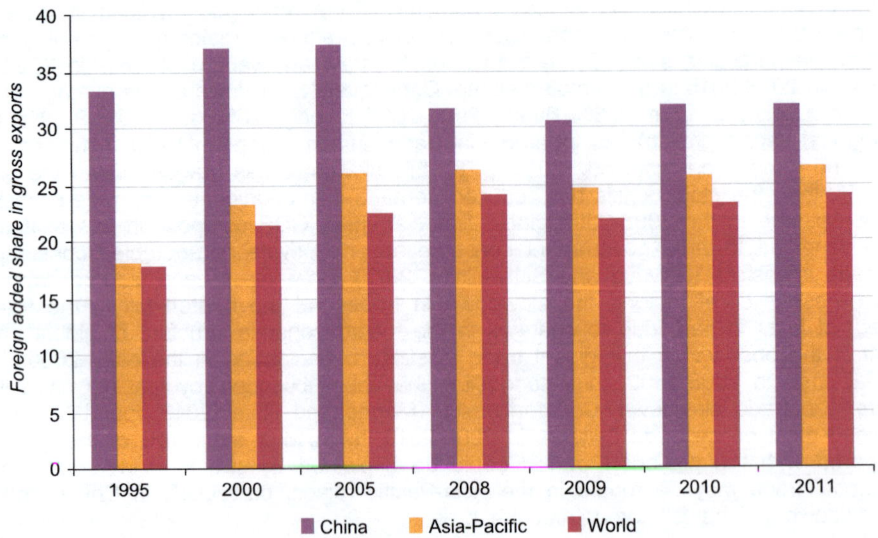

Source: ESCAP calculation based on OECD Trade in Value-Added (TiVA) data (accessed August 2016). Data are only available for 1995, 2000, 2005 and 2008-2011. The Asia-Pacific category excludes several economies for which data are unavailable.

A final argument often made to explain the apparent slowdown in trade is a recent increase in protectionism, within and outside the region. While Constantinescu, Mattoo and Ruta (2015) argued that there had only been a minor increase in formal measures of protectionism since the 2008 crisis,[20] other authors have argued that informal methods of protectionism, in particular export subsidies, may have cut least developed country exports by 5.5% annually, on average, since 2008 (Evenett and Fritz, 2015). Further, protectionist measures, both formal and informal, may have increased by as much as 50% in 2015 (Evenett and Fritz, 2016), which may be an explanatory factor for the slump in global trade shown in previous sections of this chapter. Even without a rise in protectionism, it may be the case that rapid trade growth in the 1990s and early 2000s was spurred by a rapid liberalization of trade, which has stalled with the continued failure of the WTO Doha Round.

5. Implications of a trade slowdown, and long-term regional performance

The main implication of the reduced elasticity of trade is that as the prolonged economic downturn in developed countries lifts, and global income returns to a higher level of growth, global trade may not reach the high growth rates seen throughout the 1990s and early 2000s. This is particularly important, especially for the Asia-Pacific region, as fast-growing developing countries in recent years have often utilized an export-led growth model in which they increased production to meet foreign demand. While levels of trade will remain high as long as trade growth is positive after 2015 declining trade growth means that there will be fewer opportunities for new countries to grow through an export-led strategy. In turn, countries will be less able to incorporate foreign technology and knowledge, which tends to flow with trade. In particular, the Chinese move to produce their own intermediate goods may lessen the potential for low-income countries in the region to kick-start growth through entering global value chains.

However, there are several reasons why new structural changes may increase the elasticity of trade once again, even if not to the level seen previously. First, trade growth in new areas within and outside the region (e.g. South Asia and Africa) may boost world trade growth as obstacles to trade are removed and trade openness levels reach similar heights to those in integrated countries. Second, certain technological advances (e.g. in transport and communications) may allow even greater specialization across countries. Third, an increased move to the trade in services provides scope for the impact of further liberalization, as services typically face larger trade barriers (Hoekman, ed., 2015). Consequently, there is potential for trade to expand once again in the coming years, although it is unlikely to return to pre-financial crisis levels for some time.

E. NEAR-TERM PROSPECTS AND CONCLUSION

The Asia-Pacific region has continued to face threats to its trade prospects in 2016, and is expected to once again see a reduction in the value of imports and exports. This is especially the case for commodity exporting countries, particularly those in North and Central Asia as well as those tied to China through global value chains. The expected declining growth rates within the region and in key world importing economies in 2016, alongside falling price indices, means that a regional trade recovery is not expected until 2017.

ESCAP estimates that the Asia-Pacific region as a whole is expected to exhibit a 5.2% and 4.9% decline in nominal export and import values, respectively, in 2016, before bouncing back in 2017 with 4.5% growth in nominal exports and 6.1% growth in nominal imports (table 1.5). These estimates are based on a lingering uncertainty with regard to the movement of oil and commodity prices. If these estimates materialize they might again cause export and import price indices to fall substantially by 5.9% and 5%, respectively. In other words, countries that export primary commodities, largely low income economies, are still exposed to the risks of declining commodity prices, due to declining global demand – especially in China – for energy and non-energy commodities.[21] The volume of trade in the region is expected to grow in 2016, although only feebly, by 0.7% and 0.1% for exports and imports, respectively; this is far from the heights of around 7% seen globally in the early 2000s. The 2017 expansion of trade will be due to a mixture of expected increased prices and expected real growth; export and import price indices are expected to grow by 3% and 2.3%, respectively, while export and import volumes are projected to increase by 1.5% and 3.8%, respectively. Thus, as discussed in section D, trade (nominal and real) is expected to bounce back in the coming years, but not to the heights seen prior to the 2008-2009 global financial crisis.

Table 1.5 **ESCAP forecasts for merchandise trade growth, by selected Asia-Pacific economy, 2016-2017**

(Annual percentage change)

	Exports						Imports					
	2016[a]			2017[a]			2016[a]			2017[a]		
	Value	Price	Volume	Value	Price	Volume	Value	Price	Volume	Value	Price	Volume
Australia	-0.98	-3.80	2.93	11.58	10.30	1.16	-2.24	-3.20	0.99	9.56	4.20	5.14
Bangladesh	5.00	4.20	0.77	5.50	3.80	1.64	4.10	3.20	0.87	5.60	0.80	4.76
China	-6.13	-6.40	0.29	3.34	0.80	2.52	-8.80	-8.50	-0.32	5.51	3.40	2.04
Hong Kong, China	-3.53	-2.30	-1.26	3.11	0.80	2.29	-3.62	-1.70	-1.96	3.78	1.60	2.15
India	-0.29	-3.70	3.54	8.38	5.60	2.63	-1.67	-0.60	-1.08	9.14	-7.30	17.73
Indonesia	-6.43	-5.80	-0.67	3.00	2.30	0.68	-8.13	-7.30	-0.90	3.85	1.90	1.92
Islamic Republic of Iran	10.85	-6.10	18.05	21.27	10.80	9.45	14.00	24.20	-8.21	19.00	25.20	-4.95
Japan	4.84	3.60	1.20	2.56	7.30	-4.42	0.43	-1.30	1.75	1.86	-1.90	3.83
Kazakhstan	-23.16	-18.60	-5.60	18.38	17.00	1.18	-25.72	-3.30	-23.19	7.19	4.10	2.97
Malaysia	-4.78	-6.70	2.05	2.25	0.10	2.15	-5.55	-4.90	-0.68	2.11	0.60	1.50
New Zealand	-6.66	-5.30	-1.44	4.32	4.80	-0.46	-3.29	-4.30	1.06	7.47	4.20	3.14
Pakistan	-7.81	-1.40	-6.50	5.44	1.90	3.48	-2.65	-7.90	5.70	5.97	4.20	1.70
Philippines	-6.09	-8.80	2.98	3.14	-0.50	3.66	-1.17	-5.60	4.70	8.96	3.50	5.28
Republic of Korea	-7.25	-6.70	-0.59	1.44	0.60	0.83	-5.47	-8.80	3.65	7.57	3.90	3.53
Russian Federation	-23.69	-21.70	-2.54	11.61	9.80	1.65	-13.91	-2.60	-11.61	5.59	0.90	4.65
Singapore	-6.45	-8.00	1.68	3.22	3.80	-0.56	-6.84	-6.60	-0.25	4.67	4.30	0.35
Sri Lanka	-0.50	-5.30	5.06	8.58	2.60	5.83	4.08	-1.30	5.45	7.54	0.70	6.79
Taiwan Province of China	-8.46	-7.20	-1.36	-0.33	-1.70	1.39	-8.31	-9.00	0.76	1.51	1.90	-0.38
Thailand	-10.43	-9.50	-1.03	3.81	2.60	1.18	-3.38	-1.20	-2.20	8.95	8.30	0.60
Turkey	-0.21	-3.70	3.62	5.05	0.80	4.22	0.24	-6.50	7.21	8.99	2.60	6.23
Viet Nam	4.45	-3.20	7.91	18.68	10.20	7.69	4.58	-4.70	9.74	19.78	7.50	11.42
Asia-Pacific[b]	-5.21	-5.89	0.68	4.53	3.03	1.49	-4.90	-5.03	0.13	6.09	2.26	3.83
Developed Asia-Pacific[b]	3.07	1.53	1.54	4.56	7.34	-2.78	-0.36	-1.91	1.55	3.88	-0.21	4.10
Developing Asia-Pacific[b]	-6.46	-6.99	0.53	4.52	2.30	2.22	-5.73	-5.56	-0.17	6.51	2.74	3.78

Source: ESCAP calculation based on the Economist Intelligence Unit, as of August 2016.

Note: The estimated growth rates are calculated based on constant prices (in 2013 terms).

a Projections.

b Regional trade growth is the trade-weighted, time-varying average growth rate.

However, there is also substantial heterogeneity in the trade prospects for Asia-Pacific economies, highlighting the different environments that they face. The clearest distinction is between developing and developed economies in the region. While developing economies are expected to see only a small increase in real exports (0.5%), a small decrease in real imports (0.2%) and a sharp contraction in nominal trade, exports for developed Asia-Pacific countries are expected to grow in both real and nominal terms, and imports are expected to grow in real terms and fall in nominal terms. The trend for developed countries is mainly due to the expected strong real export performance by Australia, and an increase in the export price index in Japan, for which nominal exports are expected to recover from a sharp contraction. Developing economies within the region – most notably India and Viet Nam – with strong trade connections to the United States as well as the advanced economies in the European Union are expected to see better trade growth performance than countries trading intensively with China. While the growth of the United States and European economies is still not at pre-financial crisis levels, and is expected to fall slightly in 2016, reasonable growth recovery in these regions will benefit their close trading partners.[22]

In contrast, countries tied to China through global value chains (e.g. Thailand, the Philippines and the Republic of Korea) are expected to experience large export (and smaller import) contractions in 2016, before witnessing a smaller than average rebound in 2017. China's economic slowdown and transition to a new growth strategy, which is focused on domestic demand rather than exports and investment, has helped lower its own trade forecast, which gives an expected nominal contraction of 6.1% and 8.8% for exports and imports, respectively, with real trade almost unchanged. Thus upstream GVC members, in turn, face export contractions, exacerbated by the "bullwhip effect", during which downturns upstream manufacturers run down inventories rather than importing new parts.

Finally, countries in North and Central Asia are expected to see the largest trade contractions in 2016, although strong growth is expected in 2017. Due, in large part, to falling export prices (particularly in the case of fuel-based commodities), nominal exports from the Russian Federation and Kazakhstan are expected to collapse by 23.7% and 23.2%, respectively. In turn, this is expected to cause a sharp contraction in real imports of 11.6% for the Russian Federation and 23.2% for Kazakhstan, with relatively little change in the import price index.

Therefore, the recent trade slowdown is expected to continue throughout 2016 as the post-financial crisis recovery in developing countries remains sluggish and developing countries are experiencing deep structural changes. A projected continued fall in prices (if that materializes), matched with sluggish real trade will lower the nominal value of trade in 2016, before improvements in both prices and real trade bring about a projected recovery in 2017. Therefore, countries within the region face challenges to export-led growth in the near future; therefore public policies for improving trade environments, including bilateral, regional and multilateral trade agreements, are more essential than ever.

Endnotes

1 The numbers for merchandise trade were compiled by the ESCAP secretariat, based on data available from the World Trade Organization and International Monetary Fund at the time of preparing this report. More recent revisions of trade data by those data sources may result in different trade balance values. The numbers include trade data for Taiwan Province of China, which is not a United Nations ESCAP member, but represents 4.3% of merchandise exports in the Asia-Pacific region. The use of other sources of trade data may produce different estimates. Individual economic data for ESCAP member States are available from the ESCAP online statistical database.

2 A possible explanation can be that the growth recovery was still driven by household spending which is relatively less import intensive compared to private investment which is still on a sluggish path (Bussière and others, 2013). As discussed later in the chapter, both the global and regional economies are experiencing falls in trade elasticity, thereby indicating less chance of trade recovery even with a revival of the economic growth.

3 Data from the IMF World Economic Outlook Database, accessed July 2016. More recent revisions of GDP growth data by IMF may result in different growth rate estimates.

4 The nineteenth Global Trade Alert Report (Evenett and Fritz, 2016) calculates that there was a 50% increase in protectionist measures in 2015 compared with 2014, largely by G20 countries and largely affecting G20 countries.

5 Data from IMF Primary Commodity Prices track a 37% and 17% decline in fuel and non-fuel prices, respectively, in 2015.

6 Data from the IMF World Economic Outlook Database, accessed July 2016. More recent revisions of data by the IMF may result in different growth rate estimates.

7 ESCAP calculations based on data from the Economist Intelligence Unit, accessed August 2016, show that for the Asia-Pacific region as a whole, export prices fell by 10% and import prices by 12%, in 2015.

8 The IMF estimates that exports contribute about 30% in terms of value-added to output growth of China, up from 15% in the 1990s. This large contribution reflects rapid growth in exports (on average by 18.5% since the end of the 1990s until before the 2008-2009 global financial crisis and an increase in the domestic content of exports (Guo and N'Diaye, 2009).

9 The import-export ratio consistently trended upwards in 2014 and 2015, from 1 to 1.18 in January 2014 to 1 to 1.47 in December 2015.

10 Pre-copy edited version of the Report was finalized on 15 September 2016.

11 The IMF projected growth figures are taken from IMF July 2016 World Economic Outlook update. These figures have been used, rather than the more comprehensive April 2016 World Economic Outlook database, in order to account for the impact of the United Kingdom of Great Britain and Northern Ireland's vote to withdraw from the European Union. Growth estimates have mainly been revised downwards as a result of this decision. The estimate for the United Kingdom itself has been lowered from April to June by 0.2 percentage points for 2016 and 0.9 for 2017, while the projection for advanced economies fell by 0.1 and 0.2 percentage points, respectively; the projection for emerging and developing economies remained constant overall.

12 ESCAP (2016) projects the declining growth of China from 6.5% in 2016 to 6.3% in 2017. In addition, according to the IMF, the economic turmoil in other major developing countries is also expected to continue (the Russian Federation is projected to remain in recession until 2017, and Brazil until 2018).

[13] This includes both intraregional trade flows and flows with the rest of the world.

[14] See Russell (2016), Sanctions over Ukraine: Impact on Russia, European Parliament Briefing, available from http://www.europarl.europa.eu/EPRS/EPRS-Briefing-579084-Sanctions-over-Ukraine-impact-Russia-FINAL.pdf (accessed 15 July 2016).

[15] This number is larger than that given in figure 1.3 (12.6%) as figure 1.3 includes exports from China, lowering the amount. Exports to China from all Asia-Pacific countries excluding China amount to 19.8 % of these economies' total exports.

[16] Indian imports from South and South-West Asia fell by 33%, while those from South-East Asia fell by 6.6%. Those from East and North-East Asia rose by 2.9%. Imports by the Russian Federation from North and Central Asia fell by 37.2%, while those from East and North-East Asia fell by 34%, and those from South-East Asia declined by 16%.

[17] Following the UNCTAD-Stages of Processing provided in WITS, international trade is classified, based on the Broad Economic Categories (BEC) classification, into four major economic categories, depending on the stage of processing and use. Primary products comprise raw materials and resources used in the productive process. Intermediate products comprise semifinished goods that are used in the production of other products. Consumer products are those that are intended for final consumption. Capital goods are manufacturing goods such as machinery that are intended to be used in the production of other goods.

[18] Decomposing export growth to analyse the contribution of different constituent parts involves weighting the average annual growth rates of each part by the share of that part in the total level of exports. Thus, if two constituent parts have the same growth rate, the part with the largest share of exports will contribute more to overall growth.

[19] Trade elasticity with regard to GDP refers to the percentage change in global trade given a 1% change in global GDP. See further details in box 1.1.

[20] Constantinescu, Mattoo and Ruta (2015) stated that the increase in various measures of protectionism had been only "modest" and that adding a variable for protectionism into their core Error Correction Model barely changed the core coefficients, while the coefficient on protectionism was not significant.

[21] As China accounts for 18% of world economic activity in 2016 (IMF estimate), its demand for commodities has been a key factor in commodity prices in the past two decades. Falling GDP growth in China has been considered a key factor in falling prices in recent years. See www.ft.com/cms/s/2/30441208-b548-11e5-b147-e5e5bba42e51.html#axzz4HkYkfLUm.

[22] These predictions were made prior to the presidential election in the United States.

REFERENCES

Bussière, M., and others (2013). Estimating trade elasticities: Demand composition and the trade collapse of 2008-2009. *American Economic Journal*: Macroeconomics, vol. 5(3), pp.118-151.

Constantinescu, C., A. Mattoo and M. Ruta (2015). The global trade slowdown: cyclical or structural? IMF Working Paper No. 15/6. Washington, D.C. Available from https://www.imf.org/external/pubs/ft/wp/2015/wp1506.pdf.

Economic and Social Commission for Asia and the Pacific (2016). *Economic and Social Survey of Asia and the Pacific 2016: Nurturing Productivity for Inclusive Growth and Sustainable Development*. Sales No. E.16.II.F.10

European Commission (2015). *European Economic Forecast Winter 2015*. Available from http://ec.europa.eu/economy_finance/publications/european_economy/2015/pdf/ee1_en.pdf.

Evenett, S., and J. Fritz (2015). Crisis-era trade distortions cut LDC export growth by 5.5% per annum. In B. Hoekman, ed., *The Global Trade Slowdown: A New Normal?* Chapter 15. Available from http://voxeu.org/content/global-trade-slowdown-new-normal.

______ (2016). *Global Trade Plateaus: 19th Global Trade Alert Report*. London: Centre for Economic Policy Research. Available from www.globaltradealert.org/gta-analysis/global-trade-plateaus.

Gangnes, Byron, Alyson C. Ma and Ari Van Assche (2015). Global value chains and the trade-income relationship: implications for the trade slowdown. In B. Hoekman, ed., *The Global Trade Slowdown: A New Normal?* Chapter 6. Available from http://voxeu.org/content/global-trade-slowdown-new-normal.

Guo, K., and P. N'Diaye (2009). Is China's export-oriented growth sustainable? IMF Working Paper No. 09/172. Washington, D.C. Available from https://www.imf.org/external/pubs/ft/wp/2009/wp09172.pdf.

Hoekman, B., ed. (2015). *The Global Trade Slowdown: A New Normal?* Available from http://voxeu.org/content/global-trade-slowdown-new-normal.

International Monetary Fund (2016a). *World Economic Outlook Update July 2016*. Washington, D.C. Available from https://www.imf.org/external/pubs/ft/weo/2016/update/02/pdf/0716.pdf.

______ (2016b). *World Economic Outlook October 2016: Subdued Demand, Symptoms and Remedies*. Washington, D.C. Available from www.imf.org/external/pubs/ft/weo/2016/02/pdf/text.pdf.

McKinsey Global Institute (2016). *Digital Globalization: The New Era of Global Flows*, McKinsey and Company. Available from www.mckinsey.com/business-functions/digital-mckinsey/our-insights/digital-globalization-the-new-era-of-global-flows

Ollivaud, P., and C. Schwellnus (2015). Does the post-crisis weakness of global trade solely reflect weak demand? OECD Economics Department Working Paper No. 1216, Paris: OECD. Available from http://dx.doi.org/10.1787/5js1qvnff3hk-en.

Pei, Jiansuo, Cuihong Yang and Shunli Yao (2015). Trade impact of China's transition to the new normal. In B. Hoekman, ed., *The Global Trade Slowdown: A New Normal?* Chapter 14. Available from http://voxeu.org/content/global-trade-slowdown-new-normal.

Russell, M. (2016). Sanctions over Ukraine: Impact on Russia. European Parliament Briefing. Available from www.europarl.europa.eu/EPRS/EPRS-Briefing-579084-Sanctions-over-Ukraine-impact-Russia-FINAL.pdf.

Thorbecke, W. (2015). The global trade slowdown: lessons from the East Asian electronics industry. In B. Hoekman, ed., *The Global Trade Slowdown: A New Normal?* Chapter 12. Available from http://voxeu.org/content/global-trade-slowdown-new-normal.

ONLINE DATABASES

International Monetary Fund (2016). World Economic Outlook database. Available from https://www.imf.org/external/pubs/ft/weo/2016/01/weodata/index.aspx.

______ (2016). Primary Commodity Prices Database. Available from www.imf.org/external/np/res/commod/index.aspx.

______.Direction of Trade Statistics database. Available from http://data.imf.org/?sk=9D6028D4-F14A-464C-A2F2-59B2CD424B85.

World Bank. World Integrated Trade Solutions (WITS) database. Available from http://wits.worldbank.org/.

World Trade Organization. International Trade Statistics (ITS) database. Available from https://www.wto.org/english/res_e/statis_e/statis_e.htm.

______.Online Short-Term Trade Statistics database. Available from https://www.wto.org/english/res_e/statis_e/short_term_stats_e.htm.

CHAPTER

2

TRADE IN COMMERCIAL SERVICES SLIDING DOWNHILL

While service trade exhibited more resilience to negative shocks during the great financial crisis, together with less volatility historically, the uninterrupted weak performance of merchandise trade over the past five years and the struggle of the major developed and emerging economies to return to a higher growth path appear to have contributed to a decline both in the global and the Asia-Pacific region's services trade in 2015.

As repeatedly emphasized in the previous issues of APTIR, development of the services sector is crucially important to economic diversification and inclusive trade in the Asia-Pacific region. Therefore, with other areas of international exchange in trouble, the focus on service trade performance only sharpens and expands the need for more information on services performance. However, the monitoring of trade in services, especially in developing countries, suffers from several weaknesses including, most importantly, the lack of reliable and complete statistics.[1,2] Given these issues with the availability of data, the analysis in this chapter remains mostly at the aggregate level. Nevertheless, it is possible to derive some important trends. First, services trade for which statistical data are available (which arguably is not more than half of the total international service transactions) remains below 30% of merchandise trade with a very mild rising trend during this period of slowed growth of both GDP and trade. Second, in contrast to global services trade, in the Asia-Pacific region services capture a lower share of merchandise trade, and even less (under 20%) on export side. Third, the Asia-Pacific region doubled the value of imports and exports of services between 2006 and 2015. Consequently, its share in global services trade has been increasing; however, it is still below the region's share in merchandise trade – just below 33% on import side and reaching 30% on the export side. These findings from a descriptive statistic go along with a picture of a perceived role of Asia as the manufacturing producer and exporter (i.e. factory Asia). Fourth, while overall services trade fell in in 2015, both for the global economy and for Asia and the Pacific, larger declines were either recorded in services closely linked to merchandise trade (e.g. transport) or reflect the level of general economic activity (e.g. construction) than in other services sectors. Unfortunately, a lack of statistical data prevents tracing the sectoral performance at the intraregional or intra-subregional levels, but aggregate data show a mild recovery in some services activities, especially travel services. A more detailed exploration of selected sectoral trends is made wherever data allow, as in the case of the tourism sector.

A. THE RETURN OF SERVICES TRADE CONTRACTION

Despite the services trade exhibiting higher resilience to external shocks back in 2008/2009, the continued economic slowdown, and worsening economic and political uncertainty in 2015 triggered a strong contraction in commercial services trade flows. At the global level, growth of commercial services exports moved into a negative area when it fell by 6.1% for the first time after the 2009 global trade collapse.[3] The Asia-Pacific region followed this global trend by recording a drop in its commercial services exports and imports of 4.5% and 4.9%, respectively, in 2015 (figure 2.1). According to the WTO quarterly statistics database,[4] the downward trend of commercial services exports and imports of the region has been tampering off as export growth was -0.2% in the second quarter after a worse performance at -2.5% in the first quarter of 2016. Following four negative quarterly performances in 2015, in contrast to merchandise trade, imports started to grow at 2.7% and 4% in the first and second quarters of 2016, respectively.[5] As discussed in more details below, 2016 exports globally and in the region was affected by the transport services falling by more than the combined positive growth of other services categories.

> *"The global economic slowdown has had a strong impact on commercial services trade in Asia and the Pacific in 2015."*

Figure 2.1 **Growth in commercial services trade in Asia-Pacific economies and the world**

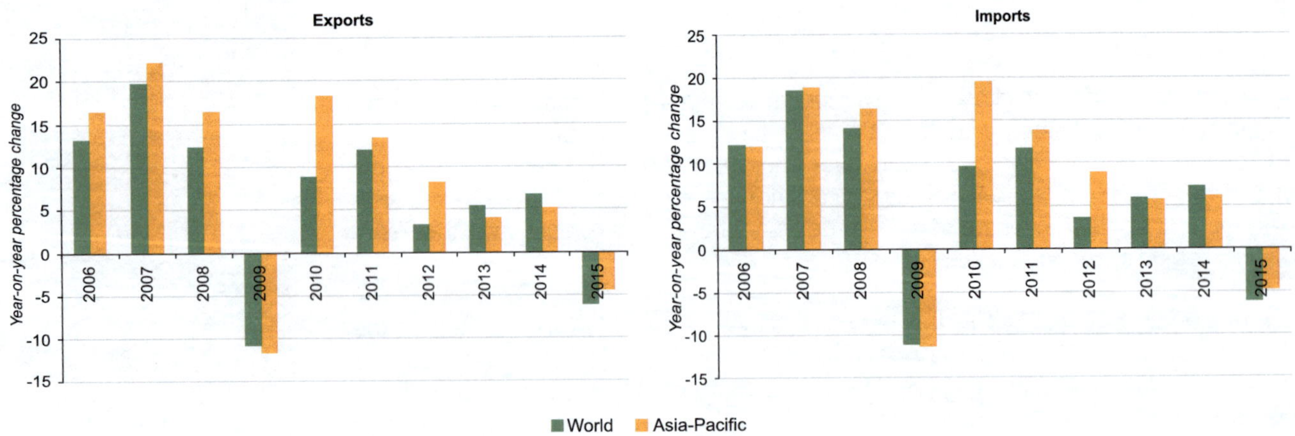

Sources: ESCAP calculation based on the WTO International Trade Statistics Database.

The region remains a net importer of commercial services, accounting for almost 33% of world imports, while contributing 29% to world exports in 2015. China alone represents more than a quarter of the region's total imports (figure 2.2). In terms of exports, China, India, Japan and Singapore account for about a half of the region's total exports.

> *"The region accounts for about a third of global services trade but remains a net importer of commercial services."*

In 2015, the global economic slowdown has started to have a more serious impact on services exporters. Most of the major exporters in the region faced significant export deterioration (figure 2.3). Weak business activity worldwide led to a drop in demand for transport services, financial services and other business services (consulting and technical/trade-related services). In addition, economic slowdown has threatened the prospects of travel services because tourists tend to reduce their expenditure during times of economic (and political) uncertainties, while business travel also declines proportionately to the economic slowdown (see more details in section D). Although the region's largest exporter, China, registered an increase in exports, its growth rate dropped more than five-fold from 12.4% in 2014 to 2.2% in 2015,[6] thus contributing to the weak results for the region as a whole. Exports fell mildly for India, Japan and Taiwan Province of China. Most of the other major exporters experienced a marked export contraction, including Macao, China (24.9%), the Russian Federation (21.3%), the Republic of Korea (12.7%), Turkey (10%), Australia (9.4%) and Singapore (7.4%).

There were also glimpses of positive performances. Thailand and the Philippines, for example, recorded an improvement in their services export performance with growth of about 10%. This was driven by a recovery of growth in the tourism sector of Thailand while dynamic growth in "other business services"[7] was recorded in the case of the Philippines. Several small emerging economies also shared in this positive picture by managing to register relatively high growth in contrast to the region's mediocre performance. Tonga (21.5%), Sri Lanka (14.2%) and Mongolia (12.8%) are some examples; however, their export volumes were small, relative to other economies in the region and thus their successful export growth could not improve the region's average.

Intraregional demand for services has severely declined, reflecting the regional economic recession. Only three major importers – China; Hong Kong, China; and Taiwan Province of China – were able to maintain modest import growth in 2015 (3.4%, 0.2% and 3.8%, respectively), while others experienced import contraction – the Russian Federation (27%), Australia (14%), Malaysia (12%), Japan (8.7%), Indonesia (8.6%), Singapore (7.7%), Thailand (4.6%), India (3.5%) and the Republic of Korea (2%).

WTO (2016) has argued that exchange rate movements in 2015 – particularly the appreciation of the United States dollar against major world currencies, and the fact that trade statistics are recorded in United States

Figure 2.2 **Share of commercial services exports and imports in Asia-Pacific economies, 2015**

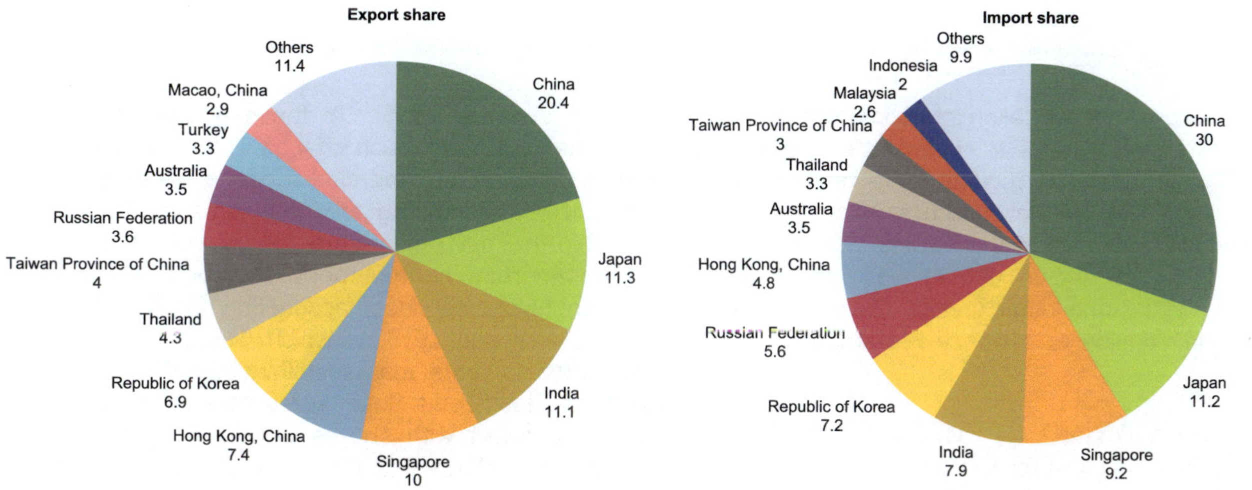

Sources: ESCAP calculation based on available data from WTO International Trade Statistics Database. Data on individual economies are available online in the ESCAP statistical database.

Note: "Others" is an aggregate of remaining Asia-Pacific economies with an individual share of less than 1.5% of total Asia-Pacific trade.

Figure 2.3 Growth of services exports and imports, by Asia-Pacific economy, 2015

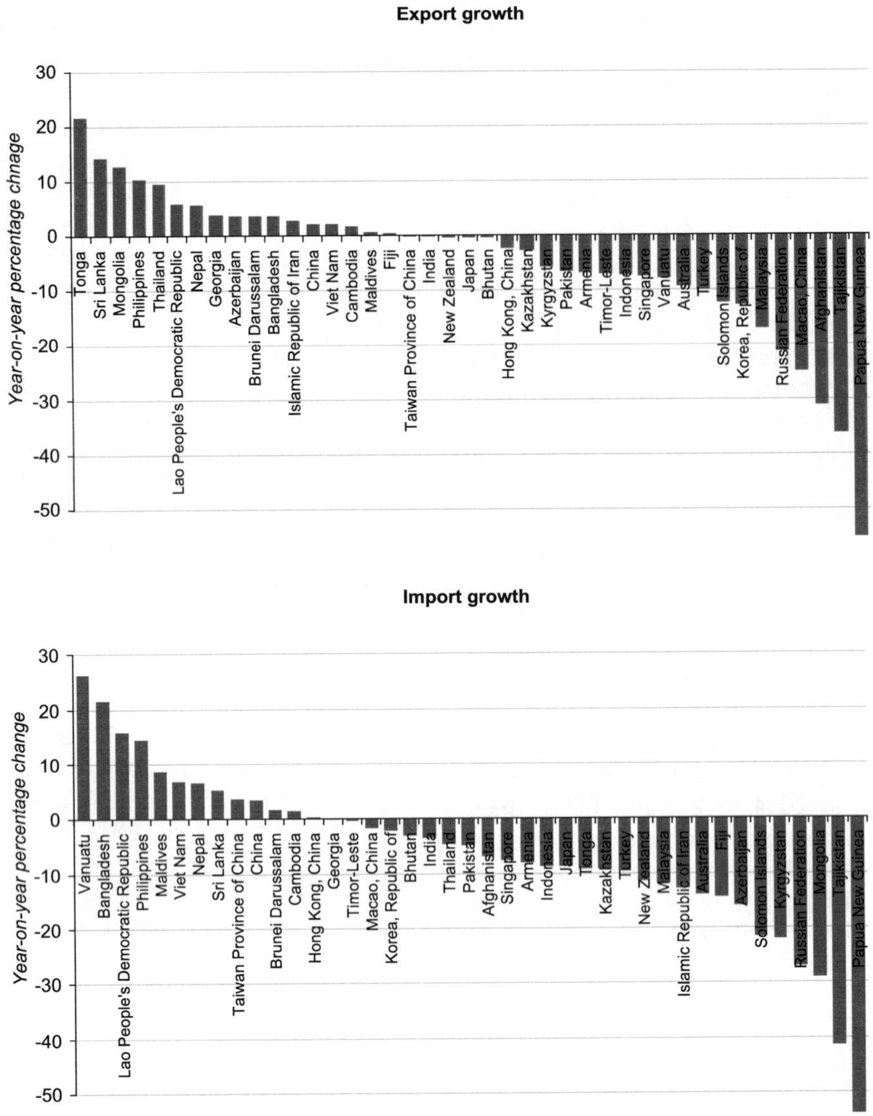

Sources: ESCAP calculation based on available data from WTO International Trade Statistics Database. Data on individual economies are available online from the ESCAP statistical database.

dollars – should also be taken into consideration when identifying factors that have influenced services trade performance. While all regions have been affected by exchange rate fluctuations, in several economies of the Asia-Pacific region the decline in both exports and imports (as shown above) was rather steep, indicating that some other factors might have been involved in addition to currency movements.

B. REPOSITIONING OF MAIN PLAYERS IN SERVICES TRADE CONTINUES

Figure 2.4 provides a geographical breakdown of commercial services trade among the subregions of Asia and the Pacific. At these aggregate levels, there has not been much change in the geographical composition of commercial services trade in Asia and the Pacific during the past decade. The East and North-East Asia subregion is still by far the most important contributor to the region's exports in commercial services, accounting for nearly 53% by this sector in 2015, of which China's contribution amounted to more than one third. South-East Asia, and the South and South-West Asia (dominated by India) followed with shares of 21.4% and 16.2%, respectively. North and Central Asia as well as the Pacific played a relatively minor role with shares of 4.8% and 4.6% of the region's exports, respectively. The subregional distribution of imports is similar.

Figure 2.4 Shares of commercial services trade, by subregion

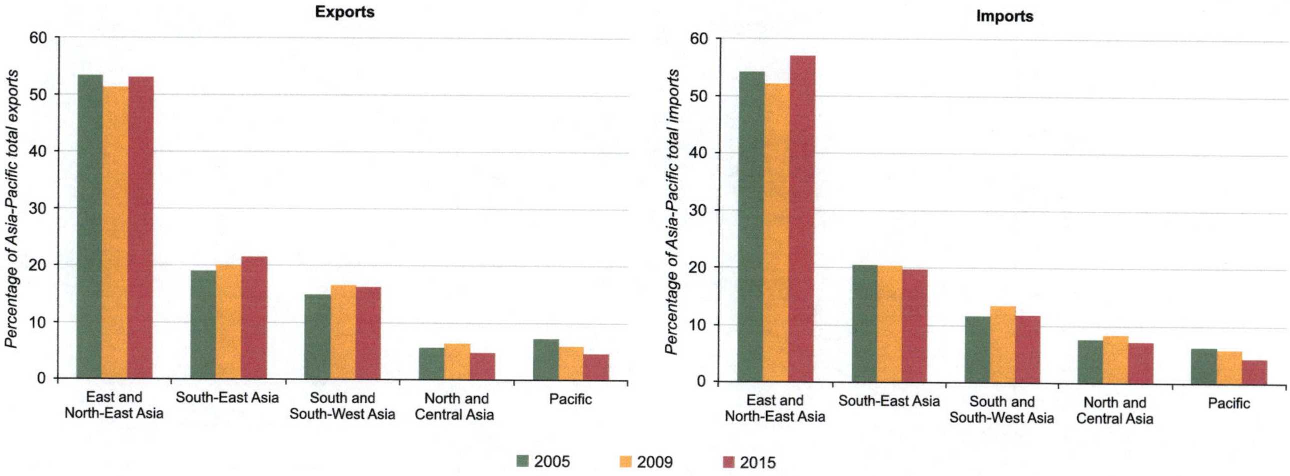

Sources: ESCAP calculation based on available data from WTO International Trade Statistics Database (accessed June 2016). Data on individual economies are available online from the ESCAP statistical database.

However, to see any changes in the pattern one has to look at the details at the country level. In other words, there are changes in terms of country positioning. During the past decade, the importance of services exports for developing Asia-Pacific countries, especially China and India, has been growing. From 2005 to 2015, the share of China's exports increased from 14.8% to 20.4% of the region's total services exports, while India's share grew from 8.6% to 11.1%.

The growing share of China and India has been at the expense of some other traditional exporters, especially large ones, in the same subregion. In East and North-East Asia, the share of Japan in the subregion's total exports decreased substantially from 31.2% in 2005 to 21.3% in 2015, while the export shares of China and Macao, China increased from 27.7% and 2.7% to 38.5% and 5.4%, respectively. The other countries in East and North-East Asia maintained the same export shares. In South and South-West Asia, the rising share of India, from 58.2% to 68.3% of the subregion's exports, was mainly the result of a decrease in the export shares of Turkey (30.9% to 20.2%). The combined export share of the subregion's least developed countries (Afghanistan, Bangladesh, Bhutan and Nepal) as well as Maldives accounted for 3%.

Similar to trade in goods, large economies dominated subregional service trade performance in the Pacific as well. In 2015, Australia and New Zealand accounted for approximately 97% of the total exports and imports of the subregion's commercial services trade. While the Russian Federation contributed 76.2% of the exports from North and Central Asia, the remaining two subregions, South-East Asia, and East and North-East Asia had a more even distribution among their economies. In South-East Asia, the largest contributor of exports of services was Singapore (46.4%).

C. DIVERGENT PERFORMANCE ACROSS SERVICE SUBSECTORS

For the purposes of statistical monitoring, commercial services trade is divided into four broad categories: (a) transport; (b) travel; (c) other commercial services;[8] and (d) goods-related services.[9] To identify changes in sectoral performance and repositioning of these services categories, it is necessary to observe their trade flows for longer than a year or two. However, because the above classification is still in the process of implementation by a number of countries, statistics shown under a "new" category of goods-related services are estimates that are considered preliminary and should be considered with caution. Furthermore, while it is possible to analyse the first three categories over a longer period, goods-related services statistics is available only for more recent years.

Taken as an aggregate, over the past decade, services trade performance in the Asia-Pacific region was robust in contrast to its weak performance in 2015 (and, partly, in 2016). Asia and the Pacific performed better than the world average in all major categories of commercial services (figure 2.5). Historically, the strong export-growth performance was driven in particular by other commercial services and travel services. From 2005 to 2015, the region's exports of travel services and other commercial services grew on average by 11% per year.

Figure 2.5 **Average export-growth rate, by subsector, 2005-2015, Asia-Pacific region compared with the rest of the world**

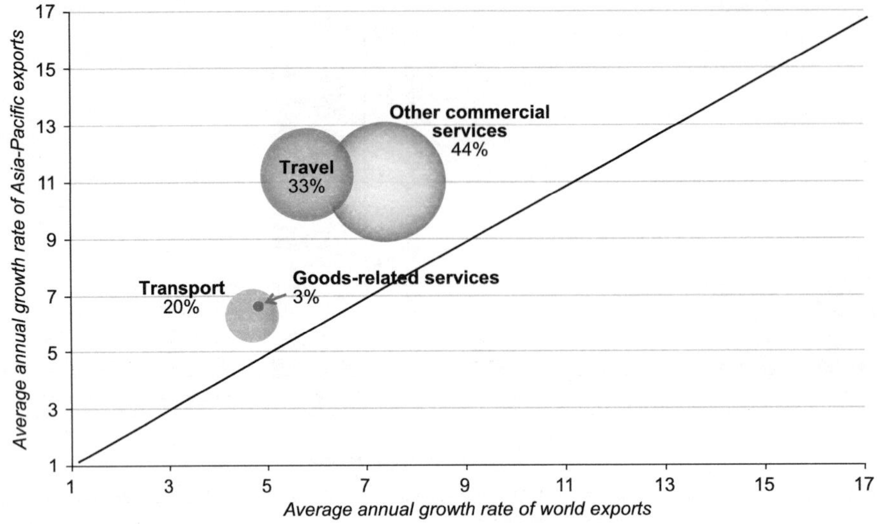

Sources: ESCAP calculation based on available data from WTO International Trade Statistics Database. Data on individual economies are available online from the ESCAP statistical database.

Note: A geometric average is used. The size of the bubbles represents the share of the respective service sector in Asia-Pacific total exports of commercial services in 2015. The equal growth rate between exports by the world and the Asia-Pacific region is represented by the diagonal, so the figure shows that export growth of the Asia-Pacific region was higher than that of the world.

During that period, the strong expansion of intraregional demand for imports from China was a key factor in this growth. Concerning the global exports, the region's share of travel services went up from 24% in 2005 to 37% in 2015. Similarly, the region captured an increased share of global exports of other commercial services, growing from 19% to 24% during the same period. In the case of transport services, the region's exports grew by 6% per year, almost two percentage points higher than the world average. The region's average export growth of goods-related services (seen as linked to the participation in global value chains) was about 7% per year, which was higher than the regional growth of goods export of about 5% during that period.

Imports of travel services by the region grew much faster than the world average, while the region's imports of other commercial services lagged slightly. The Asia-Pacific growth in imports of travel services was 14% annually on average from 2005 to 2015, compared with less than 7% for the world. The regional imports driver is found in the rising travel demand from China (see section D for more details). As a result, the region doubled its share of global imports of travel services, from 20% in 2005 to 39% in 2015. In contrast, the region's average import growth of other commercial services was around 4% per year while the average global import growth of these services was 7% per year. In the case of transport services, the region's imports grew by approximately 7% per year, slightly higher than the world average. The goods-related services category captured only 2% of commercial services imports by the region.

> *"Asia and the Pacific performed especially strongly in travel services as well as other commercial services exports, which were dominated by business services."*

As mentioned above, the new category of goods-related services has not been recorded properly in a number of countries, including relatively large service exporters and importers of the region such as New Zealand or Thailand.[10] The goods-related services cover maintenance and repairs, processing, assembly, labelling and packing, and as such focuses on a relatively narrow segment of service activity. First, this has made the share of goods-related services very small in most of the reporting countries, at about 2% to 3% of all commercial services trade, and second, the trade is concentrated on a handful of countries. In fact, 15 countries account for 95%-96% of total goods-related services exports and imports; with the European Union having a stake of more than 45% (WTO, 2016). On the export side, China held third place while another six regional economies were included in the top 15 globally, including one least developed country (Myanmar). On the import side, 10 out of the top 15 importers were from Asia (WTO, 2016).

However, cross-country comparisons reveal that for the top Asian exporter, China, goods-related services exports represented 8% of the country's commercial services exports in 2015 while accounting for only 0.3% of the country's commercial services imports. China was ranked eighth out of the top 15 importers and accounted for only 1.5% of total global goods-related services imports. This is in contrast to the findings for Hong Kong, China, where goods-related services imports accounted for 15% of services imports and only 0.3% of the services exports. Hong Kong, China was also second among the top 15 importers and did not even feature among the top 15 exporters. This divergent pattern between the two economies clearly reflects the position of China as an assembly centre for manufacturing products that are then exported to Hong Kong, China for packaging and re-export.

Box 2.1 **Least developed countries of Asia and the Pacific and commercial services trade**

Commercial services have been shown to have an important positive effect on development of industrial exports, economic efficiency and diversification (APTIR, 2015 and earlier issues). However, the share of services trade in total trade of least developed countries continues to be negligible. Several factors are involved here, most of which are related to the level of these countries' development, reinforcing a vicious circle. For example, poor infrastructure and a lack of skilled labour prevent the establishment and expansion of many technology and knowledge-intensive services; in turn, a lack of such services impairs the industrial and development prospects of a country. A similar impact comes from the lack of financial resources or inappropriateness of a regulatory regime. Furthermore, these economies are categorized by high share of informal activities, especially in this sector. Finally, lack of statistical capacity plays an important role too. Most least developed countries have lower statistical capacities to measure trade in commercial services, which are increasingly difficult to measure not only because of new international classification but because of the impact of digital trade as well. Hence their low share in commercial services trade is at least partly attributed to their difficulties in capturing all the services trade.

In the past decade, the share of least developed countries in world exports of commercial services doubled from 0.4% in 2005 to 0.8% in 2015 while on the import side the share rose from 1% to 1.6% (WTO, 2016). At the same time, the services trade of least developed countries grew on average much faster than for the rest of the world. According to WTO (2016), during 2005-2015, commercial services exports grew by 14% and imports by 11%, more than twice the rate of the rest of the world.

This growth was fuelled by only a few least developed countries and in a limited number of sectors. Most notably, in 2015 Asia-Pacific least developed countries contributed 36% of the exports by the whole group of least developed countries. Two Asian least developed countries with extraordinary growth in tourism, i.e. Cambodia and, in more recent years, Myanmar, have been largely driving the overall services export growth of the group of least developed countries. Furthermore, Bangladesh has become an emerging exporter of information and communications services, and it is seen as an attractive information technology (IT) and business processing outsourcing location (WTO, 2016). The country has emerged as a hub for freelance IT services, including simple data entry to more complex IT services, via online sites.

Overall, in 2015, least developed countries in the Asia-Pacific region exported commercial services worth $13 billion, with Myanmar being the largest services exporter in the group with a share of 32%, followed by Cambodia at 30%. While tourism plays an important role in both countries, Myanmar services exports are more balanced across four services categories. Particularly notable is Myanmar's export of goods-related services with an above-average share, even from the perspective of more advanced developing country exporters.[a]

Globally, the least developed countries are net importers of commercial services, and recently their services trade deficit widened to reach $39 billion in 2015, up from $16.3 billion in 2005. Services categories record a very different balance. The transport sector and "other commercial services" sectors have experienced persistent trade deficits. In contrast, travel (tourism) has recorded an expanding surplus since 2005. Tourism is also the leading services sector in island least developed countries, accounting for more than 80% of total services exports by in some of them (see table next page).

Box 2.1 *continued*

Table. Exports of commercial services of the least developed countries, by category, 2015

(Millions of United States dollars and percentage)

	Value of exports	Share in commercial services							
		Goods-related services		Transport		Travel		Other com. services	
Country	2015	2010	2015	2010	2015	2010	2015	2010	2015
Afghanistan	799	...	0	10.1	4.5	4.2	13.2	85.7	82.3
Bangladesh	1 684	3	4.6*	14.2	24.2*	6.6	9.4*	76.2	61.8*
Bhutan	122	...	...	35.3	21.4	60	75.7	4.6	2.8
Cambodia	3 775	...	...	13.8	11.8	79.2	82.9	7	5.2
Kiribati	11*	...	...	17.1	10.3	37.3	26.5*	45.2	63.3*
Lao People's Democratic Republic	790	...	...	11.4	...	78.1	...	10.5	...
Myanmar	4 127*	17.2	28.4*	43.9	5.5*	21.3	39.1*	17.6	27*
Nepal	1 139	...	...	6.8	...	59	47	34.2	...
Solomon Islands	95	...	0	36	27.5	48.7	49.7	15.4	22.9
Timor-Leste	57	...	...	2.6	2.7	78.1	89.4	19.3	7.9
Tuvalu	...	...	...	9.1	...	73.7	...	17.2	...
Vanuatu	295	...	...	11.6	14.1	80.1	80.4	8.3	5.5
Least developed countries total	36 000	0.5	3.7	19.5	20.8	50.2	52.6	29.8	22.8
World	4 754 000	3.6	3.2	21.5	18.4	25	25.9	49.9	52.5

Source: Table A13 in WTO (2016), p. 103.

Notes: * refers to 2014.

The improvement of the quality of data in recent years may have resulted in changes relating to the breakdown of exports of commercial services by category of services.

As a number of economies are currently in the process of implementing international recommendations on the compilation of goods-related services, these estimates are to be considered preliminary and should be taken with caution

a However, since the statistics for this category of services are still under development, all reports of goods-related services exports and imports should be considered with caution.

1. Changing composition of commercial service trade

While the region's total exports of commercial services increased more than twofold between 2005 and 2015 (figure 2.6), the share of other commercial services, dominated by business services, increased from 38% to 44% while the share of travel services climbed from 28% to 33%. The relatively faster growth of other subsectors has put pressure on transport services the demand for which has been threatened by the global trade slowdown during the recent past. The share of transport services thus declined from 29% to 20% between 2005 and 2015.

Commercial services imports increased at a slower rate than their exports in the observed period, (128% in total). Travel services have been a major import growth driver. The share of travel in imported services doubled from 16% in 2005 to 33% in 2015. In contrast to developments in the composition of exports (discussed above), the share of travel services grew much faster on the import side[11] and ended up squeezing out the "other commercial services", which declined from 60% in 2005 to 40% in 2015. In addition, the largest component of "other commercial services" imports shifted from insurance and pension services to business services in the same period.

2. Trends within the other commercial services category

Given the dynamic growth of other commercial services, and its importance to the rest of the economy and trade (as discussed in APTIR 2014 and 2015) a detailed analysis of the components of this services category is made here. The breakdown of the exports and imports of other commercial services into seven subcategories is shown in tables 2.1 and 2.2. First, the changes in other commercial services exports are discussed. From 2005 to 2015, exports by this sector increased more than twofold from $235 billion to $609 billion. The Asia-Pacific region increased its overall share in global exports

Figure 2.6 Commercial services trade of the Asia-Pacific region, by sector, 2005 and 2015

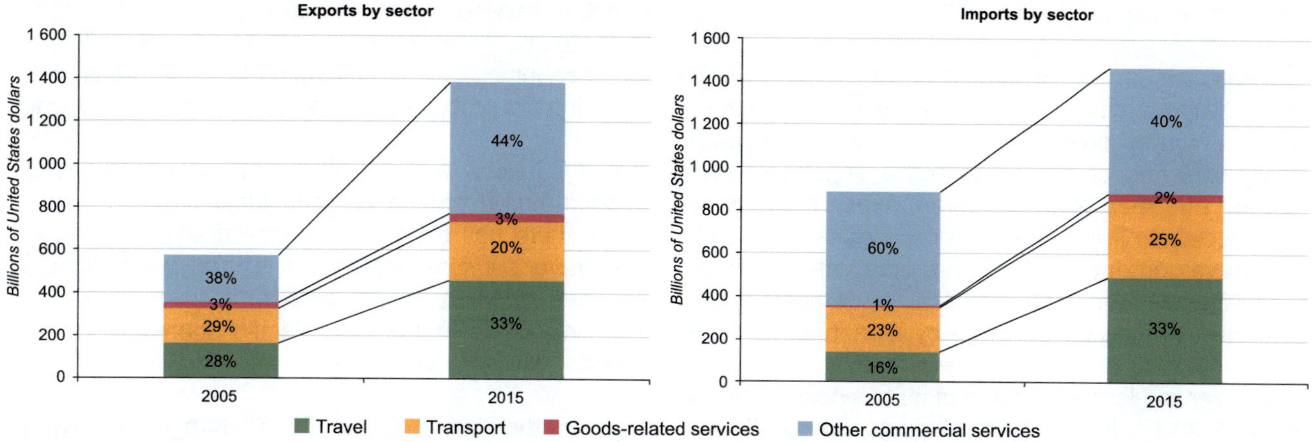

Sources: ESCAP calculation based on available data from WTO International Trade Statistics Database (accessed June 2016). Data on individual economies are available online from the ESCAP statistical database.

Table 2.1 Commercial services and other commercial services exports breakdown

Services category	Export value (billions of United States dollars)		Growth in Asia-Pacific exports (%)		Share in Asia-Pacific exports (%)		Asia-Pacific share in world exports (%)	
	2005	2015	2014	2015	2005	2015	2005	2015
Goods-related	19	39	-2.0	-0.01	3.5	2.9	22.1	25.7
Transport	141	256	-0.2	-2.8	25.9	18.9	24.3	29.2
Travel	150	449	3.5	13.5	27.5	33.2	21.8	36.5
Other commercial services	235	609	10.2	-4.5	43.1	45.0	18.9	24.4
• Other business services	123	279	9.8	-12.4	22.6	20.6	23.4	26.6
• Telecommunications, computer and information services	32	113	8.1	2.0	5.9	8.4	16.1	23.7
• Financial services	23	67	11.4	0.6	4.2	5.0	10.5	16.1
• Charges for the use of intellectual property, n.i.e.	22	51	14.9	-0.8	4.0	3.8	13.5	17.0
• Construction	23	51	6.9	-15.6	4.2	3.8	48.8	57.2
• Insurance and pension services	6	19	20.8	-3.5	1.1	1.4	9.8	14.9
• Personal, cultural, and recreational services	5	8	17.8	-5.5	0.9	0.6	19.7	20.6

Source: ESCAP calculation based on WTO International Trade Statistics Database.

Table 2.2 Commercial services and other commercial services imports breakdown

Services category	Import value (billions of United States dollars)		Growth in Asia-Pacific imports (%)		Share in Asia-Pacific imports (%)		Asia-Pacific share in world imports (%)	
	2005	2015	2014	2015	2005	2015	2005	2015
Goods-related	9	33	1.9	-12.5	1.6	2.3	13.8	33.7
Transport	184	327	2.6	-16.0	33.0	23.1	27.1	30.0
Travel	133	475	33.4	8.6	23.8	33.5	20.4	39.1
Other commercial services	232	583	5.7	-10.0	41.6	41.1	20.9	26.4
• Other business services	17	286	6.4	-13.1	3.0	20.2	23.1	27.3
• Telecommunications, computer, and information services	21	55	25.3	-6.0	3.8	3.9	7	11.6
• Financial services	9	32	5.4	-12.8	1.6	2.3	4.4	7.6
• Charges for the use of intellectual property n.i.e.	44	93	2.9	-13.1	7.9	6.6	26.4	31.2
• Construction	14	39	3.4	-9.0	2.5	2.8	37.8	43.0
• Insurance and pension services	120	39	-3.0	-30.8	21.5	2.8	31.5	31.4
• Personal, cultural, and recreational services	5	10	10.0	-1.3	0.9	0.7	21.6	25.5

Source: ESCAP calculation based on WTO International Trade Statistics Database.

of other commercial services from 18.9% to 24.4%. In terms of subsectors, it still claims half of all global construction services exports.

However, this is not the largest or the most dynamic sector when it comes to importance to the region's exports. Other business services, while growing slowly in terms of value, still make up almost one half of the Asia-Pacific region exports of other commercial services. This category includes research and development, professional and management consulting services, and technical, trade-related and other business services. Rising by an annual average of around 10% since 2005, the share of developing economies in global exports of other business services reached 29.1% in 2015. Developing Asia continued to play the main role at 22.9%, with exports from India and China alone accounting for 10.2% of world exports. These two economies ranked first and second as preferred offshoring services locations. India's exports to foreign clients included a wide range of services, such as finance and accounting, auditing, book keeping and tax consulting services, customer services, medical transcriptions and various types of engineering services (embedded solutions, product design, industrial automation and enterprise asset management). Other Asian economies play a key role in business process outsourcing. The Philippines, for example, has specialized in call centres but it has also expanded into higher value-added services. Its exports of other business services increased by 15% in 2015 (WTO, 2016).

Telecommunications, computer and information services, while not the largest, are among the most dynamic export sectors. The rapidly growing exports of these services have resulted in the Asia-Pacific region gaining a significant increase in its share of global exports, from 16.1% in 2005 to 23.7% in 2015.

The region also gained a rising market share in world exports of finance and insurance services. The Asia-Pacific region's share in global exports of those categories increased by almost 5 percentage points to reach 16.1% and 14.9% in 2015, respectively. Export income from royalties and license charges for the use of intellectual property doubled, which translates into an increase of approximately 3 percentage points of the Asia-Pacific share in global exports. In terms of exports of personal, cultural and recreational services,[12] the region has maintained its share of global exports, which was slightly higher than 20% in 2015.

Despite overall growth, the share of developing economies in exports of commercial services continues to lag behind in higher-skilled services, such as charges for the use of intellectual property, or insurance and pension services, and financial services. The lack of adequate high-skill labour points to the difficulty these countries face in competing in these areas, and resolving this problem is crucial to national development.

Travel services was also the only sector reporting positive import growth in 2015 (table 2.2). Yet, since 2005, there has been a dramatic development in not only travel services imports but also in goods-related services imports, which account for approximately 20% increases in the Asia-Pacific shares of global imports of both categories.

Despite the fact that the 2015 changes in every subcategory of other commercial services imports were negative, their growth over the past decade has been robust, with the total imports by this sector increasing by more than twofold from $232 billion in 2005 to $583 billion in 2015. The Asia-Pacific region increased its share of global imports of all other commercial services from 20.9% to 26.4% during that period. In terms of subsectors, it claims 43% of all global construction services imports. Other business services, the subcategory in other commercial services that showed the most dynamic growth of imports from 2005, comprise 20% of the region's imports of commercial services. Telecommunications, computer and information services imports increased more than double in terms of value, and gaining an increased share of global imports, from 7% in 2005 to 11.6% in 2015.

D. INTERNATIONAL TOURISM IN ASIA AND THE PACIFIC

The 278 million international tourist arrivals to Asia and the Pacific recorded in 2015 captured 26.5% of global tourist arrivals.[13] The largest share of those tourist arrivals was gained by East and North-East Asia (40.2%), followed by South-East Asia (29.5%), North and Central Asia (10%), South and South-West Asia (16.4%) and the Pacific (4%). Most Asia-Pacific subregions have been net exporters of tourism services since 2006. The tourism-trade surplus is particularly high in South-East Asia as well as South and South-West Asia. Although East and North-East Asia is the only Asia-Pacific subregion with a trade balance in tourism services it is, in fact, the largest exporter and importer of tourism services with shares of 44.3% and 56.3%, respectively, of the region's total exports and imports, respectively, based on 2014 data on tourist receipts and expenditures.

> *"Although the number of tourist arrivals in Asia and the Pacific continues to grow, spending by tourists has declined."*

However, the recent decline of tourism receipts has put the net export position of Asia-Pacific tourism services at risk. Followed the persistent slowdown of the global economy and, more recently, China's economic rebalancing, there is a clear sign that tourists coming to the region are spending less in total. In 2015, while the numbers of tourist arrivals were still growing at 5.4%, the region's total tourism receipts fell by 1.6% (figure 2.7). Among the Asia-Pacific subregions, North and Central Asia faced the

Figure 2.7 International tourist receipts and expenditures in Asia and the Pacific, by subregion, 2005-2015

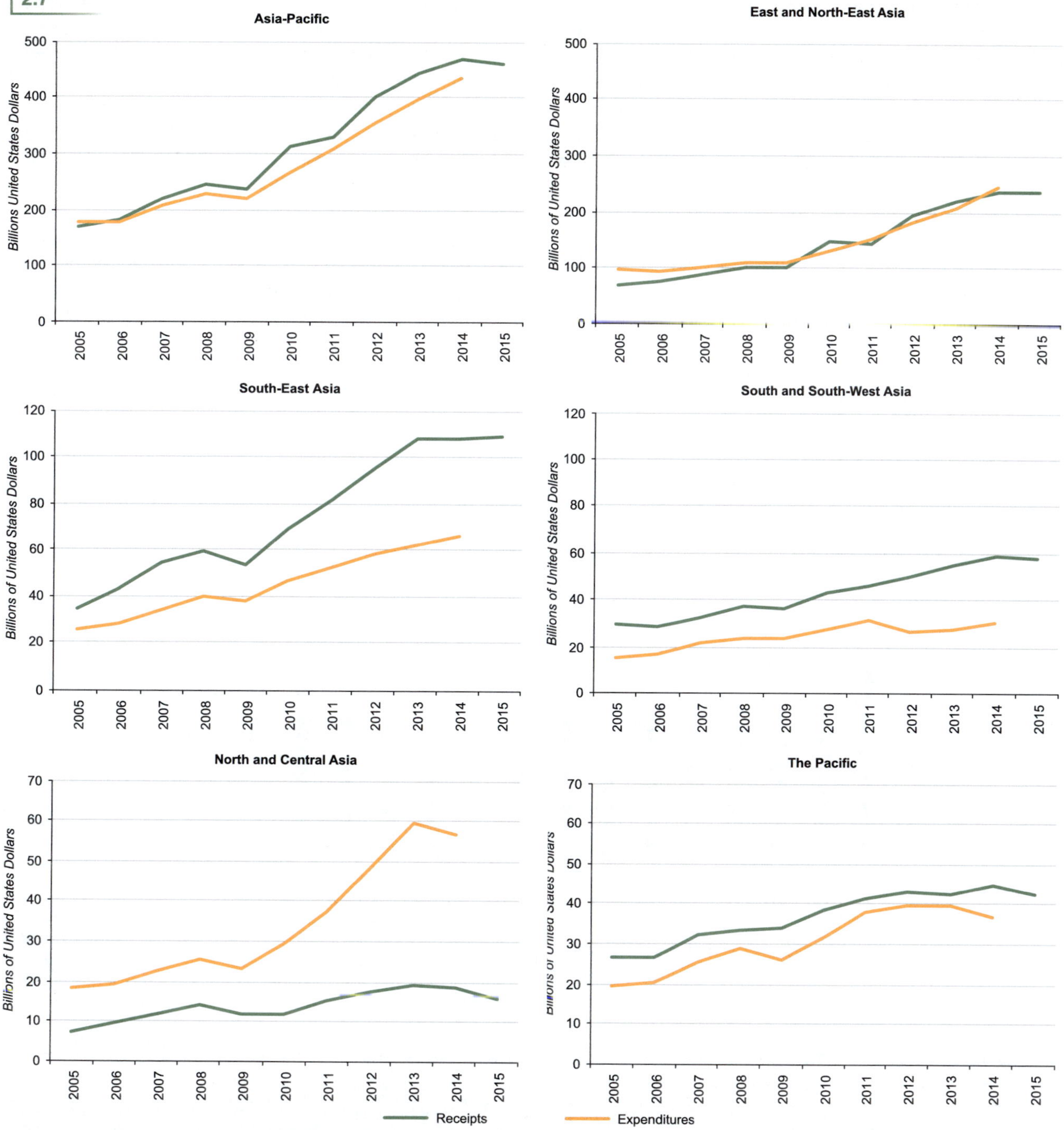

Sources: WTO, World Bank database (most recently accessed on 14 June 2016).

Note: Data on international tourist expenditures in 2015 have not been reported at the time of report preparation. Data on tourism receipts in 2015 are not available for Afghanistan, Bangladesh, Iran, Brunei Darussalam, Lao People's Democratic Republic, Myanmar, Tonga, Tuvalu, Cook Islands, French Polynesia, Kiribati, Marshall Islands, Federated States of Micronesia New Caledonia, Palau, Papua New Guinea and Vanuatu.

largest drop in tourism receipts (16.6%), followed by the Pacific (5.3%).

In 2016, the region made a promising start by leading all other regions with an 8.3% growth rate in tourist arrivals during the first few months.[14] It remains to be seen whether the region will be able to maintain such dynamic growth through the remainder of the year, given that the economic slowdown in China and the Russian Federation – which have been major intraregional sources of tourist arrivals with the share of 16% and 9% of total inbound flows in the region in 2015 – persists. However, it is likely that intraregional demand for tourism services will soften during the rest of the year. According to the United Nations World Tourism Organization (UNWTO), projections for tourist arrivals at Asia-Pacific destinations remain generally positive at between 4% and 5%. Although China, the major source of tourism income for various Asia-Pacific destinations, is expected to maintain double-digit growth of its outbound tourism, it could be capped by the country's sluggish economic recovery in 2016.

Nine out of 10 most popular tourist destinations were found to be in two subregions of East and North-East Asia, and South-East Asia (table 2.3).[15] China was the most popular tourist destination in Asia and the Pacific, accounting for approximately 20% of international tourist arrivals in the region in 2015. However, China's share of major tourist destinations in the region has been decreasing since the post-financial crisis period of 2008-2009; in the meantime, its share of tourist arrivals has been increasing. This could be a reflection of China's shifting role from that of being a main destination for tourists to becoming a major source of tourists visiting other countries in Asia and the Pacific (particularly Japan and Thailand). According to UNWTO, Chinese outbound tourists based on departures increased 10% in 2015. Since 2013, China has become the most important source of tourists in the region, with a 29% share in 2014, instead of Hong Kong, China.

In general, international tourists visiting East and North-East Asia grew 4.3% in 2015, a significant decline from 7.3% in 2014. A major factor was the reduction of tourists visiting Hong Kong, China (-3.9%), Macao, China (-1.8%) and the Republic of Korea (-6.8%). These economies together comprised a 38% share of the subregion. In contrast, Japan experienced a significant

Figure 2.8 **Growth and projection of international tourist arrivals**

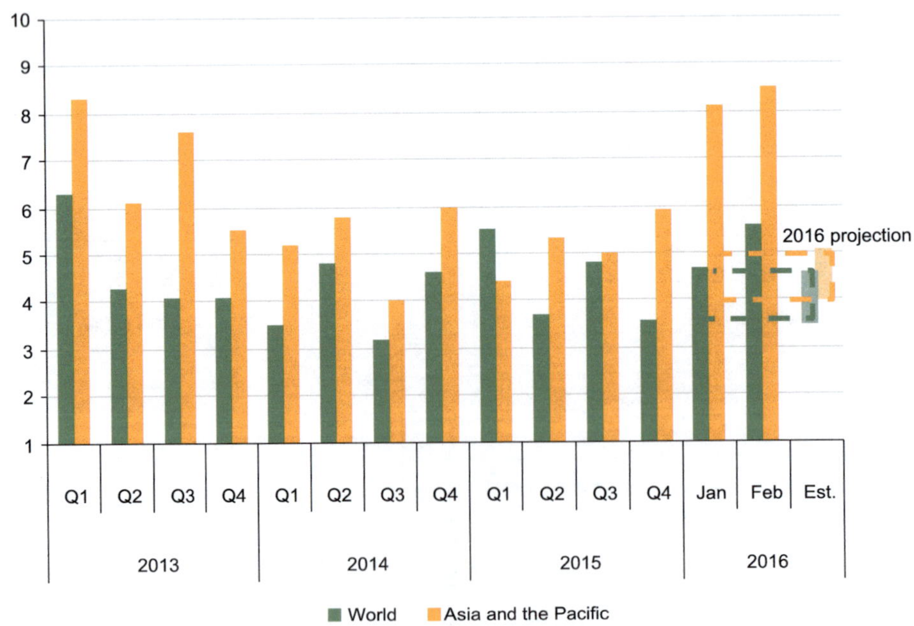

Sources: UNWTO (2016), as of 12 June 2016.

Note: Number estimated by UNWTO under its classification of Asia-Pacific countries, excluding North and Central Asia.

According to the UNWTO classification, Asia and the Pacific includes four subregions: (a) North-East Asia (China; Japan; Republic of Korea; Mongolia; Hong Kong, China; Macao, China; and Taiwan Province of China); (b) South-East Asia (Brunei Darussalam, Cambodia, Indonesia, Lao People's Democratic Republic; Malaysia; Myanmar; Philippines; Singapore; Thailand; Timor-Leste; and Viet Nam); (c) Oceania (Australia; Fiji; French Polynesia; Guam; Kiribati; Marshall Islands; Federated States of Micronesia; New Zealand; Niue; Palau; Papua New Guinea; Samoa; Solomon Islands; Tonga; Tuvalu; Vanuatu; American Samoa; Cook Islands; New Caledonia; and the Northern Mariana Islands); and (d) South Asia (Bangladesh; Bhutan; India; and the Islamic Republic of Iran). The current analysis is based on a limited selection of countries, with no reports of 2016 data yet for various key destinations around the world including the Russian Federation and Malaysia.

Table 2.3 **Major tourist destinations in the Asia-Pacific region**

(Percentage of tourist arrivals in the Asia-Pacific region)

	2008	2009	2010	2011	2012	2013	2014	2015
China	28.8	28.1	27.1	26.3	24.7	22.3	21.0	20.4
Russian Federation	11.7	10.7	9.9	10.4	11.0	11.4	11.3	11.3
Thailand	7.9	7.8	7.8	8.8	9.6	10.7	9.4	10.7
Hong Kong, China	9.4	9.3	9.8	10.2	10.2	10.3	10.5	9.6
Malaysia	12.0	13.0	12.0	11.3	10.7	10.3	10.4	9.2
Japan	4.5	3.7	4.2	2.8	3.6	4.1	5.1	7.1
Macao, China	5.8	5.7	5.8	5.9	5.8	5.7	5.5	5.1
Republic of Korea	3.7	4.3	4.3	4.5	4.8	4.9	5.4	4.7
Singapore	4.2	4.1	4.5	4.8	4.8	4.8	4.5	4.3
Taiwan Province of China	2.1	2.4	2.7	2.8	3.1	3.2	3.7	3.7
Other Asia-Pacific economies	9.8	10.7	11.9	12.2	11.8	12.4	13.2	13.8

Source: ESCAP's estimation based on country data from UNWTO database, 2016.

expansion of tourist arrivals (47%), followed by Taiwan Province of China (5.3%) and China (2.3%) (figure 2.9). The depreciation of the yen and the easing of visa requirements have boosted the dynamic growth of international tourist arrivals to Japan. According to Otake (2016), for Japan 2015 was the first time in 45 years that the number of inbound tourists surpassed that of outbound tourists. For the South-East Asia, growth picked up dramatically to 7.2% in 2015. This increase was mainly driven by the robust growth of Thailand (21.4%), which holds the largest share of tourism in the region, while emerging destinations such as Myanmar still registered dynamic growth of 51.9%. Thai tourism bounced back to high growth in 2015 mainly because of an influx of Chinese tourists and the support of the Thai Ministry of Tourism with campaigns such as "Discover Thainess" and the promotion of second-tier cities and local cultures as well as traditions as well as ensuring tourist safety, reducing illegal tourist businesses and encouraging intraregional tourism, particularly with neighbouring countries (Ngamsangchaikit, 2015).

For other subregions, tourist arrivals have tended to concentrate in the hub economy of the respective subregions. In South and South-West Asia, India attracted 69.2% of tourists travelling to the subregion (with the exclusion of Turkey) in 2015. In North and Central Asia, the Russian Federation was the dominant destination with an 89% share of total tourist arrivals in the subregion. Similarly, in 2015, 52.4% of the tourist arrivals in the Pacific came from Australia. Those key destinations experienced moderate growth rates of between 4.4% and 8.2% in 2015. However, small economies such as Sri Lanka and Palau recorded a relatively dynamic growth of inbound tourism in 2015, with growth rates of 17.8% and 15%, respectively.

Figure 2.9 **Growth of tourist arrivals, by Asia-Pacific subregion and selected economy, 2015**

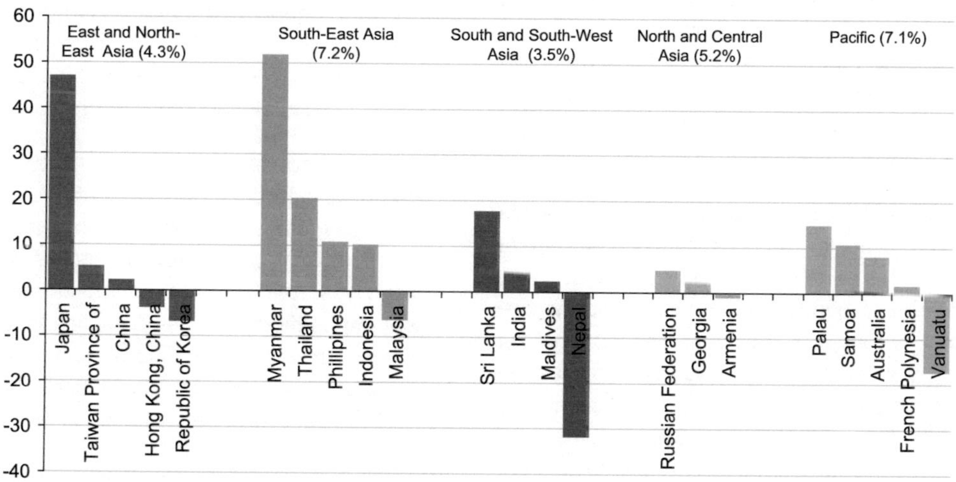

Sources: UNWTO (2016) as of 12 June 2016.

E. CONCLUSION

The performance of the Asia-Pacific region's commercial services sector, following the global trend, dropped dramatically in 2015 compared with the previous year due to the global economic slowdown and global uncertainty. Export growth declined from 5.1% in 2014 to -4.5% in 2015, while import growth fell from 6.1% to -4.9% during the same period. However, the Asia-Pacific region maintained its share of global exports and imports (29.2% and 32.8%, respectively). Trade in Asia and the Pacific commercial services was dominated by a small number of countries, especially China, Japan, India and Singapore, that represented more than half of the region's trade. Specifically, business and travel services together accounted for about 53.4% of total commercial services exports. However, the continuation of China's economic slowdown together with global trade stagnation continue to create gloomy prospects for services exports in 2016 and beyond, especially in the tourism sector.

Endnotes

1 APTIR 2015 summarized the ongoing adjustments to collection and recording of international trade statistics to improve a capture of trade in services. The current classification used by UNCTAD and WTO as well as UN Service Trade Data Collection, aggregates the commercial services flows into four major categories (transport, travel, other commercial services, and goods-related services). These categories capture only trade realized through limited modes of supply defined in the General Agreement on Trade in Services (GATS), mostly through Modes 1 (cross border supply) and 2 (consumption abroad). Mode 3, also known as commercial presence, in principle is captured by so-called Foreign Affiliates Statistics (FATS), which are available only for a limited number of countries and only for recent years; thus, such services flows are not provided in this report. (for further details see http://unstats.un.org/unsd/tradekb/Knowledgebase/50667/UN-ServiceTrade-Data-Collection).

2 The commercial services category in this report is defined as being equal to services minus government services, n.i.e. The commercial services category is further subdivided into goods-related services, transport, travel and other commercial services. The commercial services and their subcategories in this report are based on the newly-available classification in the sixth edition of the *Balance of Payments and International Investment Position Manual* (BPM6), published by IMF. Due to different editions of BPM being used, the numbers presented in the Asia-Pacific Trade and Investment Report 2016 may differ from those presented in the previous volumes of APTIR. In order to deal with the lack of data on trade in commercial services in many economies in Asia and the Pacific, the analysis in this chapter uses data compiled from different sources, including mirror data. Data presented in this chapter are mainly sourced from data released by the WTO International Trade Statistics Database during the preparation of this report.

3 Data related to Asia and the Pacific in this chapter include Asia-Pacific members of ESCAP as well as Taiwan Province of China, which is not a member of United Nations and ESCAP. Taiwan Province of China has been added to the data for the East and North-East Asia subregion.

4 https://www.wto.org/english/res_e/statis_e/daily_update_e/qrtly_comm_serv_web_e.xls.

5 Countries with no reported quarterly 2016 data on trade growth of commercial services are: Afghanistan, Bhutan, Cambodia, Fiji, Islamic of Iran, Kiribati, Kyrgyzstan, Democratic People's Republic of Korea, Lao People's Democratic Republic, Myanmar, Maldives, Marshall Islands, Federated States of Micronesia, Nauru, Palau, Papua New Guinea, Samoa, Solomon Islands, Tajikistan, Turkmenistan, Tuvalu, Uzbekistan and Vanuatu.

6 China has always been the largest service exporter in Asia and the Pacific. In 2015, China's share of services exports in the region was approximately 20%, which was about nine percentage points higher than those of Japan and India in the region.

7 See notes below on the classification of commercial services.

8 Other commercial services comprise the following subcategories: construction; insurance and pension services; financial services; charges for the use of intellectual property, n.i.e.; telecommunications; computer and information services; other business services; and personal, cultural and recreational services.

9 Goods-related services include manufacturing services using physical inputs owned by others, and maintenance and repair services that are not included elsewhere. According to WTO (2016), a number of economies are currently in the process of implementing international recommendations on the compilation of goods-related services, and statistics shown under this category are estimates that are considered preliminary and should therefore be considered with caution.

10 A number of countries are still not reporting goods-related services as a separate item. In 2015, countries that

reported exports in commercial services in BPM6, but not exports in goods-related services, included: Bangladesh; Bhutan; Brunei Darussalam; Cambodia; Kyrgyzstan; Lao People's Democratic Republic; Maldives; Nepal; New Zealand; Papua New Guinea; Solomon Islands; Sri Lanka; Timor-Leste; Thailand; Tonga; Vanuatu; Viet Nam; and Macao, China. For the countries that reported this service item, the service category represented only a marginal share in total exports and imports of commercial services, in many cases less than 1%.

[11] This could be in line with the growing purchasing power of the region's middle class, many of whom now travel and shop abroad.

[12] According to the IMF definition, personal, cultural, and recreational services involving transactions between residents and non-residents are subdivided into two categories: (a) audio-visual and related services; and (b) other cultural and recreational services. The first category comprises services and associated fees related to the production of motion pictures (film or video tape), radio and television programmes (live or on tape), and musical recordings. Included are: receipts or payments for rentals; fees received by resident actors, directors, producers etc. (or by non-residents in the compiling economy) for productions abroad; and fees for distribution rights sold to the media for a limited number of showings in specified areas. Fees to actors, producers etc. involved with theatrical and musical productions, sporting events, circuses etc., and fees for distribution rights (for television, radio etc.) for these activities are included. The second category comprises other personal, cultural, and recreational services such as those associated with museums, libraries, archives and other cultural, sporting and recreational activities. Also included are fees for services, including provision of correspondence courses, rendered abroad by teachers or doctors.

[13] Countries with no 2015 data reports of international tourist arrivals are: Turkey, New Zealand, Bangladesh, Iran, Bhutan, Pakistan, Timor-Leste, Kiribati, Marshall Islands, Federated States of Micronesia, Niue, Papua New Guinea, Tuvalu, Azerbaijan, Kazakhstan, Kyrgyzstan and Uzbekistan.

[14] The analysis of Asia-Pacific tourism in 2016 is based on the limited number of countries reporting to UNWTO in May 2016. This excludes various key economies including the Russian Federation and Malaysia. Data at the time of report preparation are available only for the first few months of the year, which, for many countries, are low-season months, with some 80 million arrivals a month worldwide, and are often not representative of the full-year trend.

[15] The Russian Federation is the only country that is not in these subregions.

REFERENCES

Economic and Social Commission for Asia and the Pacific. *Asia-Pacific Trade and Investment Report*, various issues. Available from www.unescap.org/publications/asia-pacific-trade-investment-report

Ngamsangchaikit, W. (2015). Thailand tourism makes gain. *TTR Weekly*, 7 May. Available from www.ttrweekly.com/site/2015/05/thailand-tourism-makes-gains/

Otake, T. (2016). Visitors to Japan surge to record 19.73 million, spend all-time high of ¥3.48 trillion. *Japan Times*, 19 January. Available from www.japantimes.co.jp/news/2016/01/19/national/japan-sets-new-inbound-tourism-record-2015-comes-just-short-20-million-target/#.V1-naxvVzct.

United Nations World Tourism Organization (2016). *World Tourism Barometer*, vol. 14. Madrid. Available from www.e-unwto.org/loi/wtobarometereng.

World Trade Organization (2016). *World Trade Statistical Review*. Available from https://www.wto.org/english/res_e/statis_e/wts2016_e/wts2016_e.pdf.

ONLINE DATABASES

Economic and Social Commission for Asia and the Pacific. ESCAP online statistical database. Available from www.unescap.org/stat/data/statdb/DataExplorer.aspx.

World Trade Organization. International Trade Statistics Database. Available from http://stat.wto.org/Home/WSDBHome.aspx?Language=

United Nations World Tourism Organization. UNWTO database. Available from www2.unwto.org/content/data-0

CHAPTER

3

FOREIGN DIRECT INVESTMENT MAKES A MODEST COME-BACK

A. OVERVIEW OF RECENT TRENDS IN FOREIGN DIRECT INVESTMENT

1. Global trends

Global foreign direct investment (FDI) inflows, at $1.76 trillion in 2015, reached their highest level since the financial crisis of 2008-2009. This amounted to a 38% increase compared with 2014. However, this rise in FDI was mainly attributed to a surge in cross-border mergers and acquisitions (M&A) that were, to a large extent, used for corporate reconfiguration including tax inversions.[1] After discounting for these flows, the increase in 2015 was about 15% (UNCTAD, 2016). The rise in FDI inflows was more prominent in developed economies, which received $962 billion in 2015, i.e. 84% more than in 2014. This is in contrast to the past three years, when developed economies experienced declining FDI inflows and a smaller share in global FDI flows. On the other hand, developing economies received $800 billion in 2015, a mere 5.9% increase, due to the continued decline in commodity prices, especially of crude oil, metals and minerals, which made investment in the primary sector less attractive (UNCTAD, 2016).

"The Asia-Pacific region recorded only a 5.6% increase in FDI inflow in 2015, resulting in a 10 percentage point fall in the region's share of global FDI inflows from its 2014 share of 42%."

2. Regional trends

The Asia-Pacific region continued to receive a significant amount of FDI inflows, totalling $559 billion in 2015, an increase of 5.6% over 2014 level. However, this increase paled in comparison to jump of global FDI inflows. Therefore, the region's share in global FDI inflows declined from 42% in 2014 to 32% in 2015 (figure 3.1).

The economies of the Asia-Pacific region have also contributed less to FDI outflows. The region invested $435 billion in 2015, a 22% decrease compared with the previous year (figure 3.2). The low level of investment to and from the region once again reflects the fragile global economy, volatility of global financial markets, and weak aggregate demand at the global and regional levels. In addition, the decrease in FDI outflows registered in 2015 may be attributable to a return to the "historical" average level of outflows – i.e. in 2013 and 2014 there was an unprecedented high

Figure 3.1 **FDI inflows to the Asia-Pacific region and their share in global FDI inflows, 2010-2015**

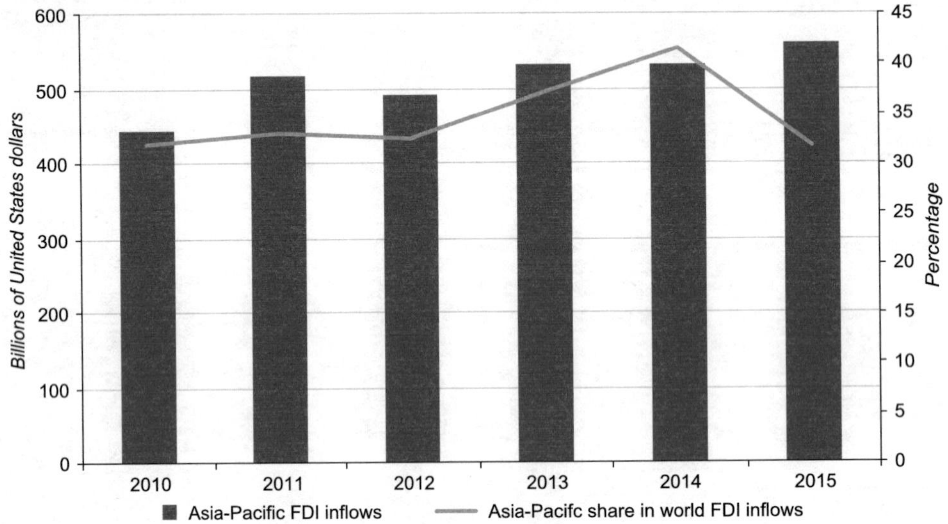

Sources: ESCAP calculation based on UNCTAD (2016).

Figure 3.2 **FDI outflows from the Asia-Pacific region and their share in global FDI outflows, 2010-2015**

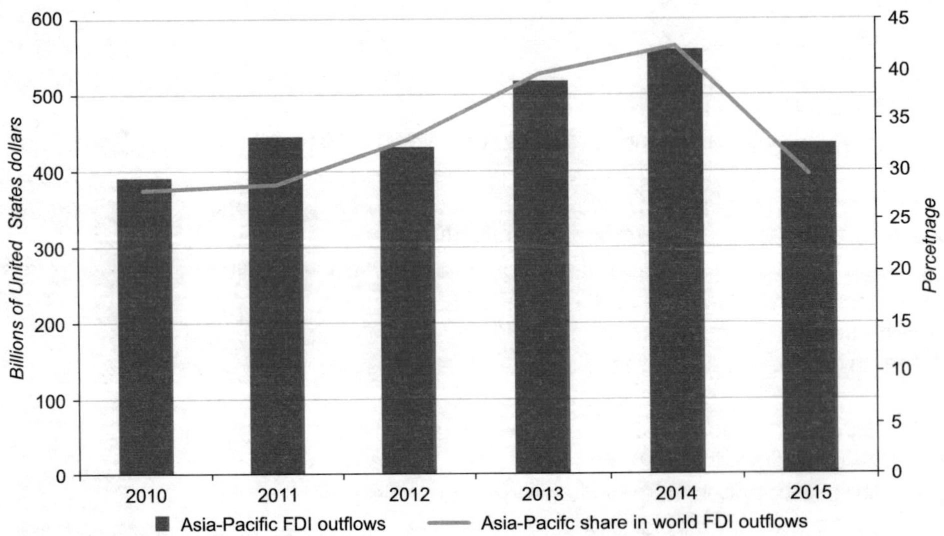

Sources: ESCAP calculation based on UNCTAD (2016).

increase in FDI outflows from the region, specifically from India and Hong Kong, China, which did not reoccur in 2015. The outflows in 2015 were thus close to the region's average recorded since the recovery after the financial crisis, ignoring the 2013 and 2014 outliers.

Greenfield FDI inflows to the Asia-Pacific region increased by 26% in 2015, which was a significantly higher growth when compared with that of global inflows, which increased by only 6%. The region received $352 billion in total greenfield FDI, which accounted for 40% of the global total. Greenfield FDI outflows from the Asia-Pacific region in 2015 also increased by 15% to $263 billion. Announced greenfield FDI data (figure 3.3) are considered as demonstrating the contribution of FDI to local economic growth, measured by capital expenditures using firm-level data (Investment Consulting Associates, 2016).

B. ASIA-PACIFIC SUBREGIONAL TRENDS

1. FDI inflows

Within the Asia-Pacific region, FDI inflows during 2013-2015 varied among the subregions and individual economies (figure 3.4).

Figure 3.3 Greenfield FDI flows in the Asia-Pacific region, 2010-2015

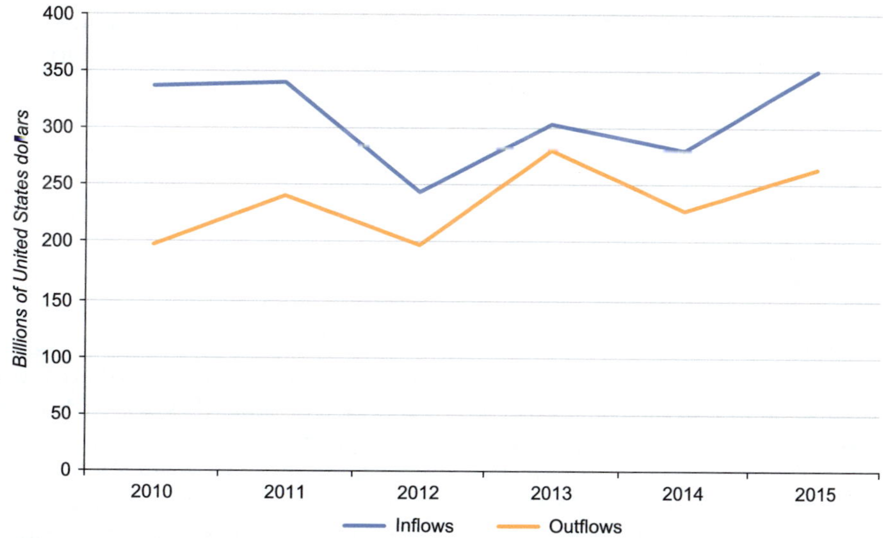

Sources: ESCAP calculation based on fDi Intelligence data, 2016.

Figure 3.4 FDI inflows to Asia-Pacific developing subregions and developed economies, 2013-2015

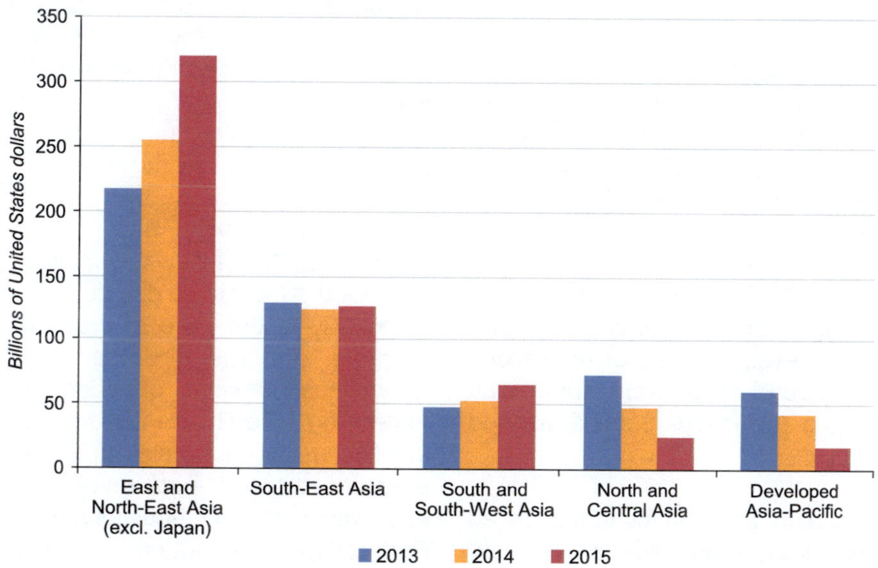

Sources: ESCAP calculation based on UNCTAD (2016).

Note: Due to the small share of outflows from the Pacific small island developing States, that subregion is not included in this figure.

(a) Developing East and North-East Asia

Developing East and North-East Asia showed a significant increase in the level of FDI inflows compared with 2014. A 53% increase in FDI inflows to Hong Kong, China was the primary reason. This increase was partly due to corporate reconfigurations. These reconfigurations could involve a large movement in the balance of payments but little change in actual operations. For example, in the restructuring of the conglomerate Cheung Kong Holdings and Hutchison Whampoa they became incorporated in the Cayman Islands, which led to a significant increase in FDI inflows into Hong Kong, China (UNCTAD, 2016).

In China, which accounts for more than 40% of the subregion, FDI inflows increased modestly in 2015 by 6% to $136 billion. The slowdown in FDI inflows is in line with that of China's economic growth. However, this moderate economic growth, which President Xi Jinping has called the "new normal", is perceived as being inevitable and in the long term more sustainable; similarly, the slowdown in FDI is considered to be inevitable to some extent (World Bank, 2015).

China is losing its significant edge in manufacturing in general and in labour-intensive production in particular, due to rising wages. The country is going through structural adjustments aimed at shifting from an export-led investment-driven growth model to a consumption-driven one, in order to expand the services sector in the economy (Drysdale, 2015a). As China is strategically moving away from manufacturing and labour-intensive production, these industries could experience decreased levels of FDI inflows. The intensity and direction of reforms could have an impact on the level and nature of FDI inflows in the coming years.

(b) South-East Asia

With almost no change in total FDI inflows to South-East Asia, Indonesia experienced a steep decline of 29% in FDI inflows in 2015 compared with 2014, while accounting for more than 10% of the FDI inflows of the subregion. One factor is that the Government of Indonesia implemented a ban on unprocessed exports of raw minerals, introduced by the Mineral and Cola Mining Law (2009) that came into force in 2014. Subsequently, in the first quarter of 2014, FDI fell significantly; however, a series of regulations relaxing the laws followed, which went some way to recovering FDI flows (Parisotto, Santibáñez and Heal, 2016).

FDI inflows to Thailand in 2015, in contrast, tripled compared with 2014, although the amount was still much lower than that recorded in 2012 and 2013. However, other small and low-income economies, including the Lao People's Democratic Republic, Myanmar and Viet Nam, all continued to perform well, with low labour and other production costs, and their Governments' push to liberalize and promote FDI. In 2015, FDI inflows to Myanmar almost doubled, while FDI inflows to the Lao People's Democratic Republic and Viet Nam were also significantly higher by 69% and 28%, respectively, compared with 2014.

(c) South and South-West Asia

The South and South-West Asia subregion received an increased level of FDI inflows, which mostly went to India, the biggest economy in the subregion. India received $44 billion in 2015, which was a 28% increase over 2014. India is certainly improving the environment for investment and regulatory settings. Under the Government's economy strategy, including "Make in India", India is pursuing a strategy of liberalizing investment restrictions further. Also, the Reserve Bank of India (RBI) has successfully kept inflation under 6%, lower than the historical average, which further contributed to investors' confidence in the country (*Economist,* 2016).

The increase in greenfield FDI inflows to India in 2015 was even more striking: they more than doubled in 2015, received the biggest flows after the financial crisis, and surpassed the inflows to China for the first time (Panda, 2016). However, there is still potential for India to perform even better.[2] In particular, improvement of the private investment environment, especially that of infrastructure, would position India for playing a much larger role in global and regional value chain production networks. In addition, there is scope to adopt more flexible labour laws and improve coordination between the central and state Governments and their investment promotion agencies (Drysdale, 2015b). Thanks to rising FDI in labour-intensive manufacturing, inflows to Bangladesh also jumped by 44% to $2.2 billion in 2015, a historically high level.

(d) North and Central Asia

In contrast, FDI inflows to North and Central Asia continued to contract due to low commodity prices (especially in the case of crude oil), weak domestic markets, and the direct and indirect impacts of geopolitical tensions affecting mainly the Russian Federation. The Russian Federation and Kazakhstan, the two major economies in the subregion, received severely reduced investment inflows in 2015. The economic crisis and regulatory changes in the Russian Federation also reduced the scale and scope of round-tripping FDI, depressing FDI inflow figures.

(e) Pacific developing economies

The Pacific developing economies received $2.3 billion FDI inflows collectively in 2015, an increase of 16%. However, FDI inflows to the subregion are very volatile, possibly due to the structural characteristics that continue to limit FDI options, such as the lack of adequate transport, communications and energy infrastructures, low productivity capacities and the concentration on a narrow set of commodities/sectors (ESCAP, 2015). Several economies are aiming to achieve, or have pursued, economic diversification that could attract sustainable FDI flows. However, progress in these efforts is uneven and would be long-term processes that need to be incorporated in the economic policies of these economies (Asian Development Bank, 2016; Dornan and Cain, 2015; and Fingar, 2016).

(f) Developed Asia-Pacific economies

The developed Asia-Pacific economies also experienced a sharp decline in FDI inflows in 2015. FDI inflows to Japan fell to a net divestment as European TNCs withdrew investments (UNCTAD, 2016). This could be due to the high costs of doing business and pursuing M&As in Japan, as pointed out in a recent survey (Urata, 2015). Australia and New Zealand also continued to experience decreased FDI inflows, as in the case in the past few years, with continued depressed commodity prices.

2. FDI outflows

Most FDI outflows from the Asia-Pacific region are from East and North-East Asia. That subregion accounts for 78% of total FDI outflows from the region as a whole, but almost exclusively from China, followed by Hong Kong, China, and Japan (figure 3.5). Also, these outflows are increasingly invested intraregionally (see section C for more details). It should also be noted that the subregion captures most of intraregional trade flows, on both the import and export sides (see chapter 1 for more details).

China has continued to expand its outward FDI, on the one hand, to secure mineral and petroleum resources, and on the other hand for efficiency seeking due to rising labour costs at home. Since the Government initiated its "going out" strategy in 1999, China has focused its FDI in areas that contribute directly to China's development, such as natural resources, lower production costs and, most recently, strengthening its technological base as the country is facing over-capacity in the labour-intensive manufacturing sector. It is aiming to move towards attracting FDI in technologically advanced sectors (Sauvant and Nolan, 2015). China remains the third-largest outward investing country worldwide and has emerged as a leading investor in developing economies, particularly in Africa and increasingly in countries that are part of the Belt and Road Initiative (UNCTAD, 2016). After a surge of outward FDI in 2014, investment from Hong Kong, China has more than halved as it has been affected by divestment due to strategic corporate restructuring (UNCTAD, 2016).

With regained confidence and traditionally facing limited prospects in the home market, Japan continued to seek growth opportunities abroad. Japan recovered

Figure 3.5 **FDI outflows from Asia-Pacific developing subregions and developed economies, 2013-2015**

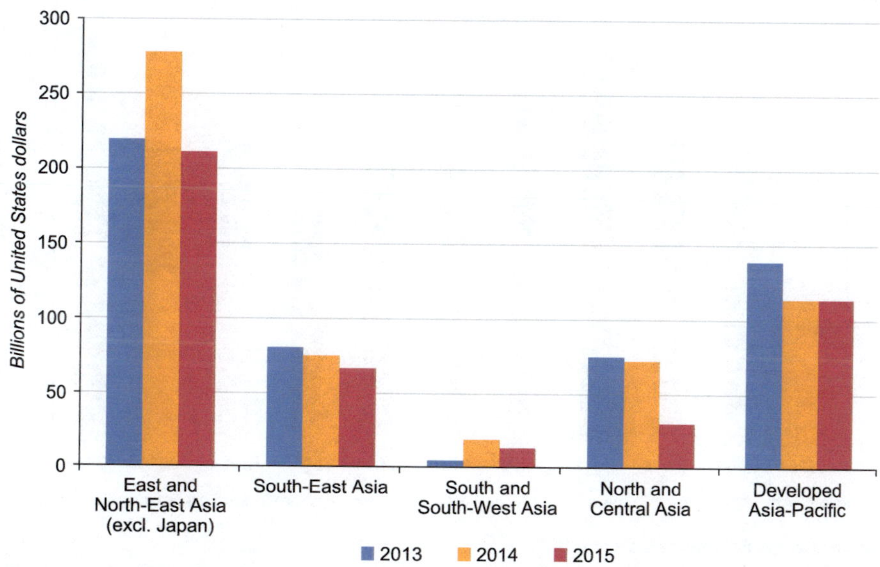

Sources: ESCAP calculation based on UNCTAD (2016).

Note: Due to the small share of outflows from the Pacific small island developing States, that subregion is not included in this figure.

its FDI outflows to the levels existing prior to the financial crisis in 2008-2009, recording $129 billion in FDI outflows in 2015, which was a 13% increase over 2014.

C. INTRAREGIONAL FOREIGN DIRECT INVESTMENT FLOWS

> *"The share of intraregional greenfield FDI inflows in total greenfield FDI inflows to the Asia-Pacific region has continuously increased during the past few years, accounting for 52% in 2015."*

As the economic relevance and dynamism of the Asia-Pacific region increases, intraregional greenfield FDI flows are replacing those from the traditional big investors such as the United States and countries in Europe (ESCAP, 2013). After the financial crisis in 2009-2009, in particular, the share of intraregional greenfield FDI inflows in total greenfield FDI inflows to the Asia-Pacific region has continuously increased, accounting for 52% in 2015 (figure 3.6).

Increasing intraregional FDI flows can be, at least partially, attributed to continuous efforts for regional and subregional integration within the Asia-Pacific region.

The Association of Southeast Nations (ASEAN), which includes all economies in South-East Asia except Timor-Leste, has become a popular destination for intraregional FDI, thanks to its continuous collaborative efforts on subregional integration with outward-oriented focus approach, and further developments on investment environment. In 2015, $83 billion was received from countries in the Asia-Pacific region, which amounted to 46% of total intraregional inflows.

As production costs are rising in labour-intensive industries in China, the smaller and less developed countries in ASEAN are benefiting from a shift of FDI to these industries despite their overall poor investment climate. Specifically, development challenges in CLMV countries (Cambodia, Lao People's Democratic Republic, Myanmar and Viet Nam) were noted and efforts are ongoing through the Initiative for ASEAN Integration and other aid programmes (OECD, 2016). Possibly because of these factors, CLMV countries have received steady and increasing FDI inflows since 2011. The total FDI inflows have reached $18 billion in 2015, an increase of 70% compared with 2011. In this regard, it appears that ASEAN is attracting a significant portion of FDI inflows from its neighbours, mainly China, Japan and Republic of Korea, and some other countries in the region, which together accounted for 72% of total greenfield FDI inflows to ASEAN during 2013-2015 (figure 3.7).

> *"Intraregional greenfield FDI flows are gradually replacing those from the traditional big investors in Europe."*

Figure 3.6 **Asia-Pacific intraregional greenfield FDI inflows and their share in total greenfield FDI inflows, and major destinations, 2005-2015**

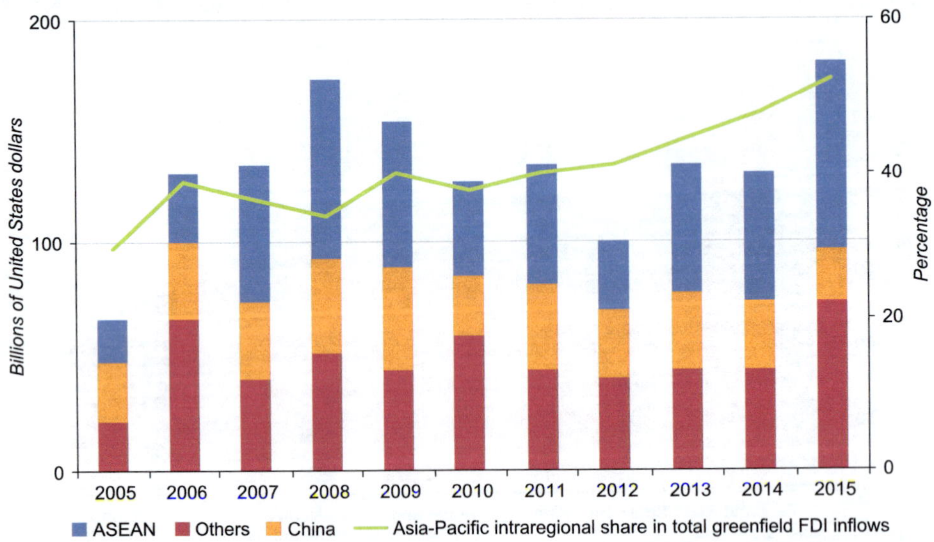

Sources: ESCAP calculation based on fDi Intelligence data, 2016.

Note: "intraregional" in the context of the above figure implies flows in a country or a subregion from the rest of Asia and the Pacific.

Figure 3.7 **Intraregional greenfield FDI flows between selected economies, and total intraregional inflows and outflows to and from those economies, 2013-2015**

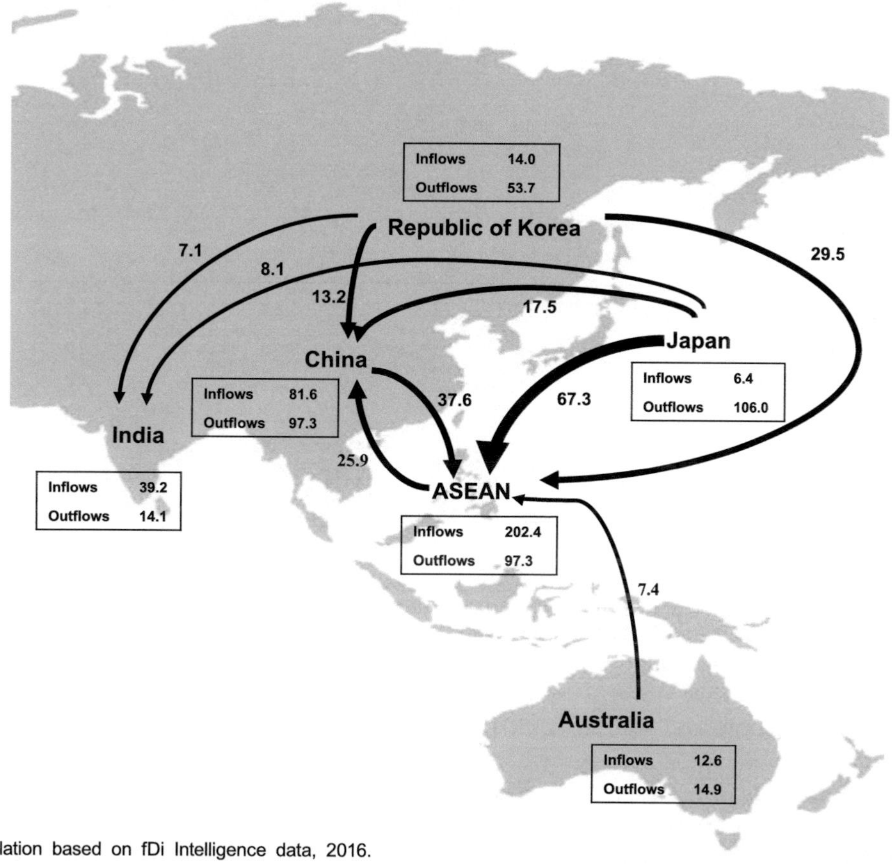

Sources: ESCAP calculation based on fDi Intelligence data, 2016.

Note: In order to even out the volatile annual FDI flows, the total invested FDI flow during 2013-2015 is used instead of annual flows.

It should also be noted that major investors are highly concentrated in one or two key industries and sometimes also in certain economies. For example, Chinese companies dominate the FDI in manufacturing (48% of total manufacturing FDI), and are the largest investors in the Lao People's Democratic Republic at 62% of FDI flows, mainly focused on infrastructure. For Viet Nam, 67% of FDI flows in 2015 were in manufacturing and were led by investors from the Republic of Korea (ASEAN Secretariat and UNCTAD, 2016).

> *"While FDI inflows to China are slowing down, more FDI is directed towards economies in ASEAN instead."*

D. SECTORAL FOREIGN DIRECT INVESTMENT FLOWS

The Asia and Pacific region continued to receive significant FDI in both the manufacturing and the services sectors. However, in 2015, greenfield FDI inflows to the primary sector increased noticeably. The coal, oil and natural gas industries received $67 billion in 2015, 2.6 times more than in the previous year; the metals sector received $28 billion in 2015, more than double than the previous year (figure 3.8). Taking a closer look reveals that the following industries received a significant portion of greenfield FDI flows in 2015: fossil fuel electric power, petroleum refineries; iron and steel mills, and ferroalloy, and natural, liquefied and compressed gas. The increase of greenfield FDI in the primary sector differs from the decreased level of overall FDI flows to developing economies. However, it is in line with the significant increase in overall greenfield FDI flows to the region. Also, the fact that companies are still investing in the primary sector in the region despite the low commodity prices could be an indication of a potential rebound in FDI as macroeconomic and financial conditions improve in the Asia region (UNCTAD, 2016). Also, it is worth noting that greenfield FDI inflows are on an announcement basis only; thus, there could be time delays between the announcement and actual transactions.

Figure 3.8 **Greenfield FDI inflows to the Asia-Pacific region by sector, 2010-2015**

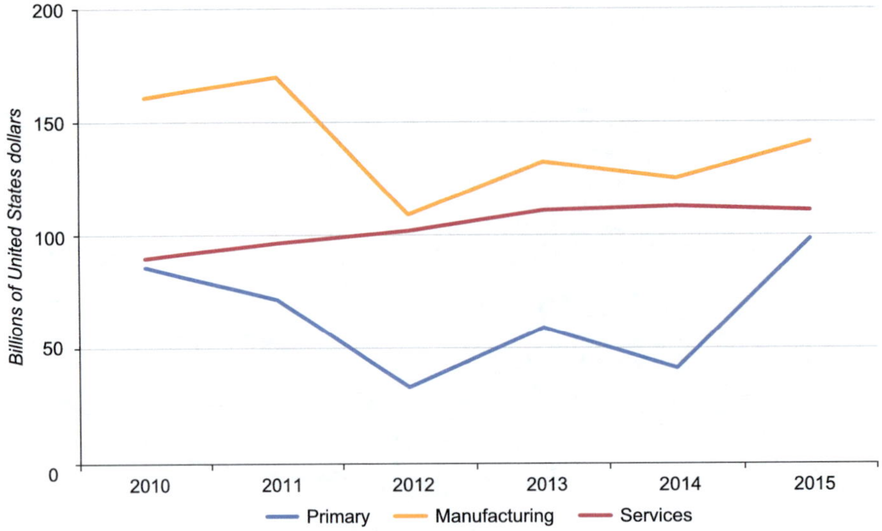

Sources: ESCAP calculation based on fDi Intelligence data, 2016.

During 2013-2015, the industries listed in table 3.1 received the biggest FDI inflows. Among them, real estate and alternative/renewable energy received almost double the amount compared with 2010-2012.

Many economies in the region are paying more attention to attracting FDI in technologically more advanced industries in order to move away for reliance on labour-intensive manufacturing as they believe that such FDI would bring desired spillover effects to the economy alongside capital inflows and contribute to sustainable development (box 3.1).

In addition to FDI inflows to technologically more advanced industries, investment in infrastructure serves important roles as catalyzers. Not only the physical infrastructure such as railroads, ports, and highways, but also soft infrastructure such as financial services and information and communications technology would be critical for attracting further FDI investment in host countries (ASEAN Secretariat, 2015b). FDI inflows in these sectors are also encouraged by regional integration efforts such as recently announced the Belt and Road Initiative and Asian Infrastructure Investment Bank (AIIB), and existing initiatives such as the Eurasian Development Bank (EDB), with its focus on regional integration and economies ties. Therefore, countries have paid special attention to promote and/or control investment in infrastructure industries, through investment policies and other means.

Table 3.1 **Greenfield FDI inflows to top 10 industries, 2013-2015**

(Millions of United States dollars)

Top 10 industries (ranking in 2010-2012)	Total greenfield FDI inflows, 2013-2015
Coal, oil and natural gas (1)	125 701
Real estate (6)	100 896
Metals (3)	63 522
Financial services (2)	54 264
Alternative/renewable energy (new)	52 814
Automotive OEM (5)	46 886
Transportation (7)	43 129
Communications (10)	41 952
Chemicals (4)	39 010
Food and tobacco (9)	36 658

Source: ESCAP calculation based on fDi Intelligence data, 2016.

Box 3.1 Attracting FDI for sustainable development

Increasingly, economies are putting much effort into attracting the FDI that would enable sustainable growth. Originally, it was believed that FDI inflows would automatically result in growth and, hence, many economies pursued outward-oriented growth strategies that not only focused on increasing international trade but also encouraging high levels of FDI. However, empirical evidence has revealed that these FDI inflows by themselves do not automatically translate into growth, and particularly what is considered to be sustainable growth. The following prerequisites as well as required host country characteristics are necessary for attracting FDI for sustainable development.

First, absorptive capacities are needed to ensure positive spillovers, which arise when resources, notably knowledge, are spread and transferred (Meyer, 2004). These positive spillovers lead to productivity growth via enhanced knowledge and skills (Görg and Greenaway 2004). Absorptive capacities and host country characteristics matter in making a difference in the extent or speed with which spillovers occur. Some of well-discussed absorptive capacities include research and development (R&D) capacities, human resources, technological capacity and infrastructure (Guimón 2013; and Görg and Greenaway 2004). These positive spillover effects, in turn, enhance the attractiveness of host countries for FDI and, therefore, contribute to retained and continuous inflows of FDI with long-lasting positive effects.

Second, national FDI policies and regulations should seek to balance investors' rights with the public interest in order to ensure that FDI will bring growth in the three pillars of sustainable development (i.e. economic, social and environmental). With the 2030 Agenda for Sustainable Development and the 2015 Addis Ababa Action Agenda on Financing for Development reaffirming the importance of sustainable development, more attention is given to this area. For example, FDI in extractive industries can certainly generate government revenue, foreign exchange earnings and employment; however, they also can aggravate or cause serious environmental, health and social problems, including conflict and war (Liebenthal, Michelitsch and Tarazona, 2003). FDI in high-tech industries can potentially bring technology transfer and technological spillovers. However, it can also lead to pollution, such as e-waste or other negative externalities.

It is therefore important that Governments ensure that efforts are put in place to enhance absorptive capacities as well as ensure that encouraging FDI should not deter domestic policies and regulation in the public interest. Governments, therefore, should balance the economic, social and environmental dimensions of FDI and demand corporate responsibility from investors, in accordance with internationally accepted principles and standards.

E. NATIONAL INVESTMENT POLICIES

National investment policies continue to be geared towards investment liberalization and promotion. According to UNCTAD (2016), 46 countries and economies adopted 96 policy measures affecting foreign investment in 2015. Of these measures, 71 were related to liberalization, promotion and facilitation of investment, while 13 introduced new restrictions or regulations on investment.

> *"Asia-Pacific countries lead with investment liberalization and promotion policies accounting for almost half of such measures adopted in 2015."*

Asian and Pacific countries are in the lead with investment liberalization and promotion policies. According to the same report (UNCTAD, 2016) the region adopted 46 investment policies affecting foreign investment, accounting for almost half of the global total (figure 3.9). Of these measures, 43 were related to liberalization, promotion and facilitation of investment, while only 3 introduced new restrictions or regulations on investment. These investment policy changes removed restrictions on foreign investment, strengthened investment promotion and facilitation, and further ensured the rights of investors. Two areas of investment policy changes earn special attention, i.e. liberalization of industry sectors and special economic zones (SEZs).

1. Liberalization of industry sectors

For many years, emerging Asian economies have been pursuing economic development by emphasizing their openness and integration into the global economy. In particular, two of the largest emerging economies in Asia, China and India, were the most active in opening up various industries to foreign investors in 2015.

Figure 3.9 **Investment policy changes in Asia-Pacific countries, 2015**

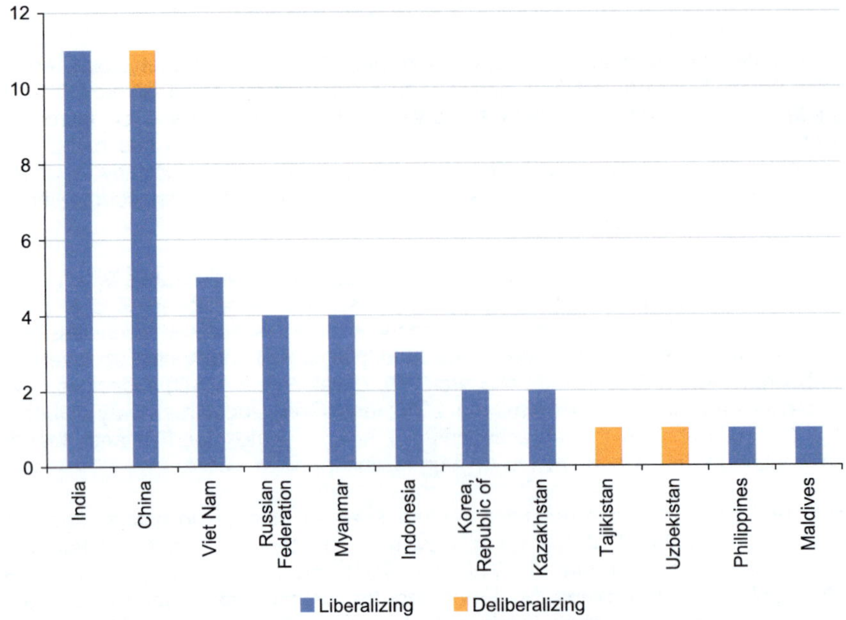

Sources: ESCAP calculation based on the UNCTAD Investment Policy Monitor Database, 2016.

For many years, emerging Asian economies have been pursuing economic development by emphasizing their openness and integration into the global economy. In particular, two of the largest emerging economies in Asia, China and India, were the most active in opening up various industries to foreign investors in 2015.

In China, with the announcement of the draft Foreign Investment Law (FIL) from the Ministry of Commerce (MOFCOM), a comprehensive reform of the legal system for foreign investment in China is anticipated. The FIL is intended to move the focus from supervision of the organizational structures and business activities of foreign companies investing in China to post-investment supervision, which mainly concerns reporting obligations and national security (Yang and Huang, 2016). This is contrary to the current pre-establishment system, which regulates foreign investment with a positive list approach, approving investment on a case-by-case basis. While seeking public opinion and in anticipation of enacting the FIL, China is piloting the foreign investment negative list in the Shanghai, Tianjin, Guandong and Fujian Free Trade Zones (FTZs). As indicated in a recent government statement, China intends to open more sectors to foreign investors, such as education, finance, culture and manufacturing (Bloomberg News, 2016).

Despite a clearly intended move towards liberalization in general, China is also protecting core industries in terms of national security. MOFCOM and the National Development and Reform Commission (NDRC) jointly released an updated version of the Guiding Catalogue on Foreign Investment in Industry in March 2015, which lifts restrictions on foreign investment in several areas, but remains largely unaltered in industries that have traditionally faced heavy restrictions, such as banking, telecommunications and cultural industries (United States Department of State, 2016a). A recent National Security Law, enacted in July 2015, has also raised concerns that the Law may be used to restrict foreign investment in some sensitive sectors (Wong, 2015).[3]

India has also taken up major reforms since 2014, including various liberalization measures such as:

(a) Permitting FDI up to 100 per cent ownership under the automatic route (instead of government approval route) in the manufacturing of medical devices, telecommunications, railway infrastructure and non-banking finance companies;
(b) Increasing the FDI cap from 26% to 49% for foreign ownership in the insurance and defence sectors;
(c) Relaxing sourcing norms for single-brand retail trading for high-tech segments;
(d) Increasing the thresholds of inward FDI projects that require prior approval from INR 20 billion to INR 50 billion[4] (UNCTAD, 2016; ENS Economic Bureau, 2016; and D.H. Law Associates, 2015).

India also introduced a comprehensive FDI liberalization strategy and relaxed FDI rules in 15 major sectors, including agriculture, civil aviation, construction, defence, manufacturing and mining (UNCTAD, 2016). India is also continuing its liberalization measures in other sectors such as, for example, e-commerce, which is expected to further encourage FDI inflows to India (box 3.2).

Box 3.2 **India: liberalizing e-commerce**

Among the sectors recently opened up to FDI in India is e-commerce. The Government of India announced that FDI of up to 100% would be permitted in the marketplace-based model of electronic commerce (e-commerce), in Press Note No. 3 released on 29 March 2016 (Cave, 2016). However, the liberalization comes with restrictions; according to the notification, e-commerce companies would not be allowed to influence prices of the goods sold on their website, and not more than 25% of goods sold can come from a single merchant (Reuters, 2016).

E-commerce, referring to the trading or facilitation of trading in goods and services using computer networks, poses a huge opportunity to trigger growth, especially for developing countries. E-commerce has become essential for many industries that have globally dispersed value chains. The existence of sophisticated platforms for e-commerce could significantly enhance the attractiveness of economies as investment destinations and trade partners. Together with many other countries – including China, which allows full foreign ownership of e-commerce business[a] – India has followed suit. While India has taken steps in the right direction, greater clarification of the restrictions is needed. In addition, India needs to develop the supporting infrastructure for e-commerce, including basic Internet connectivity, trade facilitation, streamlining non-tariff measures, and to improve the regulatory regime for services (Johns, 2016).

[a] The Ministry of Industry and Information Technology of China issued Announcement No. 196 (2015) on 19 June 2015, allowing full foreign ownership of e-commerce business. On 20 June 2015, the State Council released policy guidelines for supporting cross-border e-commerce.

In 2015, there were also some noteworthy measures from smaller Asia-Pacific economies. For example, Viet Nam implemented a number of reforms of its investment policy, including: (a) implementation of a "negative list" approach; (b) allowing foreign investors in its airport and aviation industry; and (c) lifting a 49% cap on foreign ownership in some industries (Peel and Linh, 2015; United States Department of State, 2016b). The Philippines issued a revised negative list, removing foreign ownership restrictions in a number of sectors. In Myanmar, the Parliament approved amendments to the Foreign Investment Law and the Myanmar Citizens Investment Law in December 2015, aimed at paving the way for speedier investment approvals (Economist Intelligence Unit, 2016).

2. Special economic zones

Special economic zones (SEZs) have become popular, especially in developing economies, as modalities to attract FDI. There are more than 4,500 SEZs of various types worldwide (*Economist*, 2015). SEZs refer to "geographically limited and specially administered areas within a country that are established to attract local and foreign direct investment, trade, employment and industrial development" (UNCTAD, 2015). They typically provide certain advantages such as preferential tax or duty treatment or exemptions from restrictions on the repatriation of profits, direct subsidies and enhanced physical infrastructure as well as expedited permitting and related services. The popularity of SEZs is based on anticipated benefits such as increased FDI inflows and employment, despite mixed experiences and persisting concerns about social and environmental effects. However, SEZs can provide a platform for developing the infrastructure and regulatory environment in a geographically limited area without the need to reform relevant laws of a country/economy (UNCTAD, 2015).

In Myanmar, the country's first SEZ in Thilawa became fully operational in September 2015, aimed at attracting foreign investors with hard and soft infrastructure, and providing easier establishment procedures and other concessions. In late-2015, the Government approved the development of another SEZ in Kyaukphyu, including an industrial park and a deep-sea port. However, the Dawei SEZ has experienced many obstacles, such as private sector partners' exhausted funding and withdrawal from the project, which have delayed the project. With renewed support from the Governments of Thailand and Japan, and other private sector partners, construction is still ongoing but it will be many years before the Dawei SEZ will be fully operational. The Russian Federation is committed to opening a Free Port in Vladivostok, a customs-free zone with special tax incentives for companies operating within it. In Kazakhstan, the Government approved the Law on the Astana International Financial Centre (AIFC), a financial-oriented SEZ that streamlines employment procedures for foreign employees and offers tax exemptions such as exemption from corporate income tax as well as property and land taxes for AIFC members until 1 January 2066.

The nature of industries operating in SEZs has also evolved, moving away from being exclusively locations for business processes using low-skilled labour to locations for a variety of more complex business processes requiring more highly-skilled labour, including labour associated with finance and logistics centres. For example, in 2013, in China the Shanghai Free Trade Zone opened for business, with a focus on attracting the insurance industry (UNCTAD, 2015). In 2015, three new FTZs were opened in Tianjin, Fujian and Guangdong, providing national treatment in the pre-establishment phase, and adopting the negative list for approving investments.

F. INTERNATIONAL INVESTMENT AGREEMENTS

> *"The Asia-Pacific region has assumed a central role in the global IIA universe."*

For decades international investment agreements (IIAs) have been used to underpin the active FDI agenda in the Asia-Pacific region. This has contributed to the region's status as a major player in FDI. Although IIAs have traditionally been in the form of bilateral investment treaties (BITs), they are increasingly including other forms of agreements with investment provisions such as free trade agreements (FTAs), regional trade and investment agreements (RTIAs) and economic partnership agreements (EPAs).

Economies in Asia and the Pacific have increasingly assumed a crucial role in shaping the global IIA universe. According to the UNCTAD Investment Policy Monitor Database, in 2015 the Asia-Pacific region witnessed the signing of 14 IIAs and 13 IIAs entering into force, out of 29 IIAs being signed and 19 IIAs entered into force globally. It shows the degree that the Asia-Pacific region was very actively participating in IIAs.

Importantly, there is a movement towards the formation of so-called "mega-regional" agreements, such as the Trans-Pacific Partnership (TPP) signed on 4 February 2016. Furthermore, in South-East Asia the ASEAN Economic Community (AEC) entered into force on 31 December 2015. While commentators have remarked that this does not have a big legal significance, it marks an important milestone on the road to regional economic integration among ASEAN economies (ASEAN Secretariat, 2015a). Leading up to 2015, progress was achieved in, among others, eliminating tariffs, liberalizing and facilitating investment, and facilitating mobility of skilled labour (ASEAN Secretariat, 2016). In particular, the ASEAN Comprehensive Investment Agreement (ACIA) provides for profoundly progressive liberalization of national investment regimes in ASEAN member States.

In North and Central Asia, the Eurasian Economic Union (EAEU) entered into force on 1 January 2015, replacing the Eurasian Economic Community (EAEC) and integrating five Commonwealth of Independent States (CIS) economies – i.e. Armenia and all former EAEC members except Tajikistan – into a single market with free movement of goods, services, capital and labour, thus further enhancing regional integration in that subregion (Llosa, Ratna and Mikic, 2016).

In addition to these regional agreements, a number of bilateral IIAs have been signed and entered into force. Viet Nam is especially notable, as it has concluded agreements with a large number of countries through its FTAs with the European Union, the EAEU and the Republic of Korea as well as signing the TPP. The Republic of Korea was party to three other major FTAs that entered into force in 2015, i.e. with China, New Zealand and Canada, all of which included investment chapters.

The fact that the Asia-Pacific region has assumed a central role in the global IIA universe is a reflection of the shift in the paradigm of IIAs, moving to a more balanced investment regime that serves the interests of foreign investors and host countries. This is partly in reaction to rising disputes between investors and host countries, as IIAs used to focus on provisions for investment protection and promotion, with little or no regard for preserving the regulatory space of host countries (Berger, 2015). This has become a major concern for host countries, which rely heavily on FDI in sensitive sectors such as the extractive industry, which often faces environmental and community problems when foreign investors' interests precede the rights of local workers and communities.

Another reason behind the shift is the increasing number of developing and emerging economies that have become major destinations as well as sources of FDI. These emerging economies have pushed for a more balanced approach as they accelerate their investment abroad. For example, while China initially took the restrictive approach in its BITs, it has progressively broadened its consent to arbitration for disputes with foreign investors and increased the level of substantive protections afforded to investors; this approach has been taken in order to receive equal and reciprocal protection for its own investments abroad, as China's outward FDI has continued to increase in recent years (Sauvant and Nolan, 2015). At the same time, China has firmly restricted FDI in industries that they deem to be important for national security, as mentioned above. China and many other developing countries have become important investors, which gives them greater bargaining power when IIAs are being negotiated.

G. CONCLUSION

The Asia-Pacific region has continued to be a significant actor in the global FDI scene. The region in total received FDI inflows of $559 billion in 2015, accounting for 32% of total global inflows. However, the region experienced only a small increase in FDI inflows compared with the previous year, and accounted for a smaller share of the global FDI inflows. While this is partly due to the global economic uncertainties and volatilities affecting global FDI, it is specifically due to a sharp decline in FDI to North and Central Asia, due to low commodity prices, weakening domestic markets, regulatory changes, and the direct and indirect impacts of geopolitical tensions.

However, it is worth noting that greenfield FDI inflows to the region increased by 26% in 2015 compared with the previous year, which was significantly higher than the increase in global greenfield inflows. The region experienced a reduced level of outflows, at $435 billion in 2015. Again, economic conditions prompted the decrease, which is not very high compared with the average outward FDI flow in recent years given the unprecedented high increase in FDI outflows in 2014.

Amid varied FDI flows in different subregions and economies, there are a number of areas that stand out. First, intraregional FDI flows are continuing to be significant. The share of intraregional greenfield FDI inflows in total greenfield FDI inflows to the Asia-Pacific region has continuously increased during the past few years, accounting for 52% in 2015.

Second, while FDI inflows to China are slowing down as the country is losing its competitive advantage in traditional industries due to rising production costs, more FDI is flowing to economies in ASEAN instead. Small and low-income economies, such as the Lao People's Democratic Republic, Myanmar and Viet Nam, have continued to perform well. These countries have low labour costs and Governments that are actively pursuing liberalization and promotion of FDI. This is also reflected in intraregional FDI flows. In particular, ASEAN has become a popular destination for intraregional FDI, receiving $83 billion in 2015 from countries in the Asia-Pacific region, and accounting for 46% of total intraregional inflows.

Third, another country that has attracted higher FDI inflows is India, as the country is improving its regulatory environment for investment. The Government's economic strategy appears to be paying off well as inflation has been brought under control, and the country has become the top Asia-Pacific destination for FDI greenfield flows. With further improvements in the private investment environment, especially infrastructure, the country would enhance its attractiveness to foreign investors even more.

Many Asia-Pacific countries have actively pursued investment liberalization and promotion policies that have contributed to the success of the region, to become both an investment destination and a source. The majority (43 out of 46) foreign investment-related policies that were adopted in 2015 in the region comprised policies related to liberalization, promotion and facilitation of investment. In particular, two of the largest emerging economies in Asia, China and India, were the most active in opening up various industries to foreign investors. Other small economies were also pursuing further liberalization, such as Myanmar, the Philippines and Viet Nam.

One particular channel of liberalization has come in the form of SEZs. Some success cases of SEZs in the region have prompted many countries to follow suit; even though there have been mixed experiences and persisting concerns over the social and environmental effects of SEZs, they are still perceived as a useful means of attracting foreign investment and a testing ground for infrastructure development and regulatory reform. With the shifting nature of industries operating in SEZs, they could become more relevant as modalities for encouraging FDI for sustainable development.

Another channel of investment liberalization has come in the form of international investment agreements. The Asian and Pacific economies have assumed an increasingly crucial role in shaping the global IIA universe. It is noteworthy that many Asia-Pacific economies were, and still are active members of some mega-regional agreements, such as TPP, RCEP, and EAEU. The end of 2015 saw the entry into force of the AEC, which incorporates the ASEAN Comprehensive Investment Agreement that is a far-reaching subregional agreement that sets a standard for enhanced investment cooperation and integration among member States.

Endnotes

1 Tax inversion, or corporate inversion, is the practice of relocating a corporation's legal domicile to a lower-tax nation, or tax haven, usually while retaining its material operations in its higher-tax country of origin.

2 The World Bank's Doing Business Index, the World Economic Forum's Global Competitiveness Index and the Milken Institute's Global Opportunity Index point out that India still ranks lower than China. (Sauvant and Allman, 2016).

3 Also referred to in www.amcham-shanghai.org/ftpuploadfiles/insight/ Security%20Reviews%20and%20Neg%20List.pdf.

4 The Government of India, through the Ministry of Commerce and Industry recently issued its consolidated Foreign Direct Investment Policy Circular of 2015 that updates the FDI regulations.

REFERENCES

ASEAN Secretariat (2015a). *A Blueprint for Growth – ASEAN Economic Community 2015: Progress and Key Achievements*. Jakarta. Available from www.asean.org/storage/images/2015/November/aec-page/AEC-2015-Progress-and-Key-Achievements.pdf.

______ (2015b). ASEAN *Investment Report 2015: Infrastructure Investment and Connectivity*. Jakarta, November 2015. Available from www.asean.org/wp-content/uploads/2015/12/ASEAN-Investment-Report-2015.pdf .

______ (2016). *ASEAN Economic Community Blueprint 2025*. Jakarta. Available from www.asean.org/storage/2016/03/AECBP_2025r_FINAL.pdf.

Asian Development Bank (2016). Economic diversification needed for sustainable, inclusive growth. Manila. Available from https://www.adb.org/news/economic-diversification-needed-sustainable-inclusive-growth-adb.

Berger, A. (2015). Financing global development: can foreign direct investments be increased through International Investment Agreements? German Development Institute Briefing Paper. Bonn, Germany. Available from www.die-gdi.de/en/briefing-paper/article/financing-global-development-can-foreign-direct-investments-be-increased-through-international-investment-agreements/.

Bloomberg News (2016). China to slash limits on foreign investment to revive spending, 23 August. Available from www.bloomberg.com/news/articles/2016-08-23/china-to-slash-limits-on-foreign-investment-to-revive-spending.

Cave, B. (2016). India relaxes rules on foreign direct investment in e-commerce. Available from http://www.lexology.com/library/detail.aspx?g=3cee6abf-8888-44f5-9305-6926de6b3786.

D.H. Law Associates (2015). Consolidated foreign direct investment policy, May-June. Available from www.dhlawassociates.com/assets/newsletters/2015/may-june-2015.html.

Dornan, M., and T.N. Cain (2015). Tourism and economic diversification in Vanuatu. Available from http://devpolicy.org/tourism-and-economic-diversification-in-vanuatu-20150616/.

Drysdale, P. (2015a). Has China's transition to 'new normal' growth stalled? East Asia Forum, 6 July. Available from www.eastasiaforum.org/2015/07/06/has-chinas-transition-to-new-normal-growth-stalled/.

______ (2015b). Can India make it without manufacturing? East Asia Forum, 26 October. Available from www.eastasiaforum.org/2015/10/26/can-india-make-it-without-manufacturing/.

Economic and Social Commission for Asia and the Pacific (2013). *Asia-Pacific Trade and Investment Report 2013 – Turning the Tide: Towards Inclusive Trade and Investment*. Sales No. E.14.II.F.2. Available from www.unescap.org/resources/asia-pacific-trade-and-investment-report-2013-turning-tide-towards-inclusive-trade-and.

______ (2015). *Asia-Pacific Trade and Investment Report 2015: Supporting Participation in Value Chains*. Sales No. E.15.II.F.15. Available from www.unescap.org/resources/asia-pacific-trade-and-investment-report-2015-supporting-participation-value-chains.

Economist (2015). Not so special, 4 April. Available from www.economist.com/news/leaders/21647615-world-awash-free-trade-zones-and-their-offshoots-many-are-not-worth-effort-not.

______ (2016). A second helping of Raghu, 18 June. Available from www.economist.com/news/leaders/21700654-governor-reserve-bank-india-should-be-asked-serve-second-term-second-helping.

Economist Intelligence Unit (2016). Myanmar: Parliament hands festive gifts to businesses. Available from http://country.eiu.com/article.aspx?articleid=223829806&Country=Myanmar&topic=Economy&subtopic=Fo_3.

Indian Express (2016). Govt eases FDI norms in 15 major sectors, including defence, civil aviation, 11 November. Available from http://indianexpress.com/article/india/india-news-india/govt-eases-fdi-norms-fipb-limit-raised-from-rs-3000-crore-to-rs-5000-crore/.

Investment Consulting Associates (2016). *AIM Investment Report 2016: the Future of FDI*. Report presented at the Annual Investment Meeting: the New World of FDI, Key Features and Best Practices, Dubai, 11-13 April. Available from http://ic-associates.com/wp-content/uploads/2016/04/AIM-Report.pdf.

Fingar, C. (2016). How island nations can make their investment potential shine. fDiIntelligence, 16 June. Available from www.fdiintelligence.com/Locations/Asia-Pacific/How-island-nations-can-make-their-investment-potential-shine.

Görg, H., and D. Greenaway (2004). Much ado about nothing? Do domestic firms really benefit from foreign direct investment? *The World Bank Research Observer*, vol. 19, No. 2 (Autumn).

Guimón, J. (2013). National policies to attract R&D-intensive FDI in developing countries. Innovation Policy Platform Policy Brief. Available from https://innovationpolicyplatform.org/sites/default/files/rdf_imported_documents/NationalPoliciesToAttractR&DIntensiveFDIInDevelopingCountries.pdf.

Johns, M.B. (2016). E-trade: national and international policy implications. Trade Post, 30 May. Washington, D.C.: World Bank. Available from http://blogs.worldbank.org/trade/e-trade-national-and-international-policy-implications.

Liebenthal, A., R. Michelitsch and E. Tarazona (2003). *Extractive Industries and Sustainable Development: An evaluation of World Bank Group Experience*. Washington, D.C: World Bank. Available from http://ieg.worldbank.org/Data/reports/extractive_industries_evaluation_overview.pdf.

Llosa, D., R. Sudesh Ratna and M. Mikic (2016). An update on the preferential trade agreements of Asia-Pacific economies. APTIAD Briefing Note, August 2016. Available from www.unescap.org/sites/default/files/APTIAD-brief-August2016.pdf.

Meyer, K.E. (2004). Perspectives on multinational enterprises in emerging economies. *Journal of International Business Studies*, vol. 34, No. 4, pp. 259-277.

Organisation for Economic Co-operation and Development (2016). *Economic Outlook for Southeast Asia, China and India 2016: Enhancing Regional Ties*. Paris. Available from www.oecd.org/dev/economic-outlook-for-southeast-asia-china-and-india-23101113.htm .

Panda, A. (2016). India takes over from China as top global FDI destination in 2015. The Diplomat, 25 April. Available from http://thediplomat.com/2016/04/india-takes-over-from-china-as-top-global-fdi-destination-in-2015/.

Parisotto, L.G., D.G. Santibáñez and A. Heal (2016). Adding value to Indonesian mining exports: time to revisit export restrictions? Trade Insights, No. 19. Bangkok: ESCAP. Available from www.unescap.org/sites/default/files/Trade%20Insight%2019%20final.pdf.

Peel, M., and N.P. Linh (2015). Vietnam scraps foreign ownership limits in investment push. *Financial Times*, 29 June. Available from www.ft.com/cms/s/0/1f44855a-1e35-11e5-aa5a-398b2169cf79.html#axzz4HTkx8PIS.

Reuters (2016). India approves foreign investment in e-commerce sector, 30 March. Available from http://in.reuters.com/article/india-ecommerce-fdi-idINKCN0WV248.

Sauvant, K.P., and D. Allman (2016). Can India emulate China in attracting and benefitting from FDI? Columbia FDI Perspective, No. 168. New York, N.Y.: Columbia Center on Sustainable Development. Available from http://ccsi.columbia.edu/files/2013/10/No-168-Sauvant-and-Allman-FINAL.pdf.

Sauvant, K.P., and M.D. Nolan (2015). China's outward foreign direct investment and international investment law. *Journal of International Economic Law*, vol. 18, No. 4, pp. 893-934.

United Nations Conference on Trade and Development (2015). *Enhancing the Contribution of Export Processing Zones to the Sustainable Development Goals: An Analysis of 100 EPZs and a Framework for Sustainable Economic Zones*. Geneva. Available from http://unctad.org/en/PublicationsLibrary/webdiaepcb2015d5_en.pdf.

_____ (2016). *World Investment Report 2016*. Sales No. E.16.II.D.4. Available from http://unctad.org/en/PublicationsLibrary/wir2016_en.pdf.

United States, Department of State (2016a). China: 2016 investment climate statements. Available from www.state.gov/e/eb/rls/othr/ics/2016/eap/254271.htm.

_____ (2016b). Vietnam: 2016 investment climate statements. Available from www.state.gov/e/eb/rls/othr/ics/2016/eap/254329.htm.

Urata, S. (2015). Revitalising sluggish FDI in Japan. East Asia Forum, 23 February. Available from www.eastasiaforum.org/2015/02/23/revitalising-sluggish-fdi-in-japan/.

Wong, C.H. (2015). China adopts sweeping National Security Law. *Wall Street Journal*, 1 July. Available from www.wsj.com/articles/china-adopts-sweeping-national-security-law-1435757589.

World Bank (2015). *China Economic Update: June 2015*. Washington, D.C. Available from www.worldbank.org/content/dam/Worldbank/document/EAP/China/ceu_06_15_en.pdf.

Yang, L., and S. Huang (2016). The pros and cons of China's new Foreign Investment Law. fDiIntelligence, 14 April. Available from www.fdiintelligence.com/Locations/Asia-Pacific/China/The-pros-and-cons-of-China-s-new-Foreign-Investment-Law?ct=true.

ONLINE DATABASES

Financial Times Ltd. fDiIntelligence, fDi Markets: The in-depth crossborder investment monitor. Available from www.fdimarkets.com/.

United Nations Conference on Trade and Development. Investment Policy Monitor Database. Available from http://investmentpolicyhub.unctad.org/IPM.

CHAPTER 4

TRADE FACILITATION IN ASIA AND THE PACIFIC: AN UPDATE

Trade facilitation and the reduction of international trade transaction costs remain an important priority for many countries of the Asian and Pacific region. Two thirds of the Asia-Pacific members of WTO have now ratified the WTO Trade Facilitation Agreement and are well on their way towards its implementation.[1] In addition, ESCAP member States, in May 2016 finalized the Framework Agreement on Facilitation of Cross-border Paperless Trade in Asia and the Pacific (Framework Agreement). This unique and innovative instrument is expected to greatly support the region in maintaining its trade competitiveness and reaping the benefits from the fast-growing digital economy. The Framework Agreement encourages continued progress by early adopters of cross-border paperless trade, while also lowering the barriers to entry for late movers. This is particularly important given the wide range of capabilities for trade facilitation and paperless trade implementation in the Asia-Pacific region.

Section A of this chapter provides a snapshot of the progress on trade cost reduction in the Asia-Pacific region, based on the ESCAP-World Bank Trade Cost Database. Section B looks at the performance of the Asia-Pacific region in relation to "hard" and "soft" infrastructure reform, by considering the Logistics Performance Index, Liner Shipping Connectivity Index and Trading across Border: Doing Business in the Asia-Pacific countries. Section C provides a brief update on trade facilitation and paperless trade initiatives in Asia and the Pacific, including a review of the progress made by ESCAP member States in ratifying the WTO Trade Facilitation Agreement as well as the adoption of the Framework Agreement. Given the disparities between the Asia-Pacific subregions with regard to trade costs and trade facilitation implementation, this chapter highlights the fact that the new regional cooperation framework can provide a useful mechanism for allowing late-movers to progress more quickly and to participate in more efficient and less costly cross-border trade.

> *"Further reductions in trade costs will have to be achieved by tackling the non-tariff sources of trade costs."*

A. PROGRESS IN TRADE COST REDUCTION

After the significant reduction – and, in many cases, elimination – of import tariffs during the past two decades, further reductions in trade costs will have to be achieved by tackling the non-tariff sources of trade costs, which now account for more than 90% of overall international trade costs.

Figure 4.1 shows the evolution of trade costs of the Asia-Pacific subregions in trading with the three largest developed economies from 2000 to 2013.[2] With the exception of the Pacific island developing economies (PIDEs), the trade cost levels in the Asia-Pacific region have typically remained similar across time. Although trade costs in North and Central Asia remain excessively high, this subregion appears to have made relatively more progress in reducing trade costs with the selected developed markets during the period. No such trend is found in the case of South or South-East Asia. In contrast, the regional group of EU-3 (considered the global benchmark) continues to reduce its trade costs over time, implying that there are possibilities for further trade cost improvement, even among the best performers.

Figure 4.1 **Trade costs of Asia-Pacific subregions with large developed economies, 2000-2013**

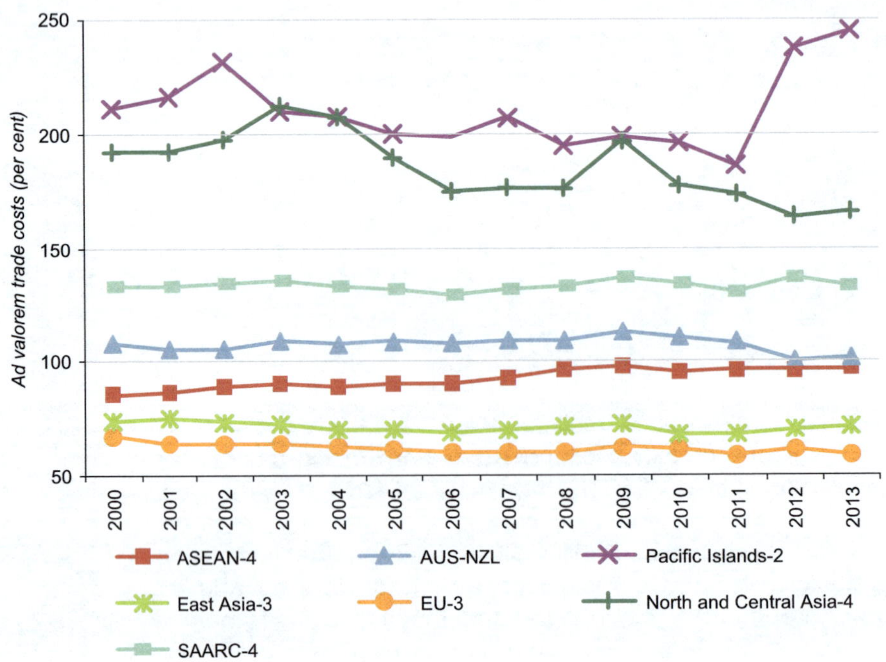

Sources: ESCAP-World Bank Trade Costs Database (accessed June 2016).

Note: ASEAN-4 – Indonesia, Malaysia, the Philippines and Thailand; AUS-NZL – Australia and New Zealand; East Asia-3 – China, Japan and the Republic of Korea; EU-3 – Germany, France and the United Kingdom; Pacific Islands-2 – Fiji and Papua New Guinea; North and Central Asia-4 – Georgia, Kazakhstan, Kyrgyzstan and the Russian Federation; and SAARC-4 – Bangladesh, India, Pakistan and Sri Lanka. Trade costs shown are tariff equivalents, calculated as trade-weighted average trade costs of countries in each subregion with the three largest developed economies (Germany, Japan and the United States).

Table 4.1 Intra- and extraregional comprehensive non-tariff trade costs in the Asia-Pacific region

(Percentage)

Region	ASEAN-4	East Asia-3	North and Central Asia - 4	Pacific Islands Developing Economies	SAARC-4	AUS-NZL	EU-3
ASEAN-4	76						
	(8)						
East Asia-3	75	51					
	(5)	(-3)					
North and Central Asia - 4	354	175	121				
	(11)	(-6)	(7)				
Pacific islands developing economies	172	175	369	132			
	(-10)	(-3)	(29)	(-10)			
SAARC-4	128	124	285	318	116		
	(1)	(-1)	(2)	(2)	(11)		
AUS-NZL	101	88	336	83	138	52	
	(4)	(-5)	(-7)	(-8)	(-5)	(-4)	
EU-3	106	85	152	209	115	108	43
	(-1)	(-3)	(-8)	(-4)	(2)	(-1)	(-5)
United States of America	86	63	177	163	110	100	67
	(10)	(0)	(-1)	(-6)	(6)	(4)	(1)

Source: ESCAP-World Bank Trade Costs Database (accessed June 2016).

Note: Trade costs shown are average trade costs during 2009-2014 and may be interpreted as tariff equivalents. Changes in average trade costs between 2003-2008 and 2009-2014 are in parenthesis. Refer to the note in figure 4.1 for details of country groupings.

As table 4.1 shows, the subregional grouping that exhibits the lowest intraregional trade costs (closest to EU-3) is East Asia-3 (51%) for 2009-2014, followed by AUS-NZL (52%). In addition, the intraregional trade costs of East Asia-3 show a 3% decrease during 2009-2014 when compared with the 2003-2008 average; at the same time, the extraregional trade costs of East Asia-3 with all the regional groups also fell. The PIDEs have the highest intraregional trade costs (132%) followed by North and Central Asia-4 (121%); both subregions have intraregional trade costs that are more than double those of the regional benchmark, East Asia-3. The two subregions also have the highest extraregional trade costs (369%).

Overall, trade costs in the Asia-Pacific region remain heterogeneous across subregions. There is no strong trend towards convergence in trade costs between subregions that experience higher intra- and extraregional trade costs and those for which trade costs are relatively lower. Furthering regional integration agendas and ensuring that international trade continues to be an engine for growth will require addressing the disparities in trade costs.

"No strong trend towards convergence in trade costs between subregions is observed."

Figure 4.2 shows the trade costs evolution of countries with special needs (CSNs) with the three largest developed economies. Trade costs of CSNs are found to be two to three times higher than those experienced by East Asia-3 (the regional benchmark). The small island developing States (SIDS) experience the highest trade costs. Of greatest concern is the fact that trade costs for this set of countries appear to have increased over time – although more detailed analysis reveals that trade costs of the larger SIDS, such as Fiji and Papua New Guinea have seen a declining trend. Landlocked developing countries appear to have fared better and exhibit a gradually declining trend over time. Asia-Pacific least developed countries, as a group, also have experienced declining trade costs in recent years (since 2009).

"Addressing the disparities in trade costs is a critical part of furthering regional integration agendas."

The costs shown in table 4.1 are broadly consistent with data published by UNCTAD on international transport costs, which show a long-term trend towards cost reductions, albeit with stark differences among regions (UNCTAD, 2015). They are also consistent with the outcomes of the 2015 Global Survey on Trade Facilitation and Paperless Trade Implementation

Figure 4.2 **Trade costs of Asia-Pacific countries with special needs and large developed economies, 2000-2013**

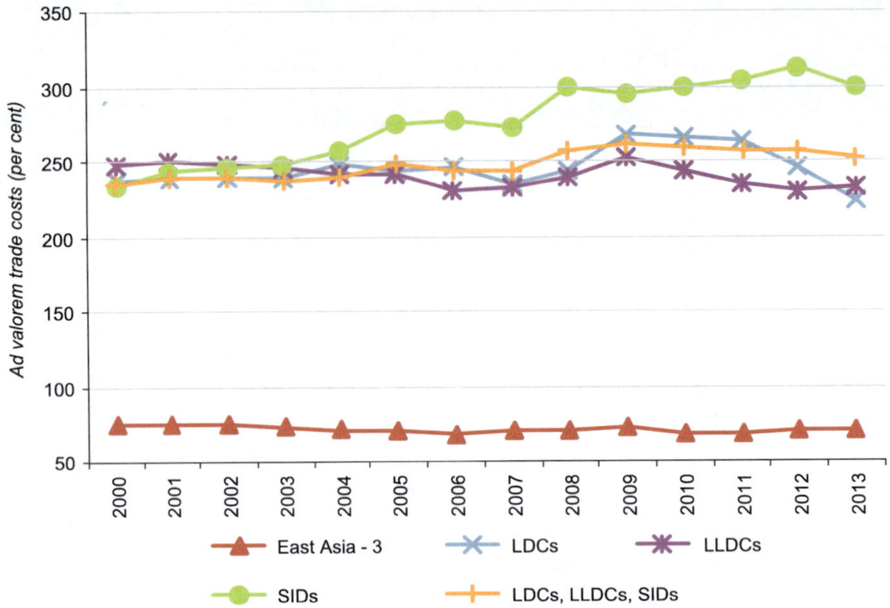

Sources: ESCAP-World Bank Trade Cost Database (accessed June 2016).

Note: The trade costs shown are tariff equivalents, calculated as trade-weighted average trade costs of countries in each group with the three largest developed economies (Germany, Japan and the United States). LDCs – least developed countries; LLDCs – landlocked developing countries; SIDS – small island developing States.

(ESCAP, 2015a), which found disparities between the subregions in their trade facilitation implementation levels. Given the strong correlation between trade facilitation and paperless trade implementation levels found in the survey and international trade costs, as explored in APTIR 2015,[3] there is a strong case for policymakers to pursue further reform in these areas in order to reduce trade costs, and ultimately enhance trade competitiveness and promote regional integration.

B. TRADE FACILITATION TOWARDS SEAMLESS SUPPLY CHAINS

In order to gain greater insight into the progress made and the remaining challenges towards trade facilitation and seamless supply chains, regional performance is analysed based on the latest data from the three metrics – the World Bank Logistics Performance Index (LPI)[4] and Trading Across Borders (TAB)[5] indicators as well as the UNCTAD Liner Shipping Connectivity Index (LSCI).[6] While the three sets of indicators are interrelated, there are also differences – LPI covers both "soft" and "hard" infrastructure aspects associated with moving goods across borders, while TAB focuses mainly on regulatory and procedural aspects at the border in terms of documentation. In turn, LSCI provides insights specifically into maritime connectivity and port efficiency, which remain an essential aspect of reducing international trade costs.

According to LPI 2016, the top trade logistics performers in the Asia-Pacific region are Singapore, which is ranked the highest, followed by Hong Kong, China in second place and Japan in third position. The LPI, through its six components captures "hard" and "soft" infrastructure elements of trade facilitation measures.

Figure 4.3 shows the relative performance of Asia-Pacific subregions for six components of LPI, i.e. efficiency of customs and border management clearance (customs); quality of trade and transport infrastructure (infrastructure); ease of arranging competitively priced shipments (international shipments); competence and quality of logistics services – trucking, forwarding, and customs brokerage (logistics quality and competence); ability to track and trace consignments (tracking and tracing); and frequency with which shipments reach consignees within scheduled or expected delivery times (timeliness).[7] The performance of ESCAP developed economies is also shown for reference purposes.

Overall, figure 4.3 shows that trade logistics performance varies greatly across the Asia-Pacific subregions. East and North-East Asia, the best performing Asia-Pacific subregion, is continuing to make progress across all components of LPI over time. The other Asia-Pacific subregions, with the exception North and Central Asia, have shown only incremental improvement between 2010 and 2016.

Figure 4.3 **Evolution of the Logistics Performance Index, by Asia-Pacific subregion, 2010-2016**

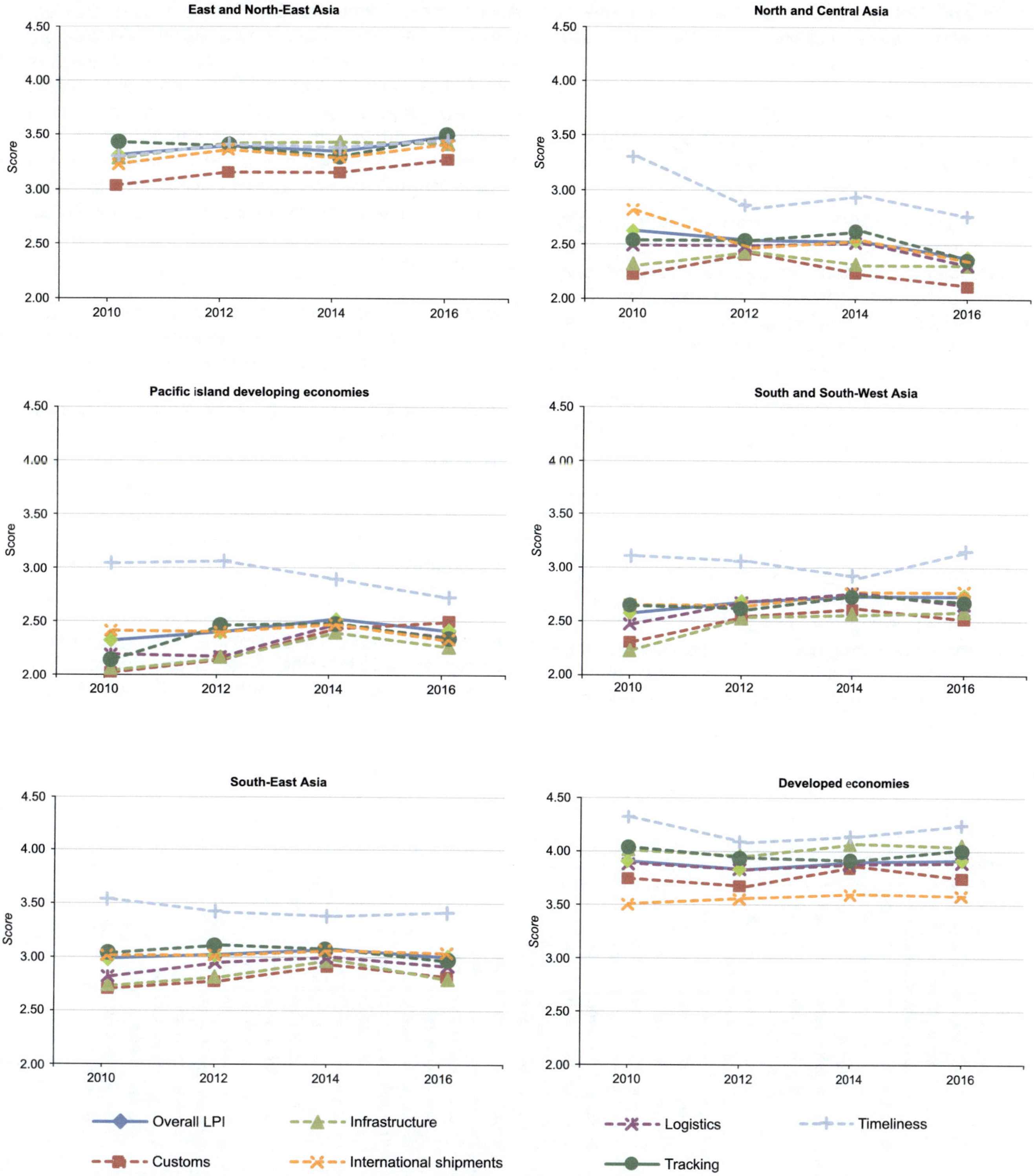

Sources: World Bank Logistics Performance Index (accessed August 2016).

Note: East and North-East Asia – China, Hong Kong, China, Republic of Korea, Mongolia; South-East Asia – Cambodia, Indonesia, Lao People's Democratic Republic, Malaysia, Myanmar, Philippines, Singapore, Thailand and Viet Nam; South and South-West Asia – Afghanistan, Bangladesh, India, Islamic Republic of Iran, Nepal, Pakistan and Turkey; Pacific island developing economies – Fiji and Papua New Guinea; North and Central Asia – Armenia, Georgia, Kazakhstan, Kyrgyzstan, Russian Federation, Tajikistan and Uzbekistan; developed economies – Australia, France, Germany, Japan, New Zealand, United Kingdom and the United States.

However, the rate of improvement and performance across indicators is mixed. A number of subregions – i.e. South-East Asia, South and South-West Asia, PIDEs and North and Central Asia – show uneven and, in some cases, declining performance in relation to the "timeliness" indicator.

> *"East and North-East Asia continue to top the Asia-Pacific region in terms of logistics and trade facilitation performance."*

The "timeliness" indicator, which provides some insights into the reliability and predictability of the supply chain, is particularly important for traders and producers. Hence, sustained improvement in this area would be beneficial to achieving overall competitiveness. The Asia-Pacific subregions show the widest range of performance in relation to the LPI "customs" and "tracking and tracing" components. Overall, "tracking and tracing" can be considered as one of the most challenging components, particularly for developing countries, due to the investments required for the technical infrastructure and solutions (World Bank, 2016a).

The seven worst logistics performers shown in figure 4.4 are all landlocked developing countries. This is unsurprising, as access to an efficient port is an important component of logistics performance. Furthermore, the requirements for transit and the frequent changes in modes of transport required by goods from the landlocked countries can adversely affect trade logistics in those countries.

A new methodology for the Trading Across Borders (TAB) of the World Bank Doing Business Indicators was introduced for the 2016 indicators. While this makes comparisons across time more problematic, the new methodology seeks to reflect the actual directions and volumes of international trade and differing regulatory burdens faced by traders (World Bank, 2016b).[8] The indicator looks at three components of the procedures required for importing and exporting, i.e. documentary compliance, border compliance and domestic transport.[9]

The time and costs of domestic transport are measured under the new methodology; however, they do not count towards the overall TAB rankings. Hence, it can be seen that landlocked countries fare much better under the new TAB methodology. In fact, in terms of overall TAB rankings (table 4.2), the top two performers in the Asia-Pacific region are landlocked Bhutan and Armenia, as they both have relatively lower times for importing and exporting, and cost of trade. The lowest ranking countries are in South and South-West Asia, i.e. Afghanistan, Bangladesh and Pakistan.

Figure 4.5 presents the subregional averages of time and cost to trade in terms of border and documentary compliance. The leading performers in the Asia-Pacific

Figure 4.4 Performance across six dimensions of trade logistics, 2016

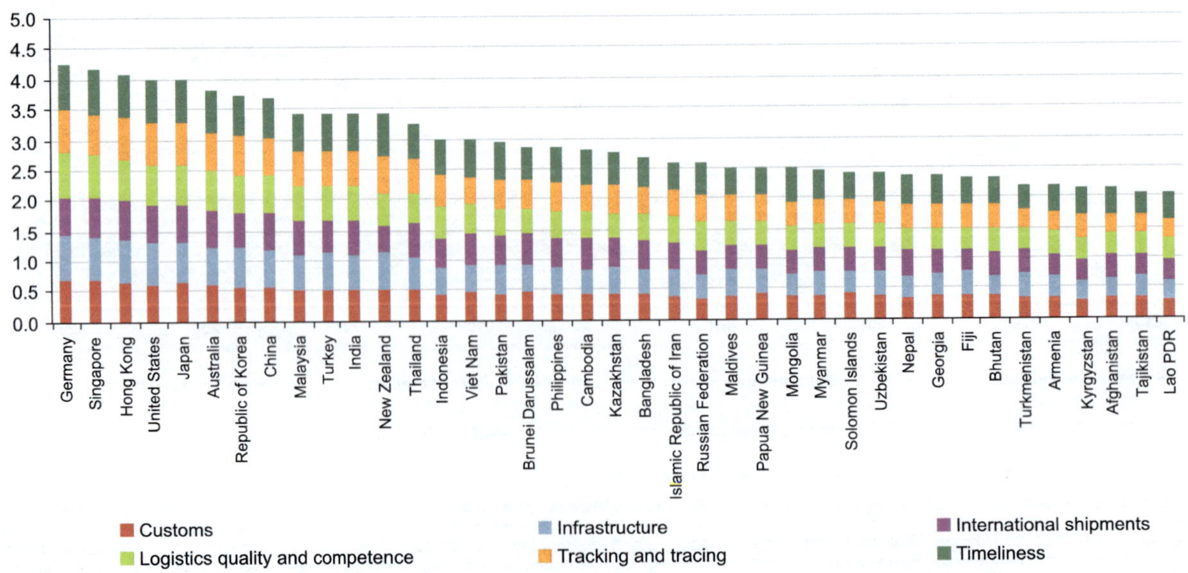

Sources: World Bank Logistics Performance Index (accessed July 2016).

Table 4.2 **Performance rankings according to LPI, TAB and LSCI, 2016**

Economy	LPI rank 2016	TAB rank 2016	LSCI rank 2016	Economy	LPI rank 2016	TAB rank 2016	LSCI rank 2016
Germany	1	35	8	Bangladesh	87	172	113
Singapore	5	41	3	Islamic Republic of Iran	96	167	88[a]
Hong Kong, China	9	47	6	Russian Federation	99	170	49
United States	10	34	7	Maldives	104	137	138
Japan	12	52	18	Papua New Guinea	105	163	139
Australia	19	89	76	Mongolia	108	74	1[a]
Republic of Korea	24	31	4	Myanmar	113	140	142
China	27	96	1	Solomon Islands	116	141	140
Malaysia	32	49	5	Uzbekistan	118	159	49[a]
Turkey	34	62	36	Nepal	124	60	43[a]
India	35	133	43	Georgia	130	78	154
New Zealand	37	55	92	Bhutan	135	21	43[a]
Thailand	45	56	46	Fiji	136	73	131
Indonesia	63	105	86	Armenia	141	29	36[a]
Viet Nam	64	99	25	Kyrgyzstan	146	83	49[a]
Pakistan	68	169	63	Afghanistan	150	174	63[a]
Philippines	71	95	101	Lao People's Democratic Republic	152	108	46[a]
Cambodia	73	98	155	Tajikistan	153	132	63[a]
Kazakhstan	77	122	49[a]	Guam	N/A	47	133
Azerbaijan	87	94	36[a]	Sri Lanka	N/A	90	24

Note: LPI rankings are based on the World Bank Logistics Performance Index Report 2016; TAB rankings are based on the World Bank Doing Business Report 2016; and UNCTAD LSCI rankings are based on data in 2016.

[a] The LSCI ranking of each landlocked country is based on the ranking of its main transit country.

Figure 4.5 **Border and trade documentary compliance, by Asia-Pacific subregion, compared with EU-3 and the United States, 2016**

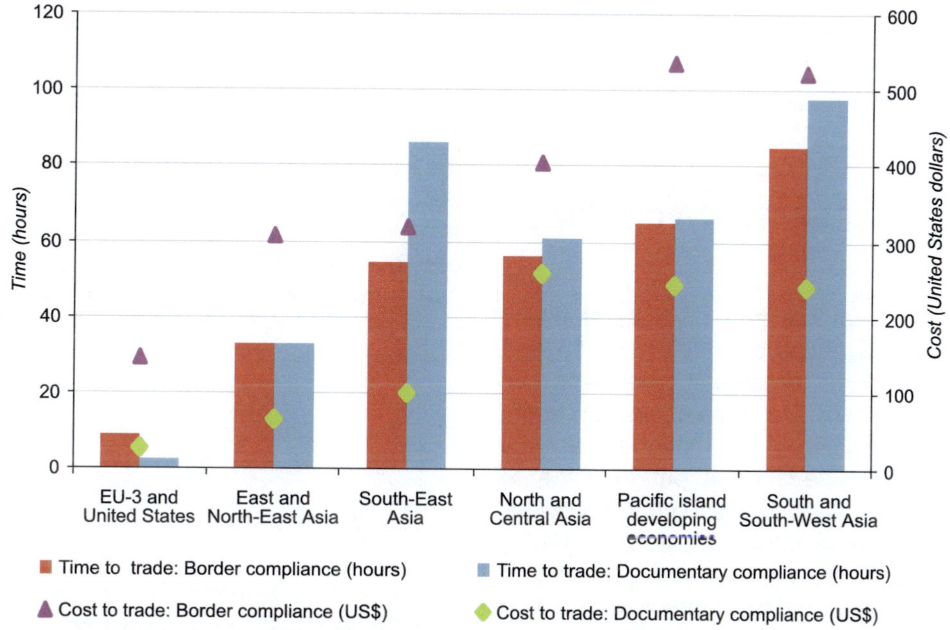

Sources: Calculation based on World Bank Doing Business Report 2016 (accessed July 2016).

Note: EU-3 and the United States – France, Germany, United Kingdom and United States; East and North-East Asia – China, Hong Kong, China, Japan, Republic of Korea and Mongolia; South-East Asia – Brunei Darussalam, Cambodia, Indonesia, Lao People's Democratic Republic, Malaysia, Myanmar, Philippines, Singapore, Thailand, Timor-Leste and Viet Nam; North and Central Asia – Armenia, Azerbaijan, Georgia, Kazakhstan, Kyrgyzstan, Russian Federation, Tajikistan and Uzbekistan; Pacific island developing economies – Fiji, Kiribati, Marshall Islands, Federated States of Micronesia, Palau, Papua New Guinea, Samoa and Solomon Islands; South and South-West Asia – Afghanistan, Bangladesh, Bhutan, India, Islamic Republic of Iran, Maldives, Nepal, Pakistan, Sri Lanka and Turkey.

region are still in East and North-East Asia with trading time associated with border and documentary compliance of 33 hours, and average cost of trade associated with border and documentary compliance of $309 and $66, respectively. While border and documentary compliance costs in South-East Asia are only slightly higher than those of North-East Asia, compliance times are much higher. In particular, documentary compliance times in South-East Asia are found to exceed those in North and Central Asia as well as the PIDEs.

The subregion with the highest average time and cost associated with border and documentary compliance is South and South-West Asia, with trading time associated with border and documentary compliance of 85 hours and 98 hours, respectively, and an average cost of trade associated with border and documentary compliance of $523 and $242, respectively. Nevertheless, within the South and South-West Asia, there is enormous variation. For Bhutan (the best subregional and the Asia-Pacific region performer), which enjoys a very open border policy with India, the trading time associated with border and documentary compliance is two hours for both measures, while the average cost of trade associated with border and documentary compliance is $84 and $50, respectively. For Afghanistan (the lowest ranking subregional and the Asia-Pacific region performer), the time associated with border and documentary compliance is 72 hours and 290 hours, respectively, while the average cost associated with border and documentary compliance is $681 and $622, respectively.

C. PROGRESS IN MULTILATERAL AND REGIONAL COOPERATION FOR TRADE FACILITATION

Cooperation at the regional and multilateral levels is required in order to effectively facilitate trade and reduce trade costs, given the cross-border nature of global production networks and value chains. In recent years a number of significant international, regional and bilateral initiatives have been put in place to enhance cooperation in trade facilitation and paperless trade. Almost all regional trade agreements (RTAs) negotiated since 2010 by economies in the region include trade facilitation provisions. Moreover, the WTO Trade Facilitation Agreement (TFA), which was finalized at the Ministerial Conference in December 2013 as part the "Bali Package", is now in the process of ratification by WTO members.[10] At the regional level, the seventy-second Commission session of ESCAP adopted the Framework Agreement of the Facilitation of Cross-border Paperless Trade in Asia and the Pacific, highlighting the fact that cooperation on progressive trade facilitation measures is an increasing priority in the Asia-Pacific region in the era of digital economy.

1. WTO Trade Facilitation Agreement

> *"The WTO Trade Facilitation Agreement provides a unique policy instrument for Governments to accelerate ongoing trade facilitation reforms."*

The objective of the WTO Trade Facilitation Agreement (TFA) is to facilitate the movement, clearance and release of goods through more efficient customs and border procedures. The TFA will enter into force once two thirds of the WTO members have completed their domestic ratification processes (or 110 members, given the current WTO membership). As of 10 November 2016, 96 WTO members – of which 26 are ESCAP regional member States and associate members – had ratified the TFA.[11] As members prepare for the implementation of the TFA, 24 developing economies in the Asia-Pacific region have already submitted notifications of relevant provisions of the TFA under Category A (figure 4.6).

Category A notifications indicate the provisions that the WTO members intend to have implemented by the time the TFA enters into force (or within a year of entry into force in the case of least developed countries). An analysis of these notifications also provides some indication of the level of trade facilitation implementation and policy priorities among the members. On average, the 24 Asia-Pacific economies have fully notified nearly 60% of all substantive provisions in the TFA. This sample includes six landlocked developing countries and four least developed countries; the results indicate that most developing countries have already made good progress in implementing many of the measures included in the TFA.

> *"Most developing countries in the Asia-Pacific region have already made good progress in implementing the WTO Trade Facilitation Agreement."*

The Asia-Pacific region is home both to the most and the least efficient economies in terms of trade facilitation. In fact, the only three economies, among all WTO members, to have fully notified all 12 articles of the TFA under Category A, are: the Republic of Korea; Singapore and Hong Kong, China. These

Figure 4.6 **Category A notifications of 24 Asia-Pacific economies (article level)**

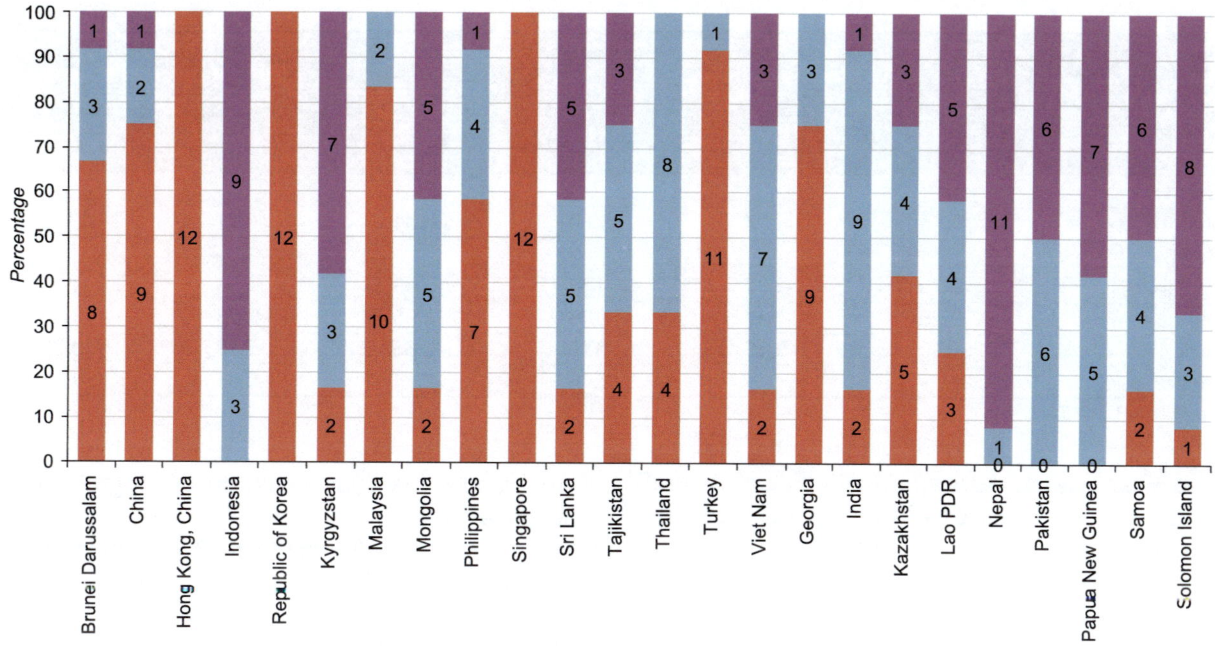

Sources: Updated from Duval and Bayona (2015).

economies are also recognized global leaders in trade facilitation. Figure 4.6 also shows that landlocked developing countries (Kazakhstan, Kyrgyzstan, the Lao People's Democratic Republic, Mongolia, Nepal and Tajikistan) have fully notified a lower percentage of the TFA than other economies (Duval and Bayona, 2015). The ability to implement trade facilitation measures is closely related to different aspects of human and institutional development, as may be captured by income, the human development index, internet access, or the corruption perception index (UNCTAD, 2016).

The TFA provides a unique and valuable tool and policy instrument for Governments in developing countries to revitalize or accelerate ongoing trade facilitation reforms aimed at reducing trade costs and enabling greater participation in global value chains (GVCs). Furthermore, the TFA can provide greater impetus for economies to adopt increasingly advanced trade facilitation reform, such as paperless trade initiatives.

Implementation both of the binding and non-binding TFA measures is expected to result in a 5% reduction in trade costs, on average, under a partial implementation scenario, and an 11% reduction under the more ambitious full implementation scenario (ESCAP, 2015c). In contrast, implementation of the binding TFA measures alone results, at best, in a 6.8% decrease in trade costs on average in the Asia-Pacific region. Under a WTO TFA+ scenario, where paperless trade measures not included in the TFA are also implemented, the average trade cost reduction across countries increases to more than 13%.

> *"Implementation of both the binding and non-binding WTO Trade Facilitation Agreement measures is expected to cut trade costs by 11%."*

Both the partial and the full implementation scenarios suggest that TFA measures, which will have the highest impact, on average, on trade costs are those related to "formalities", both in the case of binding and non-binding measures. However, analysis of the Category A notifications suggests that the provisions related to "formalities" and the "release and clearance of goods" (TFA Articles 10 and 7), including Single Window implementation, are those which will require more time and technical assistance for implementation in the Asia-Pacific region (Duval and Bayona, 2015). Beyond the TFA measures, the WTO+ scenario analysis suggests that the largest reduction of trade costs is achieved through partial or full implementation of paperless trade measures not specified in that Agreement (table 4.3).

Table 4.3 **Changes in international trade costs of the Asia-Pacific region as a result of WTO TFA implementation**

(Percentage)

	WTO TFA (Binding only)		WTO TFA (Binding + non-binding)		WTO TFA+ (Binding + non-binding + other paperless trade)	
	Partially implemented	Fully implemented	Partially implemented	Fully implemented	Partially implemented	Fully implemented
Model 1						
Overall TF	-3.15	-6.77	-5.38	-11.11	-6.71	-13.16
Model 3						
Transparency	-0.79	-1.67	-1.13	-3.09	-1.13	-3.09
Formalities	-2.25	-3.17	-2.66	-3.95	-2.66	-3.95
Institution	-0.10	-0.35	-0.10	-0.35	-0.10	-0.35
Paperless trade	-	-	-1.45	-2.34	-2.91	-4.83

Source: ESCAP (2015a).

2. The Framework Agreement on Facilitation of Cross-border Paperless Trade in Asia and the Pacific

> *"The Framework Agreement on Facilitation of Cross-border Paperless Trade in Asia and the Pacific is inclusive and designed to enable least developed and landlocked developing countries to participate."*

The recently adopted Framework Agreement is a regional United Nations treaty wholly dedicated to facilitation of paperless trade, and in particular the electronic exchange of trade-related data and documents between Governments, and between businesses and Governments, across borders. It opened for signature by ESCAP member States on 1 October 2016 at the United Nations Headquarters in New York and will enter into force 90 days after five United Nations Member States have ratified it (see box 4.1 for more details).[12]

The new regional agreement is complementary to the TFA, which focuses on more conventional trade facilitation measures. For example, while the TFA includes a provision on developing a Single Window at the national level, either paper-based or electronic, it does not address the issue of interoperability of Single Windows or cross-border paperless trade. Taking part in the implementation of the Framework Agreement is therefore expected to enable ESCAP members to more fully implement the Single Window provision of the TFA given that "[WTO] members shall, to the extent possible and practical, use information technology to support the single window".[13]

More broadly, the implementation of progressive and innovative cross-border paperless trade measures under, or related to, the Framework Agreement can be expected to bring about significant benefits in terms of new export potential and reduced trade transactions costs (box 4.1). However, taking into account the very different readiness levels of Asia-Pacific countries in trade facilitation, capacity-building and technical assistance will need to be provided to less-advanced ESCAP member States, as highlighted in the Framework Agreement itself.

> *"Adoption of new generation trade facilitation measures will be essential to competition in the digital economy."*

D. CONCLUSION

While economies in Asia and the Pacific continue to make improvements in trade facilitation, gaps among subregional economies remain. The heterogeneity in trade facilitation performance and trade cost reduction is a hindrance to full regional integration and efficient value chains. Given these disparities in development levels, access to legal and technical assistance as well as capacity-building may be required by countries with special needs in order implement more advanced trade facilitation and paperless trade measures.

In this regard the significant progress in multilateral and regional levels on trade facilitation – i.e. the WTO TFA and the Framework Agreement on Facilitation of Cross-border Paperless Trade in Asia and the Pacific – is encouraging, as these developments benefit both the trade facilitation high performers as well

Box 4.1 Innovation in trade facilitation and economic integration: ESCAP member States conclude an intergovernmental agreement on cross-border paperless trade facilitation

The Global Survey on Trade Facilitation and Paperless Trade Implementation, which was conducted in 2015 by the United Nations Regional Commissions in collaboration with other international partners, confirmed that developed and developing countries are increasingly using technological innovations to facilitate the exchange of information between traders and regulatory authorities domestically, investing in Single Window and other paperless trade systems. However, the lack of appropriate legal and technical frameworks enabling the recognition of electronic data and documents across borders by public and private stakeholders located in different countries along the international supply chain often means that international transactions cannot be completed without time and resource-intensive paper documents. Since 2012, ESCAP member States have been working together on developing cross-border paperless trade solutions, and are now negotiating a cutting-edge intergovernmental agreement dedicated to this issue.

Implementation of cross-border paperless trade measures can potentially increase Asia-Pacific exports annually by $36 billion up to $257 billion. In tandem, the time required to export would fall between 24% and 44%, and the direct costs between 17% and 31%, depending on the reform scenario considered. Furthermore, the total direct cost savings across all trade in the Asia-Pacific region would be approximately $1 billion annually for partial reform, and $7 billion annually for full implementation.

Given the large potential benefits associated with the implementation of these "next generation" trade facilitation measures, it is in the interest of countries to work together and develop the legal and technical protocols needed for the seamless exchange of regulatory and commercial data and documents along the international supply chain. Some work has already been done bilaterally as well as in several Asian subregions (e.g. the ASEAN Single Window). The implementation of the intergovernmental Framework Agreement on Facilitation of Cross-border Paperless Trade in Asia and the Pacific, adopted by the ESCAP Commission in May 2016, is expected to build upon as well as support existing initiatives, providing a "digital" complement to the WTO Agreement on Trade Facilitation. The ESCAP Framework Agreement will provide ESCAP member States who ratify the regional treaty with:

(a) A common set of general principles, based on which paperless trade systems could be implemented;
(b) A dedicated intergovernmental platform to exchange best practices, and request/offer capacity-building and technical assistance;
(c) The opportunity to multilaterally develop, adopt and implement more specific and detailed technical and/or legal protocols needed to achieve safe and secure cross-border paperless trade (e.g. the exchange and legal recognition of e-Certificates of Origin or other relevant documents).

More information about the Framework Agreement is available from:
www.unescap.org/resources/framework-agreement-facilitation-cross-border-paperless-trade-asia-and-pacific

as economies that are lagging behind by providing platforms for technology transfer, capacity-building and harmonization of international standards and tools.

Looking to the future, although regional or multilateral cooperation on trade facilitation will become increasingly important in harmonizing and simplifying trade processes and accelerating reform, policymakers will still need to work hard on enabling interagency and public-private sector cooperation domestically. This includes developing the consultation and monitoring systems necessary for identifying key bottlenecks and prioritizing trade facilitation reform accordingly.[14]

Endnotes

1 Updated information on ratification of the WTO TFA is available from www.tfafacility.org. Data on trade facilitation implementation levels in Asia-Pacific (and globally) are available from the UNRCs Trade Facilitation and Paperless Trade Implementation Survey website, http://unnext.unescap.org/UNTFSurvey2015.asp; See also Duval and Bayona (2015).

2 This is done using bilateral aggregate trade cost data from the ESCAP-World Bank Database, presented in Arvis and others (2016).

3 See figure 4.2 of the *Asia-Pacific Trade and Investment Report 2015* (ESCAP, 2015b).

4 The LPI, which seeks to assess the "logistics friendliness" of countries, is compiled based on a global survey of logistics operators – including global freight forwarders

and express carriers – of the country in which they operate in and with which they trade. The qualitative assessments of the logistics operators are supplemented with quantitative data on performance of key aspects of the logistics chain in that country. More information available at http://lpi.worldbank.org/about.

5 Trading Across Borders (TAB) is the component of the World Bank's Doing Business Indicator that records the time and cost (excluding tariffs) associated with exporting and importing goods by looking at three sets of procedures: documentary compliance; border compliance; and domestic transport. More information on TAB is available from www.doingbusiness.org/data/exploretopics/trading-across-borders.

6 LSCI comprises five components: fleet deployment – number of ships; container carrying-capacity; number of companies that deploy their container ships from a country's ports; number of liner services; and maximum vessel size.

7 The "customs" component can be considered as the performance of the "soft" infrastructure' i.e. the efficiency of border management agencies and procedures, while the "infrastructure" component captures the "hard infrastructure" requirements for trade in goods. For developing countries in particular, progress needs to be made on both of these fronts (World Bank, 2016b).

8 More information about the new methodology is available from www.doingbusiness.org/methodology/trading-across-borders.

9 Documentary compliance refers to the compliance associated with documentary requirements of all government agencies of the origin, destination and transit economies. This includes obtaining, preparing, processing presenting and submitting documents. Border compliance refers to the compliance associated with regulations or inspections that are mandatory in order for a shipment to cross a border. Such compliance extends to obtaining, preparing and submitting documents during port or border handling, customs clearance and inspection procedures. Domestic transport performance can be determined by a number of factors, including geography, road capacity, infrastructure and proximity to border. More details are available at World Bank (2016b).

10 The WTO TFA is the centrepiece of this package, thus making it the world's first truly global multilateral trade agreement concluded since the creation of WTO. The full list of countries that ratified the agreement is available from www.tfafacility.org/ratifications.

11 Thirty-six ESCAP member States and two associate members are also WTO members; of those, 12 members have not yet ratified (as of 10 November 2016) the WTO TFA, i.e. Armenia, Fiji, Indonesia, Kyrgyzstan, Maldives, Mongolia, Nepal, Papua New Guinea, Solomon Islands, Tajikistan, Tonga and Vanuatu.

12 The finalized text of the Framework Agreement on the Facilitation of Cross-border Paperless Trade is available from www.un.org/ga/search/view_doc.asp?symbol=E/ESCAP/RES/72/4&Lang=E.

13 Article 10.4.4 of the WTO Agreement on Trade Facilitation, https://www.wto.org/english/thewto_e/minist_e/mc9_e/desci36_e.htm

14 This may be done by applying the Business Process Analysis methodology developed by the United Nations Network of Experts for Paperless Trade and Transport in Asia and the Pacific (2015). Available from https://unnext.unescap.org/.

REFERENCES

Arvis, J., and others (2016). Trade costs in the developing world: 1996-2010. *World Trade Review*, vol. 15, No. 3, pp. 451-474.

Duval, Y., and P. Bayona (2015). Implementation of the WTO Trade Facilitation Agreement in the Asia-Pacific region: analysis of Category A submissions. Trade Insights, No. 7, Bangkok: ESCAP. Available from www.unescap.org/resources/implementation-wto-trade-facilitation-agreement-asia-pacific-region-analysis-category.

Duval, Y. and others (2015). Trade facilitation implementation in Asia-Pacific 2015: moving towards paperless trade. Trade Insights, No. 12. Bangkok: ESCAP. Available from www.unescap.org/publications/trade-insights-series.

Economic and Social Commission for Asia and the Pacific (2014). *Estimating the Benefits of Cross-border Paperless Trade: a Report in Support of Implementation of ESCAP Resolution 68/3*. Bangkok. Available from www.unescap.org/resources/estimating-benefits-cross-border-paperless-trade.

______ (2015a). *UNRCs Trade Facilitation and Paperless Trade Implementation Survey 2015: Asia and the Pacific Report*. Bangkok. Available from www.unescap.org/resources/unrcs-trade-facilitation-and-paperless-trade-implementation-survey-2015-asia-and-pacific.

______ (2015b). *Asia-Pacific Trade and Investment Report 2015: Supporting Participation in Value Chains*. Sales No. E.15.II.F.15. Available from www.unescap.org/resources/asia-pacific-trade-and-investment-report-2015-supporting-participation-value-chains.

______ (2015c). *Trade Facilitation and Paperless Trade: State of Play and the Way Forward for Asia and the Pacific*. Studies in Trade and Investment No. 85. Bangkok. ST/ESCAP/2742. Available from: www.unescap.org/resources/trade-facilitation-and-paperless-trade-state-play-and-way-forward-asia-and-pacific.

UNCTAD (2015). *Review of Maritime Transport 2015*. Geneva. Available from http://unctad.org/en/Pages/Publications/Review-of-Maritime-Transport-(Series).aspx .

______ (2016). *Trade Facilitation and Development*. Geneva. Available from http://unctad.org/en/PublicationsLibrary/dtltlb2016d1_en.pdf

United Nations Network of Experts for Paperless Trade and Transport in Asia and the Pacific (2015). Global Survey on Trade Facilitation and Paperless Trade Implementation: 2014-2015. Available from http://unnext.unescap.org/tfforum14-survey.asp.

World Bank (2016a). *Connecting to Compete, Trade Logistics in the Global Economy: the Logistics Performance Index and its Indicators*. Washington, D.C. Available from https://wb-lpi-media.s3.amazonaws.com/LPI_Report_2016.pdf.

______ (2016b) *Doing Business 2016: Measuring Regulatory Quality and Efficiency*. Washington, D.C. Available from www.doingbusiness.org/reports/global-reports/doing-business-2016.

ONLINE DATABASES

ESCAP-World Bank Trade Cost Database. Available from http://artnet.unescap.org/databases.html#first.

UNCTAD. UNCTADstat. Liner Shipping Connectivity Index. Available from http://unctadstat.unctad.org/wds/TableViewer/tableView.aspx?ReportId=92.

World Bank. Logistics Performance Index. Available from http://lpi.worldbank.org/.

World Bank. Doing Business – Trading Across Borders. Available from www.doingbusiness.org/data/exploretopics/trading-across-borders.

World Trade Organization. Trade Facilitation Agreement Facility. Available from www.tfafacility.org/updates.

CHAPTER 5

REGIONAL TRENDS IN TRADE POLICIES: BUILDING TALLER FENCES?

Changes in trade policies tend to mirror the overall tone and tenor of globalization. The rhetoric of protectionism that is gaining popularity among G20 economies, together with events such as "Brexit", does not bode well for the efforts towards reviving trade growth. This general "inward looking" mood in politics is also evident in the recent trends in trade policies, which is tilting towards increased restrictiveness. Liberalization efforts are increasingly limited to the "like-minded" countries and, de facto, discriminate against all others, as in some recent attempts to create mega-regional trade agreements.[1] However, since there is still considerable public resentment and angst regarding these agreements, it is possible that such efforts will be put on hold for some time. More importantly, an increasing protectionist stand does not resonate well with the universally accepted 2030 Agenda for Sustainable Development, in which trade is seen as an important means of implementation.

Against this backdrop, this chapter analyses the recent trends in trade policies that affect trade in goods and services, focusing on the region but also depicting the most important global traits. In addition to presenting the overall state of play, further details are provided concerning these trends in terms of analysing selected sectors (steel) and country groups (G20 and ASEAN). The chapter presents evidence on the continuing prominence of non-tariff measures in the trade policy portfolio of countries. Recognizing the increasing importance of the services sector, the chapter also reviews recent empirical findings relevant for the economies in the region on use of policies affecting trade in services and services sector in general.

A. RECENT TRADE POLICY DEVELOPMENTS AFFECTING TRADE IN GOODS

1. Trade policy measures under WTO disciplines

Trade policy measures can restrict and enable trade. These measures affect imports and exports of goods, and come in a form of changed tariff rates or other duties, quantitative restrictions including bans, customs procedures, taxes and a whole array of other non-tariff measures.[2] Their significant feature is the ability to discriminate among markets, products and services. This sub-section analyses the trends in trade policy measures falling strictly under the purview of WTO disciplines, based on the data collected by the WTO secretariat (WTO, 2016).

> *"The global stock of trade-restrictive measures increased by 17.5 new measures per month."*

Tables 5.1 and 5.2 present the recent trends in restrictiveness and liberalization of trade policies falling under WTO disciplines. From mid-October 2014 to mid-May 2016 (hereafter, the reporting period), the monthly increase in the global stock of trade-restrictive measures amounted to almost 17.5 new measures per month, up from 15 reported as an average during the preceding reporting period from mid-November 2013 to mid-May 2015.[3] At the same time, the number of trade-liberalizing measures also increased from 16.2 to around 19 in the current reporting period (WTO, 2015; and ESCAP, 2015).

The past seven months of the reporting period (mid-October 2015 to mid-May 2016), however, present an alarming picture with the monthly average of newly introduced restrictive trade measures amounting to 22. This constitutes the highest monthly average registered since 2011 and is larger than the monthly amount of new liberalizing measures introduced during the same period (18.6), implying the existence of a trend towards a growing stockpile of trade-restrictive measures (WTO, 2015). In the Asia-Pacific region, on average, 6.6 new restrictive measures were introduced during the full reporting period compared with 4.5 liberalizing measures. Following the global trend, during the last seven months of the reporting period the Asia-Pacific region introduced, on average, 7.7 restrictive trade measures per month. WTO estimated that since reporting began in 2008, of a total of 2,835 trade-restrictive measures worldwide, only 708 had been removed by mid-May 2016 (WTO, 2015), indicating that world has built up a considerable stock of protectionist measures.

Nevertheless, in the last reporting period, there was a very small but still a positive step towards removing some of that protectionist armoury as the world at large introduced 332 new trade-restrictive and 352 liberalizing measures. However, not all regions contributed proportionally to this result. The Asia-Pacific region introduced 125 new trade-restrictive measures compared with 85 liberalizing ones (tables 5.1 and 5.2). Asia-Pacific economies therefore accounted for 37.7% (24%) of trade-restricting (trade-liberalizing) measures introduced globally, which is somewhat less than their joint share of global exports (40%) and global imports (36%) discussed in chapter 1. India and Indonesia, by introducing 28 and 24 new measures, respectively, remain among the top economies in pursuing the use of trade-restrictive measures. At the same time, in terms of liberalization, India and China jointly earned the top rank by adding 16 new liberalizing measures each.

> *"For every trade liberalizing measure introduced, the region added one and a half restrictive measures during the reporting period."*

The impact of different trade measures varies considerably; while some may have significant commercial implications for trading partners, others cause relatively little harm, and some may actually enable trade. In order to assess the impact of individual trade measures, price and income elasticities as well as price impacts must be observed or estimated. This is often too complex due to data constraints, making it difficult to quantify commercial impacts of individual measures. While mere mapping and tracking of implemented trade measures do not suffice for an assessment of the restrictiveness of the global trade environment, they do, however, provide a good sense of

Table 5.1 **Increase in new trade and trade-related restrictive measures, mid-October 2014 to mid-May 2016 and mid-October 2015 to mid-May 2016**

Type of measure	Mid-October 2014 to mid-May 2016		Mid-October 2015 to mid-May 2016	
	World	Asia-Pacific region	World	Asia-Pacific region
Imports	252	94	116	39
of which, tariffs	**154**	**49**	**66**	**18**
Exports	55	18	24	9
Other	25	13	14	6
Total	332	125	154	54
Measures per month	17.5	6.6	22.0	7.7

Source: ESCAP calculation based on data from WTO (2016).

Note: Import measures comprise the following main categories tariffs, customs procedures, taxes, quantitative restrictions and others. Export measures comprise duties, quantitative restrictions and others.

Table 5.2 **Increase in new trade liberalizing measures, mid-October 2014 to mid-May 2016 and mid-October 2015 to mid-May 2016**

Type of measure	Mid-October 2014 to mid-May 2016		Mid-October 2015 to mid-May 2016	
	World	Asia-Pacific region	World	Asia-Pacific region
Import	295	57	103	21
of which, tariffs	**234**	**41**	**74**	**14**
Export	52	14	26	6
Other	7	14	3	4
Total	354	85	132	31
Measures per month	18.6	4.5	18.9	4.4

Source: ESCAP calculation based on data from WTO (2016).

Note: Import measures comprise the following main categories tariffs, customs procedures, taxes, quantitative restrictions and others. Export measures comprise duties, quantitative restrictions and others.

the direction in which the trend in usage of restrictive measures is going. Furthermore, as the impacts of trade-restrictive measures are cumulative, counting both new and previously implemented measures still in place allows for an enhanced understanding of an increase in total trade costs, which are mostly a reflection of the tariffs, other protectionist measures and procedures at the border, and other regulatory barriers beyond the border.

Two overall trends emerge from the previous discussions. First, even though globally trade-liberalizing measures exceeded restrictive measures during the reporting period, a build-up stock of restrictive measures is still towering over any liberalizing attempts. Moreover, the largest trading region, Asia and the Pacific, introduced many more restrictive than liberalizing measures during this period. Second, a worrying trend, globally as well as regionally, is the surge in the number of trade restrictive measures adopted per month from mid-Oct 2015 to mid-May 2016 compared with the overall reporting period. At the same time, the number of trade-liberalizing measures adopted per month remained more or less the same.

Tariff hikes remained the most widely adopted trade restrictiveness measure, contributing to 66% and 40% of the global and regional trade restrictive measures, respectively. Unilateral tariff reductions accounted for more than 66% of worldwide liberalizing trade measures and almost half of the Asia-Pacific ones (table 5.2).

To be able to respond to specific trade concerns, Governments may make use of trade remedy measures that allow them to utilize flexibility afforded by members' WTO commitments, i.e. by temporarily imposing higher tariffs on imports from individual sources. Typical trade-remedy measures come in the form of anti-dumping duties (ADs), countervailing duties (CVDs) and safeguards,[4] which allow Governments to address specific concerns arising from dumping, trade distorting subsidies and import surges. Trade remedy measures may, however, in certain circumstances be used as a protectionist tool by Governments facing pressure from domestic companies; they are actually listed as the contingent protection in the UNCTAD/WTO classification of non-tariff measures (see more details in subsection 2). Monitoring their usage therefore enables a broad assessment of the trade restrictiveness of the trading environment. An emerging trend is the utilization of trade remedies as often as, or even more often than traditional protectionist measures, as discussed above (tables 5.3 and 5.2).

"The ratio of initiations of trade-remedy measures to terminations increased significantly, both globally and regionally."

During the reporting period 283 new trade remedies were initiated, of which 106 were initiated by Asia-Pacific economies (table 5.3 and ESCAP, 2015). However, the ratio of initiations of trade-remedy measures to terminations increased significantly globally and regionally, compared with the preceding period, leading to a large increase in the overall number of barriers to trade. Metal products – particularly steel products (see box 5.2) – as well as chemicals, and plastics and rubber accounted for a large share of this increase (WTO, 2016). India was the top initiator of trade remedy cases in the reporting period, initiating 33 new trade remedies, followed by Turkey which initiated 22. India, however, was also the top terminator, ending 21 trade remedies, while Turkey ending only four. Anti-dumping duties remain the most popular form of trade remedies.

2. Trade policy measures beyond WTO disciplines

WTO reporting does not capture all potential trade-restricting measures, as members merely notify measures that fall within the WTO ruling coverage or disciplines set by WTO agreements. For example, in the aftermath of the 2008-2009 financial crisis, many Governments resorted to subsidized financing in the form of bailing out sectors (especially the banking and financial sector) that were in severe difficulties. Such measures are not part of WTO disciplines (agreements) and thus are not included among measures collected for WTO reports. However, the Global Trade Alert (GTA) initiative, gathering data from a wider range of sources and consequently capturing a larger variety of trade distorting measures, aims to close the data gap on less transparent trade distorting measures. The GTA data records all "state measure" that affects the commercial interests of a trading partner and is not confined to border measures, which is the focus of WTO data used in the previous sub-section. Measures such as domestic regulations, stimulus packages, and subsidies which affect commercial interests of a trading partner gets coverage under GTA, even though some of these measures need not be subject to WTO disciplines. Due to the more comprehensive nature of the GTA data, it is possible to obtain a more nuanced picture of the overall trend in use of trade measures.

"Bailouts, trade defence measures, import tariff increases and localization requirements constitute the majority of trade restrictive measures."

A recent GTA report confirms that resorting to protectionism – up by 50% on that observed in 2014 – has increased significantly (Evenett and Fritz, 2016). For example, in 2015, trade-restrictive measures outnumbered trade-liberalizing ones by three-to-one, a trend that will presumably prevail in 2016; in the first four months of 2016, more than 150 protectionist measures were implemented compared with the average of the first four months since 2010, which was between 50 and 100 measures. Three fifths of the trade restrictive measures taken during 2015 came in the form of the following four measures: bailouts; trade defence measures; import tariff increases; and localization requirements (Evenett and Fritz, 2016). From mid-October 2014 to mid-May 2016, the Asia-Pacific region was responsible for introducing 700 (approximately 60%) of the 1,180 trade-restrictive measures introduced worldwide. Manufacturing and agriculture were affected the most (figure 5.1).

Table 5.3 **Trade-remedy measures, mid-October-2014 to mid-May 2016, and mid-October 2015 to mid-May 2016**

Trade remedies		Mid-October 2014 to mid-May 2016		Mid-October 2015 to mid-May 2016	
		World	Asia-Pacific region	World	Asia-Pacific region
Initiation	**Total**	**283**	**106**	**118**	**46**
	Anti-dumping	218	87	88	37
	safeguards	27	11	13	4
	Countervailing	38	7	17	5
Termination	Total	188	75	56	18
	Anti-dumping	156	67	45	16
	safeguards	13	6	6	2
	Countervailing	19	2	5	0
Ratio of initiation to termination		**1.5**	**1.4**	**2.1**	**2.6**

Source: ESCAP calculation based on data from WTO (2016).

"The overall trend in policy mix of the G20 is still pointing in an increasingly protectionist direction."

According to GTA data,[5] of the economies in Asia and the Pacific region, the Russian Federation and India implemented the largest number of "red" or discriminatory measures during 2013 to mid-May 2016, when they introduced 261 and 227 measures, respectively (table 5.4), putting them on a par with the United States of America, which implemented 259. Box 5.1 highlights the case of a surge in protectionism across G20 economies, including its regional members, which could have detrimental impact on overall global economic growth prospects.

On the flip side, it is estimated that China's commercial interests were harmed 484 times, from January 2015 to May 2016, which is equivalent to China's commercial interests on average being harmed on

Figure 5.1 **Sectoral composition of new restrictions, including less-transparent measures (share of total), mid-October 2014 to mid-May 2016**

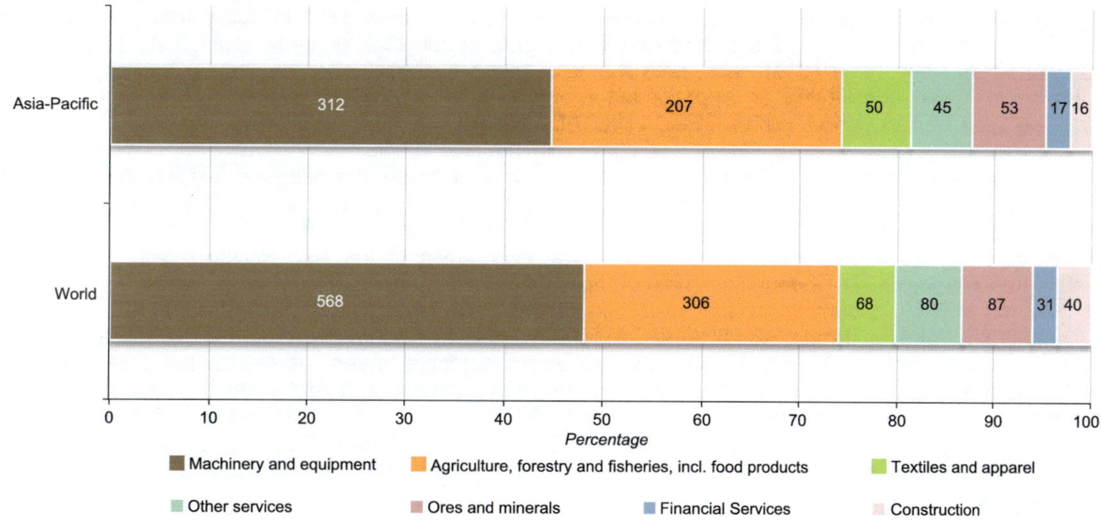

Source: ESCAP calculation based on data from Global Trade Alert, 2016.

Table 5.4 **Ranking of Asia-Pacific countries according to the overall number of red[a] measures implemented**

Implementing jurisdiction	"Red" measures		
	2013-July 2016	Mid-October 2014 to mid-May 2016	Mid-October 2015 to mid-May 2016
Russian Federation	261	119	42
India	227	87	28
Indonesia	92	43	7
Kazakhstan	76	26	7
Japan	70	47	7
Turkey	68	33	6
Australia	51	27	12
Pakistan	44	19	8
Republic of Korea	31	10	1
Viet Nam	31	11	2

Source: ESCAP calculation based on data from Global Trade Alert, 2016.

[a] GTA codes a measure as "red" if it almost certainly discriminates against a foreign commercial interest (Evenett and Fritz, 2016).

Box 5.1 **G20: Surge in protectionism**

The G20 includes the world's largest trading economies, including eight in Asia. In 2014, almost 60% of Asia-Pacific exports went to G20 members. Consequently, any trade-restrictive measures adopted by G20 members are of particular significance for the Asia-Pacific region. Since the global financial crisis, G20 leaders have repeatedly vowed to roll back existing protectionist measures and resist imposing additional ones. However, there is plenty of evidence that G20 fell short on their promises (Evenett, 2016; WTO-OECD-UNCTAD, 2016).

The latest WTO-OECD-UNCTAD overall assessment report on G20 trade measures covers mid-May 2016 to mid-October 2016. It shows that during this period, the G20 returned to the trend level for initiating new trade restrictions. The monthly average of new trade restrictions imposed came down to 17 per month – compared with 21 per month for the previous reporting period (mid-october 2015 to mid-May 2016), which was the highest counted since monitoring began in 2009. At the same time, the number of trade facilitating measures dropped 1 measure to 13 per month compared with the previous report and remained below the 2009-2015 average. Hence, the overall trend in policy mix is still pointing in an increasingly protectionist direction. Since 2008, only about 25% of trade restrictions recorded for G20 economies have been rolled back, with the total number of restrictive measures currently in place amounting to 1,671, constituting an approximate 6% growth in the overall stockpile of trade restrictions during the past review period (WTO-OECD-UNCTAD, 2016).

According to GTA data, which include a broader range of trade measures than the WTO-OECD-UNCTAD (2016) report, 736 new discriminatory measures were implemented worldwide in 2015, with G20 members being responsible for 599[a] or 81.4% of all measures, up from 76.6% in 2014 (ESCAP calculations using 2016 GTA data). In 2015, the G20 economies of the Asia-Pacific region – India, the Russian Federation, China, Indonesia, Turkey, Japan, Australia and the Republic of Korea – introduced 303 new measures, accounting for just over half of the trade-restrictive measures implemented by the G20 economies, and up from 276 (47%) in 2014. The Russian Federation, India, Indonesia and Japan, for example, implemented 86, 67, 42 and 36 new trade restrictive measures (which the GTA codes as "red" measures), respectively, in 2015, ranking them second, third, fifth and seventh most protectionist economies, respectively, in the world, compared with 84, 75, 36 and 14 measures, respectively, in 2014 (see table below). With the exception of India and China, all Asia-Pacific G20 economies increased the number of new trade restrictions introduced in 2015 compared with 2014 (ESCAP calculations using 2016 GTA data).

Despite the challenging global environment, G20 members (including those in Asia and the Pacific) must revive their commitments to maintaining and strengthening the open global trade environment, so that others may follow. For this to succeed, active steps must be taken towards untangling and dismantling the growing and complex web of trade restrictive barriers.

Table. Top 10 economies implementing "red"[b] measures, 2014 and 2015

Ranking	2014		2015	
	Economy	Number of "red" measures imposed	Economy	Number of "red" measures imposed
1	United States of America	107	United States of America	90
2	Russian Federation	84	Russian Federation	86
3	India	75	India	67
4	Brazil	54	Brazil	42
5	Germany	42	Indonesia	42
6	Argentina	39	Argentina	36
7	Indonesia	36	Japan	36
8	Italy	36	United Kingdom	36
9	China	32	Italy	34
10	United Kingdom	32	Canada	27

Source: ESCAP calculation based on data from Global Trade Alert, 2016.

a When more than one member of the relevant country group is involved in introducing a measure, then this measure is only counted once (i.e. Germany and Italy introducing a measure under the European Union counts as one measure in the aggregate, but when stating numbers for individual countries, it is counted twice).

b GTA codes a measure as "red" if it almost certainly discriminates against a foreign commercial interest (Evenett and Fritz, 2016).

a daily basis. Other G20 States such as Germany, Japan and the United States were estimated to have been hit between 300 to 360 times during the same time period (Evenett and Fritz, 2016). During 2013-2016 in the Asia-Pacific region, China, the Republic of Korea and Japan were most affected by "red" measures. While the United States, for example, was the target of 683 "red" measures, China was targeted 710, the Republic of Korea 695 and Japan 625 times (table 5.5).

3. Exploring the reasons behind the increase of protectionism

> *"The analyses of trade tensions in steel industry reveal that some of the key reasons for current increase in protectionism are past trade distorting measures and supply glut."*

There is no single reason for the cumulative increase in protectionism. However, looking at some of the key sectors affected by trade tensions can reveal some of the underlying causes. WTO (2016) highlighted the fact that metals (especially steel), followed by the plastics, rubber and chemicals sectors, saw the greatest increase in the initiation of trade remedies. In an attempt to uncover some of the factors driving this overall increase in trade restrictive measures, box 5.2 provides an analysis of the trade policy tensions in the steel industry. The key point revealed by the analysis is the long-term trade-distorting impact of measures, such as state subsidies, and how they can lead to spiralling of protectionism in future. Interestingly, this is a common phenomenon among the sectors highlighted by WTO (2016) that saw an increase in trade remedies. Trade-distorting measures of the past and present are continuing to insulate several industries from reacting to the fall in world demand following the financial crisis and the ongoing slow economic recovery. This, together with the continuing low price of oil, which is a key raw material in these sectors, has contributed to a supply glut. The recent G20 leaders' Summit in Hangzhou, China explicitly recognized the problem of "excess capacity" in industries and its negative impact on international trade (European Commission, 2016a). Further industry- and country-level research is required in order to identify other specific reasons for the increase in protectionism. Nevertheless, rising trade tensions should act as a caveat for Governments planning to take more interventionist policies in specific economic sectors or industries in future. As many countries are now realizing that, once instituted, it is often difficult to withdraw such measures.

4. Continuing prominence of non-tariff measures in trade policy portfolio

> *"With the fall in applied tariff rates, non-tariff measures are emerging as an important barrier to trade."*

Two dominant long-term trade policy trends are obvious: (a) the lowering of average applied tariffs over the past few decades; and (b) the growing importance of non-tariff measures (NTMs) as barriers to trade during the same period.

In keeping with the global trend, average applied tariff rates in the majority of Asia-Pacific countries have decreased substantially during the past few decades.

Table 5.5 Top 10 targeted jurisdictions in the Asia-Pacific region

Targeted jurisdiction	Number of "red"[a] measures		
	2013-July 2016	Mid-October 2014 to mid-May 2016	Mid-October 2015 to mid-May 2016
China	710	312	73
Republic of Korea	695	306	71
Japan	625	270	61
India	574	249	54
Russian Federation	501	222	49
Thailand	494	219	54
Turkey	441	206	51
Malaysia	422	204	52
Singapore	390	198	50
Indonesia	373	164	39

Source: ESCAP calculation based on data from Global Trade Alert, 2016.

[a] GTA codes a measure as "red" if it almost certainly discriminates against a foreign commercial interest (Evenett and Fritz, 2016).

Box 5.2 **Trade tensions in the steel industry**

Tensions in the global steel market have been growing for some time, with much of the blame being placed on Chinese producers who account for nearly half of the global steel market, according to the World Steel Association (WSA) (2016). In 2015, Chinese steel exports rose by around 20%, while exports in most other major steel-exporting economies declined, according to the Organisation for Economic Co-operation and Development (OECD) (2016). One of the main reasons cited for the excess steel production is that state-owned enterprises (SOEs) in China are insulated from the market forces by generous state subsidies. For example, in late-2015, while about 30 private steel enterprises in northern China closed their operations as a response to plummeting prices, the larger SOEs have not shown any response to market signals (Liu and Song, 2016).

The arrival of so much steel on the global market as well as the large spreads between Chinese steel prices and those in other regions have pushed down world steel prices and fuelled trade tensions. The scale of global steel production overcapacity is currently estimated to exceed 600 million metric tons. The Asia-Pacific region is especially affected by the impact of the current global steel glut due to intraregional trade; in 2014, for example, 66.6%, 81.7% and 63.3% of steel exports by China, Japan and the Republic of Korea were concentrated in Asia (WSA, 2015). Many believe that China's low-cost excess capacity – for which, to a large extent, its government subsidies are blamed – is displacing production and sales in other countries. This has provided incentives for Governments to increasingly resort to implementing trade-related policy instruments to protect the domestic steel sector. However, it is not only China that is seen as a contributor to the global steel glut, as steel industries in other countries such as the Republic of Korea, Japan, Italy, the Russian Federation and India have also become recipients of increased discriminatory trade measures.

Due to its strategic and cyclical nature, the steel industry has typically attracted a large number of trade remedy cases; from 1995 to 2014, for example, base metals (including steel) accounted for 29% of total anti-dumping (AD) initiations (OECD, 2016). Data, however, indicate that the number of AD and countervailing duties (CVD) cases reached historically high levels in 2015, with 41 new cases of AD and CVD investigations being initiated (OECD, 2016). Furthermore, the rate of new cases being picked up appears to be continuing to accelerate. In fact, metal products, and particularly steel products, accounted for the largest share of AD and CVD initiations from mid-October 2015 to the end of May 2016 (WTO, 2016).

Figure A. Global steel overcapacity and shares of global steel production, 2005-2014

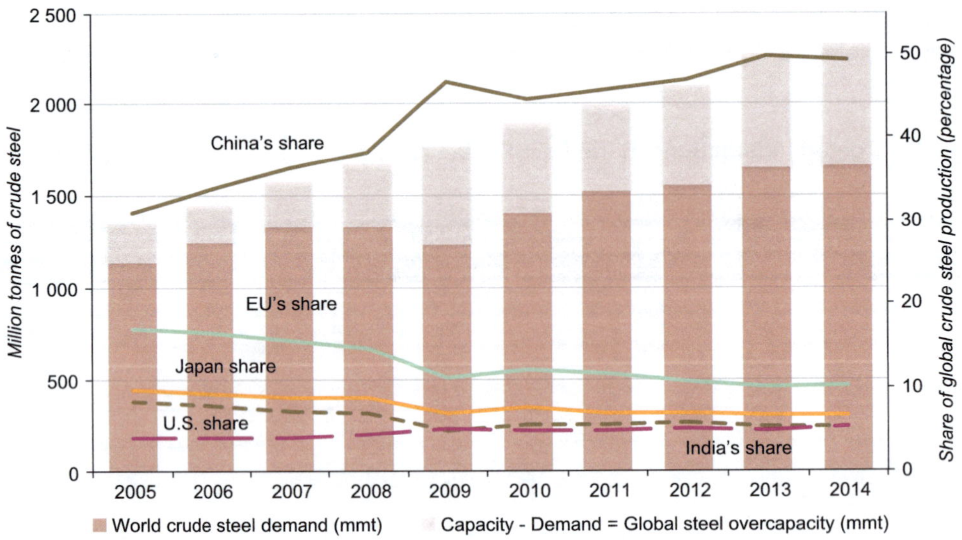

Source: ESCAP calculations based on data from WSA (2016) and OECD (2016).

Note: Data not available for 2015 world crude steel demand.

Box 5.2 ***continued***

Trade remedies, although often receiving much of attention from the media, are not the only policy measures that governments are resorting to and may not be as harmful to trade as other measures like export incentives or subsidies, which affect a larger proportion of world steel trade (Evenett and Fritz, 2016). Data indicate that since November 2008 the number of all harmful trade measures in the steel sector (including state aid measures, export incentives and investment measures) has outnumbered liberalizing measures 4.5 to 1. This figure is significantly higher than other sectors, which average 3 to 1 (Evenett and Fritz, 2016). Figure B summarizes the number of all discriminatory measures imposed in the steel sector and captured by the GTA since end of 2008, showing that the total in 2015 exceeded the total for all previous crisis-era years.

China, the Republic of Korea and Japan were the most frequent targets of steel measures during the reporting period worldwide, followed by Germany and Italy, and with many further Asia-Pacific economies following closely behind them. Most notable is China, which has been targeted by steel measures 562 times since Q4 2008 (115 times alone in 2015 and Q1 of 2016). The United States, for example, recently put tariffs of 522% for cold-rolled steel imports from China into place (United States International Trade Commission, 2016). Additionally, individual WTO members have signalled that their willingness to support market-economy status for China in the WTO later this year is dependent on it cutting back its steel production (*Wall Street Journal*, 2016).

The outlook for the global steel market continues to look weak, and while trade protectionism may provide short-term relief for domestic steel producers, it is feared that it does not provide the long-term resolution needed to support the industry and, moreover, is exacerbating the existing tensions between trading partners (OECD, 2016). It is therefore important for Governments to discuss how trade policy could be better coordinated among economies to prevent escalation of trade disputes. Ultimately, Governments should work together to remove trade-distorting policies such as subsidies and other interventions that, in their own right, promote the creation of new capacity or delay the elimination of inefficient steel production and the structural adjustment of the steel industry.

In order to specifically address the issues in the steel industry, G20 leaders' Summit in Hangzhou, China called for increased information sharing and cooperation through the formation of a Global Forum on excess steel capacity (European Commission, 2016a).

Top 10 targeted Asia-Pacific jurisdictions, steel measures, Q4 2008-Q1 2016

China	562
Republic of Korea	465
Japan	450
Russian Federation	408
India	388
Turkey	190
Thailand	179
Malaysia	158
Singapore	158
Indonesia	147

Source: ESCAP calculation based on data from Global Trade Alert, 2016.

Figure B. Number of discriminatory trade measures imposed in the steel sector, Q4 2008-Q1 2016

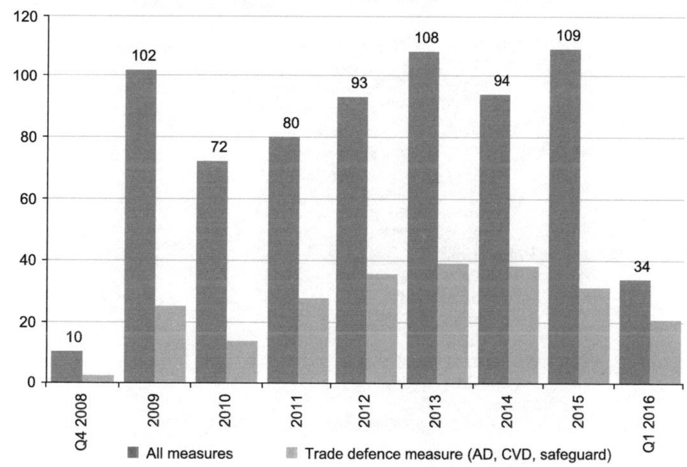

Source: ESCAP calculation based on data from Global Trade Alert, 2016

Note: Following OECD (2016), counted as steel measure if HS 7206-7302, HS 7304-7302 and/or HS 7307.02-7307.99 affected.

Reductions have been achieved through a combination of: (a) unilateral liberalization, with countries adopting more open trade-oriented development strategies; (b) preferential trade agreements, allowing greater market access to partners; and (c) multilaterally, through liberalization within the WTO framework. In 2012, average applied rates in developed countries were below 2% while those in developing countries amounted to 8%; in 1995, the equivalent rates were 6% and 17%, respectively (World Bank, 2012). These figures, however, vary substantially across sectors, with average trade-weighted tariff rates for sensitive products (e.g. agricultural products) remaining higher than those for manufactured products. In 2014, the simple average of world MFN-applied tariffs was 6% for manufacturing goods and just below 3% for natural resources, compared with 7% and 4%, respectively, in 2008. For agricultural products it was 15%, down by 2 percentage points from 2008. Widespread preferential access also contributed to the reduction in tariffs. For example, preferential liberalization in agriculture goods contributed to another 2 percentage point reduction of simple average agricultural tariffs from 2008 to 2015 (UNCTAD, 2015a). Despite the combined impact of preferential and multilateral liberalization, in 2014 developing Asia's trade-weighted average tariffs for the agriculture sector – at around 15% in East Asia and 23% in South Asia – were the highest in the world (UNCTAD, 2015a).

Despite the reduction in average tariff rates, developing countries still have substantial "policy space" – also commonly referred to as "water" in tariff rates - with their bound rates remaining considerably higher than their applied rates (figure 5.2).[6] This allows policymakers in developing countries to react in cases of import surges by increasing applied rates without violating WTO commitments; however, in some cases, Governments may also resort to safeguards. The magnitude of policy space varies substantially between Asia-Pacific economies, with, for example, Hong Kong, China and Macao, China not having any at all, while Bangladesh can increase its applied tariffs by more than 10 times and still comply with WTO rules.

Moreover, a large part of tariff lines remain "unbound" in many developing and least developed economies, even more so on "sensitive products", which are designated by the countries themselves and which are not subject to tariff binding. For example, in 2013 Bangladesh had a binding coverage of 15.5%

Figure 5.2 **Bound and applied MFN tariff rates in selected Asia-Pacific economies (all products, simple averages)**

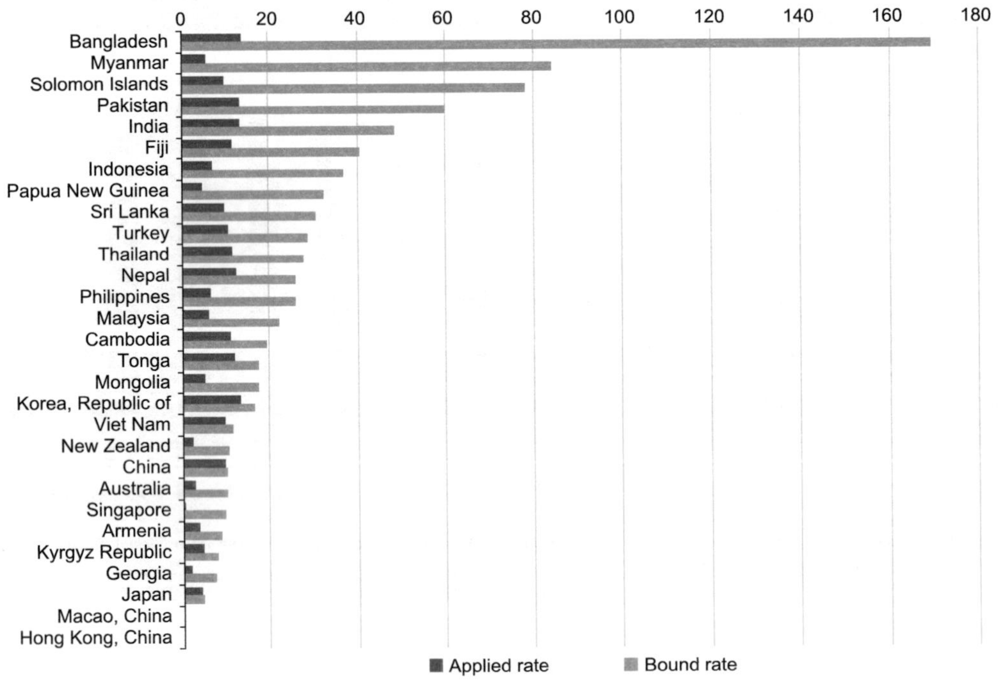

Source: WTO (2015).

compared with 74.4% in India, 99.4% in Nepal and 100% in both Cambodia and the Lao People's Democratic Republic (WTO, 2015).

In addition to tariffs, other policies and regulations determine the scope of market access, and as tariff rates and the number of products covered by tariffs have fallen over time, the latter have become relatively more important. Non-tariff measures (NTMs) cover a wide variety of regulations that may impede trade, intentionally or unintentionally. Research has found that 93% of goods exported globally and more than 75% of HS-4-digit product categories are currently potentially linked to technical regulations (Okun-Kozlowicki, 2016). "Technical NTMs" such as product-labelling standards and sanitary and phytosanitary (SPS) measures, which cover regulations on plant and animal health, have become the most common form of NTMs. Despite often fundamentally serving legitimate and important public policy objectives, these measures are occasionally misused by Governments to disguise protectionist actions. Technical NTMs are more complex, less transparent and harder to monitor than tariffs. They therefore provide a convenient means for Governments to discriminate against imported products while avoiding dispute over trade policy with their partners. This may harm trade significantly, especially in developing and least developed countries, where testing or certification facilities to ensure compliance are often lacking. Developing countries consequently have to resort to outsourcing services such as laboratory testing or certification in order to meet standards, which can erode any advantages they have (e.g. from lower labour costs) (Heal and Palmioli, 2015).

"The number of newly-initiated NTMs (TBT and SPS) within the region saw an increase in 2015, when compared with previous years."

In 2002, the number of newly-initiated NTMs notified to WTO totalled 1,200. The annual newly-initiated NTMs have increased significantly since then, and in 2015 amounted to 2,236, with more than a third of them originating from Asia-Pacific countries (up from one fifth in 2013). Some of this increase may be attributed to enhanced recording through the WTO Integrated Trade Intelligence Portal (I-TIP) platform. However, the increase in technical NTMs is also partially explained by the growth of health and environmental consciousness, especially among middle-class consumers in emerging economies (Cadot and Malouche, ed., 2012). This has pressured Governments into adopting new regulations (for example, to ensure food safety and prevent dissemination of disease). The rise in Asia-Pacific's share of new NTMs can thus be partially explained by the fast-growing middle class in many of its economies such as in China.

Figure 5.3 depicts the increasing number of SPS and technical barriers to trade (TBT) measures initiated by the economies of the Asia-Pacific region from 2002 to 2015. Particularly notable is the fact that they increased parallel to the economic slowdown caused by the 2008-2009 financial crisis. China and the Republic of Korea – important markets for other Asia-Pacific producers – were responsible for a substantial amount of the increase in the use of NTMs (Heal and Palmioli, 2015).

Figure 5.3 **Increase in the number of newly-initiated TBT and SPS measures in the Asia-Pacific region**

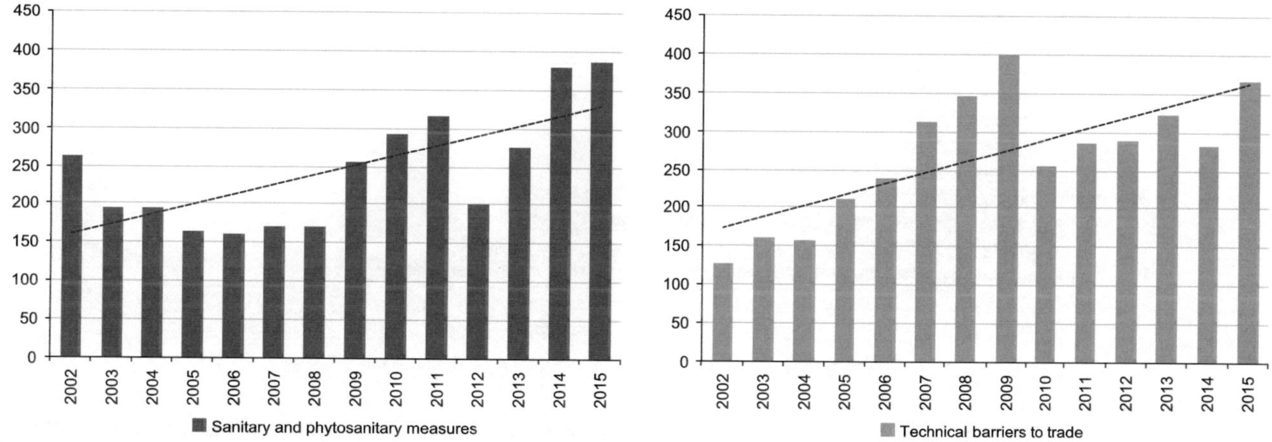

Source: ESCAP calculation using data accessed June 2016 at the WTO I-TIP Database.

NTMs are now believed to pose a greater impediment to trade as well as the cause of higher trade costs than tariffs – the traditional barriers to trade – in many sectors (UNCTAD, 2012). Most notably affected are the agricultural and food sectors. This is particularly disadvantageous to developing countries, which typically have comparative advantages in those sectors. Thus, with an increased amount of NTMs being initiated in agricultural and food product export destinations, producers in developing countries will find it difficult to export their products to lucrative global markets.

A recent study allows the comparison of ad valorem tariff equivalents (AVE)[7] of NTMs as global averages for different sectors (Cadot and Gourdon, 2015), based on data collected during 2009-2012. The average AVE across all sectors is 8.8%. However, it differs significantly between sectors, ranging from 0.8% in the case of arms and 26% – being the highest in the live animals sector where both SPS (i.e. sanitary certificates) and TBT measures (i.e. labelling requirements) are abundant.

Comprehensive and updated data availability on NTMs remains a challenge. UNCTAD and its partners have compiled a dataset for ASEAN countries.[8] Box 5.3 describes the state of play of NTMs within ASEAN economies based on this dataset. The analyses show that TBT and SPS measures dominate the NTM portfolio among ASEAN members, with Thailand, the Philippines and Malaysia emerging as the top users of NTMs within ASEAN.

Recent empirical literature underlines the increased importance of preserving an open and predictable trade policy in an environment where global value chains (GVCs) are increasingly abundant (OECD, 2013). This is due to the fact that, with production being dispersed across countries, intermediaries cross borders numerous times prior to their final assembly. Countries, instead of producing final goods in their entirety, are increasingly specializing in performing certain tasks located at different points of the supply chain, making easy access to inputs vital. Even small additional costs arising from barriers to import, such as NTMs, can harm the competitiveness of countries and their ability to participate in global value chains. Additionally, it may discourage investment by putting off multinational companies seeking to set up production bases in the country, due to inefficiencies. Measuring the exact magnitude of the impact of

Figure 5.4 **Non-tariff measures ad-valorem equivalents, by HS Section and NTM Chapter**

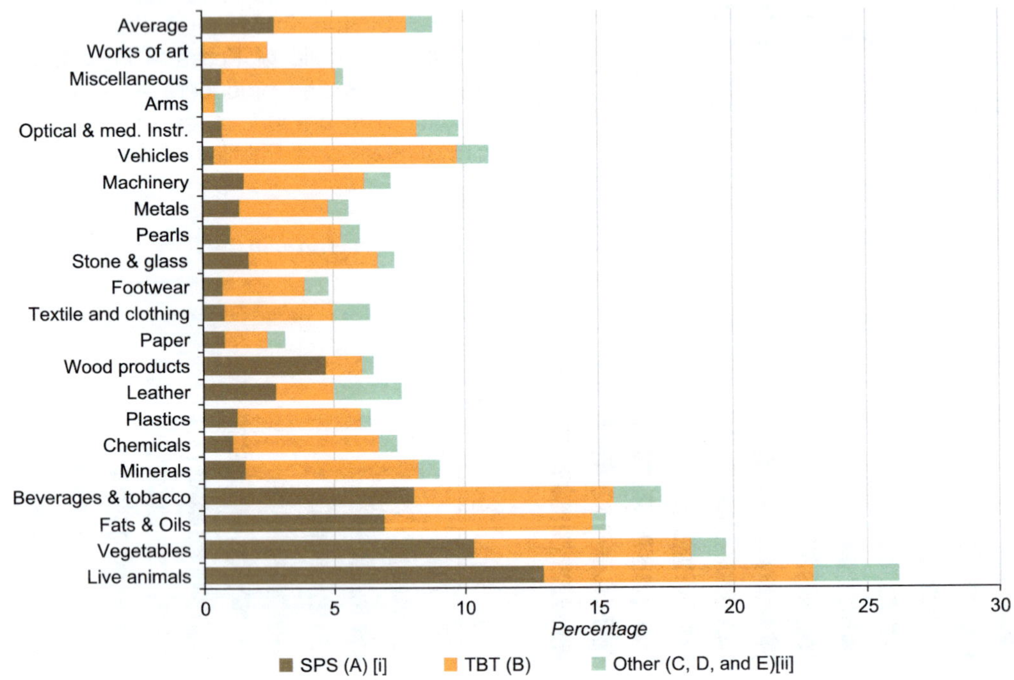

Source: Cadot and Gourdon (2015).

Notes: (a) The letters A, B, C, D and E refer to the Chapters used for classifying different types of NTMs used in the new UNCTAD classification (UNCTAD, 2015b). Technical measures (Chapters A and B) refer to product-specific properties such as characteristics, technical specifications and production process of a product. Non-technical measures (Chapters C to O) refer to trade requirements, such as shipping requirements, custom formalities, trade rules, taxation policies, etc. (b) Chapter C refers to "Pre-shipment inspection and other formalities"; Chapter D refers to "Contingent trade protective measures"; and Chapter E refers to "Non-automatic licensing, quotas, prohibitions and quantity-control measures other than for SPS or TBT reasons."

Box 5.3 **Use of non-tariff measures in ASEAN**

The establishment of a regional trade arrangement is supposed to speed up the process of economic integration in the respective region. Thus, with the establishment of the ASEAN Economic Community (AEC) and the implementation of one of its flagships, i.e. the ASEAN Trade in Goods Agreement (ATIGA), reductions of non-tariff barriers (NTBs) should be high on the agenda. Notwithstanding that, many have argued that there is still a high level of NTMs within the ASEAN region and this is reflected in the number of NTMs used by ASEAN members. The Economic Research Institute for ASEAN (ERIA) has taken the initiative to categorize NTMs in ASEAN[a] improvising the UNCTAD definition and classifications of NTMs. The data generated from the work by ERIA[b] is re-processed in this box. The NTMs are classified into contingent trade protection measures (CTPM), export-related measures (EXP), pre-shipment inspections (INSP), other measures (OTH), price control measures (PC), quantity control measures (QC), sanitary and phytosanitary measures (SPS) and technical barriers to trade (TBT).

As shown in table, each type of NTM has a different degree of frequency with regard to each and every ASEAN member.

Table. Number of NTMs, by ASEAN member and type of NTMs

ASEAN member	CTPM	EXP	INSP	OTH	PC	QC	SPS	TBT	Total
Brunei Darussalam		46	1		18	2	161	288	516
Cambodia		70	1		12	3	36	121	243
Indonesia	44	74	53	4	5	8	125	321	634
Lao PDR		82	14	1	48	26	38	82	291
Malaysia	24	72	5		12	9	260	331	713
Myanmar		35	2	1	13	5	75	41	172
Philippines	1	146	24	12	23	56	233	360	855
Singapore		49	2		35	1	127	300	514
Thailand	53	128	44	3	21	40	762	562	1 613
Viet Nam		57	5	11	7	7	121	122	330
Total	122	759	151	32	194	157	1 938	2 528	5 881

As of 21 July 2016,[c] a total of 5,881 NTMs had been taken by all ASEAN members. The type of NTMs with the highest number of use was TBT, followed by SPS measures and export-related measures. If export-related measures are excluded, a significant difference is seen in the total number of TBT and SPS cases used by ASEAN members and the rest of the NTMs. Of the total number of reported NTMs (5,881), a total of 1,938 cases were in the form of SPS and 2,528 cases in the form of TBT. In other words, 33% of all NTMs used by ASEAN members were SPS and 43% were TBT. Both SPS and TBT accounted for 76% of all NTMs in ASEAN for the period covered.

With regard to the country users of NTMs, the table above also indicates the relevant patterns of the number of NTMs that individual ASEAN members have taken as well as the types of the measures. As of 21 July 2016, Thailand was the most frequent user of NTMs with 1,613 measures, followed by the Philippines (855) and Malaysia (713). The difference between the total measures used by Thailand and those by the second- and third-highest users was significant. The difference between Thailand and the Philippines was 758 (47%) while with Malaysia it was 900 (55.7%). With regard to the types of NTMs, TBT was the most frequently used measure by ASEAN members followed by SPS. In all members except Thailand and Myanmar TBT were the most frequently used NTM; in Malaysia and Thailand SPS was the most frequently used NTM. This suggests that the move to cut down on NTM usage through the AEC will be reflected in the disciplining of the national TBT and SPS regulatory regimes of ASEAN members. This does not mean, however, that scrutinizing the other types of NTMs is not pivotal. Different types of NTMs have different natures and conditions that entail different consequences.

Source: Contributed by Dr. Haniff Ahamat, Associate Professor, Faculty of Law, National University of Malaysia.
a See De Cordoba, 2016.
b See http://asean.i-tip.org/Forms/TableView.aspx?mode=modify&action=search (accessed 21 July 2016).
c ibid (accessed 21 July 2016).

NTMs on trade, however, is highly complex, as NTMs are heterogeneous and often appear as a package of measures rather than a single measure, making cost comparison tricky (Heal and Palmioli, 2015). It is therefore vital to address the issue of NTM-based protectionism; however, a prerequisite is a continued effort to improve data availability on the impact and prevalence of NTMs.

B. TRADE POLICIES AFFECTING COMMERCIAL SERVICES

> *"Services sector restrictiveness can impede trade, both in the services and the manufacturing sectors."*

Trade in services is an important component of global trade. The phenomenon of "servicification", which refers to the increased role of services in the manufacturing production, has gained the attention of academics and policymakers alike (Cernat and Kutlina-Dimitrova, 2014). In the Asia-Pacific region, the spread of GVCs has resulted in an expansion of servicification across developing economies (Anukoonwattaka, Scagliusi and Mikic, 2015). In the aftermath of the 2008-2009 financial crisis, when compared with trade in goods, global services trade declined less during the crisis and have grown faster since the crisis (Mattoo, 2016). There is growing evidence showing that services liberalization could significantly contribute to gains in economic performance, including productivity in manufacturing and the coordination of activities both between and within firms (Francois and Hoekman, 2010). It has been found that services trade restrictiveness can have a detrimental impact not just on export and import of services but also trade in downstream manufactured goods (Nordås and Rouzet, 2015). All this suggests the importance of analysing trade policies related to the services sector.

> *"More efforts are needed to systematically collect data and analyse the restrictiveness of services sector policies, especially in developing countries."*

While quantifying trade in services is itself a difficult task, measuring its restrictiveness is even more challenging. Currently, internationally comparable and annually updated data on policies that have an impact on trade in services is virtually non-existent.[9] In 2012, the World Bank released a Services Trade Restrictions Database of 103 countries; however, the data have not been updated.[10] In 2014, OECD started an initiative to annually update the service trade restrictiveness index (STRI) for a range of sectors in selected countries (including OECD and a few non-OECD members). The database has now been updated to 2015 for seven sectors: computer services; construction; professional services, comprising accounting, architecture, engineering and legal services; and telecommunications. The analysis in this section uses data for the nine Asia-Pacific countries currently available from the database, as described in table 5.6. This list includes the top three performers in terms of total trade in the commercial service sector, i.e. China, Japan and India (ESCAP, 2015).

When compared with trade in goods, one distinguishing feature of the trade in services is clear – it is predominantly affected by "beyond the border" measures not necessarily related to trade policies. For example, these measures can range from restrictions on foreign ownership, to the degree of competition or the movement of people that affects different modes of service delivery to varying degrees. Capturing this fact, the OECD STRI includes policy measures that are categorized under five policy areas: barriers to competition and public ownership; regulatory transparency and administrative requirements; restrictions on foreign ownership and other market entry conditions; restrictions on the movement of people; and other discriminatory measures and international standards.

A higher STRI score indicates higher restrictiveness to services trade. Table 5.6 indicates the variation in service trade restrictiveness from 2014 to 2015, together with STRI scores in 2015 for seven sectors. With the exception of India and New Zealand, there was no increase in service trade restrictiveness in the region by the countries analysed. India registered an increase in trade restrictiveness in five out of seven categories analysed, while in New Zealand there was an increase in restrictiveness in telecommunications services. Overall, among the seven sectors, the telecommunications sector saw the most widespread liberalization, with five out of nine countries taking measures to liberalize the sector; other countries did not take any measures resulting in an increased STRI. During that period, the Russian Federation, followed by Japan, adopted liberalizing measures in the highest number of sectors (six and four, respectively).

For OECD members as a whole, there was a clear trend in liberalization in telecommunications and legal services between 2014 and 2015. However, in the other five sectors there were signs of increasing

Table 5.6 **Trend in STRI of selected Asia-Pacific countries, 2014-2015**

	Accounting	Architecture	Engineering	Legal	Telecom	Computer	Construction
Australia	0.167	0.134	0.103	0.145	0.229	0.122	0.137
China	0.39	0.249	0.245	0.460	0.414	0.243	0.324
India	0.887	0.610	0.286	0.946	0.457	0.357	0.318
Indonesia	0.465	0.302	0.301	0.937	0.569	0.328	0.403
Japan	0.193	0.082	0.097	0.210	0.170	0.096	0.055
Republic of Korea	0.270	0.217	0.134	0.475	0.254	0.122	0.144
Russian Federation	0.255	0.320	0.307	0.312	0.462	0.364	0.366
New Zealand	0.175	0.168	0.153	0.185	0.253	0.148	0.120
Turkey	1.000	0.161	0.134	0.485	0.236	0.182	0.193
Asia-Pacific average	0.422	0.249	0.196	0.462	0.338	0.218	0.229
OECD average	0.269	0.214	0.200	0.335	0.177	0.183	0.181

Source: ESCAP calculation based on OECD STRI dataset available from http://stats.oecd.org/, accessed July, 2016.

Note: The value of STRI corresponds to 2015. The colour of each cell corresponds to the degree of change in STRI in 2015 compared with 2014. Green = liberalization; red = increase in restrictiveness; yellow = no increase in restrictiveness. Higher STRI score represents higher restrictions to services trade.

restrictiveness in terms of the OECD average STRI score. However, this increase in restrictiveness was driven by a small group of countries, and in 24 out of 35 OECD economies there was no increase in restrictiveness in any of the seven sectors analysed. In terms of average STRI for the subgroup of Asia-Pacific countries observed, there was greater liberalization in four sectors, i.e. architecture, legal, telecommunications and construction. The ratcheting up of restrictiveness in the remaining three sectors was driven mainly by India.

In terms of services trade policies, the Asia-Pacific region is more restrictive when compared with the global average. The STRI score (based on the World Bank dataset) for the Asia-Pacific region as a whole (32.1) is higher than the world average (28.3).[11] However, there is substantial heterogeneity in service restrictiveness within the region. Gootiz and Mattoo (2015) gathered additional data specifically on ASEAN members and found that the average STRI was 60% higher than the global average. Therefore, it remains to be seen whether enhanced regional integration efforts will lead to increased liberalization in terms of services trade. Current evidence points to the fact that under the ASEAN Framework Agreement on Services (AFAS), there has not been any significant liberalization among members and, in a few instances, services trade policy has actually become more restrictive (Gootiz and Mattoo, 2015). In the ongoing negotiations of the Regional Comprehensive Economic Partnership (RCEP), service liberalization appears to have become a contentious issue among ASEAN members (Palit, 2016).

Miroudot and Pertel (2015) showed that there is considerable "water"[12] in service trade policies of countries, signifying both openness as well as a high degree of policy uncertainty. Liberalization of service sectors could facilitate cheaper import of services and would help to increase the competitiveness of domestic service providers. Recognizing the increasing importance of the services sector, the region should continuously monitor its service trade policies and the level of restrictiveness that it entails.

C. CONCLUSION

The trends in trade policies are leaning more towards restrictiveness, especially from October 2015 to May 2016. The number of trade restrictive measures adopted, both globally and within the region, has increased significantly. The G20 economies showed a surge in protectionist tendencies despite the commitment made by their leaders to ensure a more open global trade environment. Analysis of the global steel industry reveals that one of the factors driving the increase in restrictiveness belongs to trade distorting measures adopted in the past, alluding to the long-term negative impact of such measures and the challenges created by their removal.

Considering the increasing role of services in production patterns there is a need for more comprehensive efforts in the mapping of services trade policies especially for developing and least developed countries. The data available on services trade restrictiveness pertaining to some of the major economies of the region show that there has been no increase in service trade restrictiveness and that the Asia-Pacific region, based on the represented economies in the monitoring, performs better than the OECD average.

Endnotes

1 Such as the Trans-Pacific Partnership (TPP) Agreement or the Regional Comprehensive Economic Partnership (RCEP) involving Asia-Pacific region economies.

2 See UNCTAD (2015b).

3 In analysing trade policy trends the APTIR report relies on the data generated from notifications of countries to WTO and reported in the WTO Trade Policy Reviews.

4 AD measures are actions taken by Governments to protect domestic industries from unfairly low-priced exported products. CVDs can be used as a tool to counteract the effects of subsidies by national authorities on domestic industries; and safeguards – in contrast to the previous two measures this is not a reaction to unfair practices of another party – to temporarily allow the protection of domestic industries from negative effects occurring due to a surge of imports.

5 GTA codes a measure as: (a) "red" if it almost certainly discriminates against a foreign commercial interest; "amber" if its implementation is likely to discriminate against foreign commercial interests or if the measure hasn't been implemented yet – but, should that happen, it would almost certainly be discriminatory; and (c) "green" if the measure either improves the transparency of the national trade policy regime, or if it improves or has no effect on the relative treatment of foreign versus domestic commercial interests (Evenett and Fritz, 2016).

6 To bind a tariff means to make a commitment (typically through a multilateral negotiations or accession to WTO) not to increase a rate of duty beyond an agreed level. Once a rate of duty is bound, it may not be raised without compensating the affected parties. In contrast, the applied tariff rates are those actually imposed at a border. These are often considerably lower that the bound rates.

7 An ad valorem tariff equivalent is an estimate of ad valorem effect that a non-ad valorem duties or non-tariff measures have on the imports. In principle these are imperfect estimates as they depend on the price of the imported goods remaining unchanged. See more in World Tariff Profiles 2006 (WTO, 2007).

8 See New Database of ASEAN Non-Tariff Measures, available from http://unctad.org/en/pages/newsdetails.aspx?OriginalVersionID=1234&Sitemap_x0020_Taxonomy=UNCTAD%20Home.

9 See Borchert, Gootiiz and Mattoo (2012) for details on this database.

10 More information on this database is available from http://iresearch.worldbank.org/servicetrade/aboutData.htm#ScopeOfDatabase.

11 ESCAP calculation based on STRI data provided by the World Bank. Available fromhttp://iresearch.worldbank.org/servicetrade/, accessed July 2016.

12 Water in the General Agreement on Trade in Services (GATS) refers to the difference between the bound level of trade restrictivenesspermitted by GATS and the actual trade regime.

REFERENCES

Anukoonwattaka, W., M. Scagliusi and M. Mikic (2015). Servicification and industrial exports from Asia and the Pacific. Trade Insights, No 10, May 2015. Available from www.unescap.org/sites/default/files/Trade%20Insights%20Issue%20No.%2010.pdf.

Borchert, I., B. Gootiiz and A. Mattoo (2012). Policy barriers to international trade in services: evidence from a new database. *World Bank Economic Review*, vol. 28, No. 1, pp.162-188.

Cadot, O., and J. Gourdon (2015). NTMs, preferential trade agreements and prices: new evidence. CEPII Working Paper No. 2015-01. Paris: Centre d'Etudes Prospectives et d'Informations Internationales. Available from www.cepii.fr/PDF_PUB/wp/2015/wp2015-01.pdf.

Cadot, O., and M. Malouche, eds. (2012). *Non-Tariff Measures – A Fresh Look at Trade Policy's New Frontier*. Overview, pp. 1-19. Washington, D.C.: World Bank.

Cernat, L., and Z. Kutlina-Dimitrova (2014). Thinking in a box: a 'Mode 5' approach to service trade. European Commission Chief Economist's Note, No.1, March 2014. Available from http://trade.ec.europa.eu/doclib/docs/2014/march/tradoc_152237.pdf .

De Cordoba, S.F. (2016). Collecting and classifying non-tariff measures in ASEAN. In Lili Yan Ing, S.F. de Cordoba and O. Cadot, eds., *Non-Tariff Measures in ASEAN*. Chapter 1. Jakarta: Economic Research Institute for ASEAN and East Asia; Geneva: UNCTAD. Available from www.eria.org/publications/key_reports/FY2015/No.01.html .

De Melo, J., and M. Vijil (2014). *Barriers to Trade in Environmental Goods and Environmental Services: How Important Are They? How Much Progress at Reducing Them?* Fondazione Eni Enrico Mattei (FERDI) Working Paper No. 899. Available from http://services.bepress.com/feem/paper899.

Economic and Social Commission for Asia and the Pacific (2015). *Asia-Pacific Trade and Investment Report 2015: Supporting Participation in Value Chains*. Sales No. E.15.II.F.15. Available from www.unescap.org/resources/asia-pacific-trade-and-investment-report-2015-supporting-participation-value-chains.

_____ (2016). Trade as non-financial means of implementing sustainable development in Asia and the Pacific. Draft discussion paper submitted to the first meeting of the High-Level Follow-up Dialogue on Financing for Development in Asia and the Pacific, Incheon, Republic of Korea, 30-31 March 2016. Available from www.unescap.org/events/apffd-rok.

Evenett, S. (2016). Running out of tools: the G20 and the global trade halt. Geneva: International Centre for Trade and Sustainable Development. Available from www.ictsd.org/opinion/running-out-of-tools-the-g20-and-the-global-trade-halt

Evenett, S., and J. Fritz (2016). *Global Trade Plateaus: the 19th Global Trade Alert Report*. London: Centre for Economic Policy Research. Available from www.globaltradealert.org/gta-analysis/global-trade-plateaus.

European Commission (2016a). G20 Leaders' Communique Hangzhou Summit. Available from http://europa.eu/rapid/press-release_STATEMENT-16-2967_en.htm.

_____ (2016b). Report from the 15th round of negotiations for an Environmental Goods Agreement (EGA), August 2016. Available from http://trade.ec.europa.eu/doclib/docs/2016/august/tradoc_154835.pdf.

Francois, J., and B. Hoekman (2010). Services trade and policy. *Journal of Economic Literature*, vol. 48, No. 3, pp. 642-692.

Gootiiz, B., and A. Mattoo (2015). Regionalism in services: a study of ASEAN. Policy Research Working Paper No. 7498. Washington, D.C.: World Bank. Available from http://documents.worldbank.org/curated/en/616071467987821046/pdf/WPS7498.pdf .

Heal, A., and G. Palmioli (2015). Trade and non-tariff measures: impacts in the Asia-Pacific region. *Emerging Issues in Trade and Investment,* vol. 1. Bangkok: ESCAP. ST/ESCAP/2719. Available from www.unescap.org/sites/default/files/NTM%20Flagship%20-%2025%20May.pdf .

Hoekman, B. (2016) Trade and the SDGs: making 'means of implementation' a reality. Commonwealth Trade Hot Topics, No. 128. London: Commonwealth Secretariat. Available from http://www.thecommonwealth-ilibrary.org/commonwealth/trade/trade-and-the-sdgs_5jm0m93sf036-en;jsessionid=2ejs7aoe04iqs.x-oecd-live-03 .

International Centre for Trade and Sustainable Development (2016). G-20 Trade Ministers pledge "political leadership" to boost growth, prosperity. Bridges, vol. 20, No. 26. Geneva. Available from www.ictsd.org/bridges-news/bridges/news/g-20-trade-ministers-pledge-political-leadership-to-boost-growth.

Liu, H., and L. Song (2016). Reconstructing China's steel industry. East Asia Forum, 18 August. Available from www.eastasiaforum.org/2016/08/18/reconstructing-chinas-steel-industry/.

Mattoo, A. (2016). Unleashing the next engine of growth: an agenda for services trade beyond Doha and the TPP. World Bank Policy Research Talks. Available from http://pubdocs.worldbank.org/en/797541457379459380/Policy-Research-Talk-Aaditya-Mattoo-Final.pdf.

Miroudot, S., and K. Pertel (2015). Water in the GATS: methodology and results. OECD Trade Policy Paper No. 185. Paris: OECD Publishing. http://dx.doi.org/10.1787/5jrs6k35nnf1-en .

Nicita, A., and V. Rollo (2013). Tariff preferences as a determinant for exports from Sub-Saharan Africa. Policy Issues in International Trade and Commodities Research Study Series, No. 60. Geneva: UNCTAD. Available from http://unctad.org/en/PublicationsLibrary/itcdtab61_en.pdf.

Nordås, H.K., and D. Rouzet (2015). The impact of services trade restrictiveness on trade flows: first estimates. OECD Trade Policy Paper No. 178. Paris: OECD Publishing. Available from http://dx.doi.org/10.1787/5js6ds9b6kjb-en.

Organisation for Economic Co-operation and Development (2013). Trade policy implications of global value chains. Paris. Available from www.oecd.org/sti/ind/Trade_Policy_Implicatipns_May_2013.pdf .

_____ (2016). High-level symposium: excess capacity and structural adjustment in the steel sector. Background Note No. 3 – Trade and Trade Policy Developments. Paris. Available from www.oecd.org/sti/ind/Background%20document%20No%203_FINAL_Symposium.pdf.

Okun-Kozlowicki, J. (2016). Standards and regulations: measuring the link to goods trade. Washington, D.C.: International Trade Administration, Department of Commerce, Available from www.trade.gov/td/osip/documents/osip_standards_trade_full_paper_2016.pdf.

Palit, A. (2016). India & RCEP: will flexibility on tariffs get access in services? ISAS Brief No. 444, 12 August. Singapore: Institute of South Asian Studies. Available from www.isas.nus.edu.sg/ISAS%20Reports/ISAS%20Brief%20No.%20444%20%20%20India%20and%20RCEP%20Will%20Flexibility%20on%20Tariffs%20Get%20Access%20in%20Services.pdf.

United Nations Conference on Trade and Development (2012). *Non-tariff Measures to Trade: Economic and Policy Issues for Developing Countries*. Developing Countries in International Trade Studies. Geneva. Available from http://unctad.org/en/PublicationsLibrary/ditctab20121_en.pdf.

_____ (2015a). *Key Statistics and Trends in Trade Policy 2015*. Geneva. Available from http://unctad.org/en/PublicationsLibrary/ditctab2015d2_en.pdf.

_____ (2015b). *International Classification of Non-tariff Measures: 2012 Version*. Geneva. Available from http://unctad.org/en/PublicationsLibrary/ditctab20122_en.pdf.

_____ (2016). *Trading into Sustainable Development: Trade, Market Access, and the Sustainable Development Goals*. Geneva. Available from http://unctad.org/en/pages/PublicationWebflyer.aspx?publicationid=1474

United States International Trade Commission (2016). Cold-rolled steel flat products from China and Japan injure U.S. industry, says USITC. News Release 16-077, 22 June. Washington, D.C. Available from https://www.usitc.gov/press_room/news_release/2016/er0622ll621.htm.

Vossenaar, R. (2013). *The APEC List of Environmental Goods: An Analysis of the Outcome and Expected Impact*. Geneva: International Centre for Trade and Sustainable Development. Available from www.ictsd.org/downloads/2013/06/the-apec-list-of-environmental-goods.pdf

Wall Street Journal (2016). China, EU talk global steel supply, other issues at annual summit. 13 July. Available from www.wsj.com/articles/china-eu-talk-global-steel-supply-other-issues-at-annual-summit-1468413444.

World Bank (2012). *Non-Tariff Measures – A Fresh Look at Trade Policy's New Frontier*. Washington, D.C. Available from http://siteresources.worldbank.org/TRADE/Resources/NTMs_A_Fresh_Look_Complete.pdf

World Steel Association (2015). *Steel Statistical Yearbook 2015*. Brussels. Available from www.worldsteel.org/statistics/statistics-archive/yearbook-archive.html.

_____ (2016). *World Steel in Figures 2016*. Brussels. Available from www.worldsteel.org/dms/internetDocumentList/bookshop/2016/World-Steel-in-Figures-2016/document/World%20Steel%20in%20Figures%202016.pdf.

World Trade Organization (2007). *World Tariff Profiles 2006*. Geneva. Available from https://www.wto.org/english/tratop_e/tariffs_e/tariff_profiles_2006_e/tariff_profiles_2006_e.pdf .

_____ (2015). *World Tariff Profiles 2015*. Geneva. Available from https://www.wto.org/english/res_e/publications_e/world_tariff_profiles15_e.htm.

_____ (2016). Report to the TPRB from the Director-General on trade-related developments (mid-October 2015 to mid-May 2016). Trade Policy Review Body. Geneva. WT/TPR/OV/W/10. Available from https://www.tralac.org/images/docs/10027/report-to-the-trade-policy-review-body-from-the-director-general-on-trade-related-developments-july-2016.pdf .

WTO-OECD-UNCTAD (2016). Reports on G-20 trade and investment measures (mid-October 2015 to mid-May 2016). Geneva: WTO and UNCTAD; Paris: OECD. Available from https://www.wto.org/english/news_e/news16_e/g20_joint_summary_june16_e.pdf

ONLINE DATABASES

Global Trade Alert Database. Available from http://www.globaltradealert.org/ .

Organisation for Economic Co-operation and Development. Services Trade Restrictiveness Index. Available from http://stats.oecd.org/Index.aspx?DataSetCode=STRI .

World Bank. Services Trade Restrictions Database. Available from http://iresearch.worldbank.org/servicetrade/

World Bank. World Integrated Trade Solution (WITS) database. Available from http://wits.worldbank.org/ .

World Trade Organization. Integrated Trade Intelligence Portal (I-TIP). Available from https://www.wto.org/english/res_e/statis_e/itip_e.htm

CHAPTER

6

PREFERENTIAL TRADE AND AGREEMENTS: AN UPDATE

In 2016, global trade will grow by less than 3% for the fifth consecutive year, lingering behind average world economic growth (WTO, 2016a). While this extended lower trade growth is now accepted as structural in nature (see chapter 1 for more details), the efforts to revive trade growth are not withering, not least because trade is one of the key means of implementation for achieving the Sustainable Development Goals. In this context, many efforts are being directed towards reducing trade costs, which remain high for most of the countries in need of more, and more efficient, trade (see chapter 4 for more details). The autonomous liberalization, which was often credited for the "Asian miracle" in the 1980s, has for all practical purposes been abandoned due to public angst towards globalization and evidence of increasing inequalities, especially within the countries that followed these unilateral liberalization policies two decades ago. On the other hand, as shown in chapter 5, the autonomous policies are more in favour of restricting than liberalizing trade. In the absence of any reassuring signalling from WTO and negotiations at the multilateral level, Governments have turned to bilateral and regional preferential trade agreements (PTAs).

Using information from Asia-Pacific Trade and Investment Agreements Database (APTIAD),[1] this chapter maps PTAs of Asia-Pacific economies, with the focus on the number and status of PTAs, PTA partners and coverage of trade among them, and the type and scope of the agreements. Moreover, the chapter comments on the level of compliance with notification obligations under the World Trade Organization Transparency Mechanism for Regional Trade Agreements (WTO, 2006).

A. NOODLE BOWL STILL GETTING FULLER

Economies in the Asia-Pacific region continue to be drivers of preferential trade deals globally. As of July 2016, 260 PTAs[2] with membership of economies in the Asia-Pacific region were in force, signed or being negotiated. To provide a more realistic count, 32 agreements that have not been notified to WTO but have been ratified and are being implemented are also included.[3]

The numbers presented in this chapter must be seen in the context of global developments that WTO monitors. WTO recognizes only those PTAs for which official notification has been received. Given this criterion, globally there are 267 "physical" PTAs in force,[4] of which 169 (63%) involve Asia-Pacific economies. In addition, there are 12 agreements with Asia-Pacific members that have been signed with ratification still pending. Most recently, between January and July 2016, Asia-Pacific economies also signed five other agreements, most of them between economies in the region. Furthermore, 78 other PTAs are under different stages of negotiation.[5]

The Asia-Pacific "noodle bowl", a phenomenon created by the proliferation of PTAs among the same trading partners, is therefore getting fuller (figure 6.1). As argued repeatedly in the previous issues

Figure 6.1 Asia-Pacific "noodle bowl"

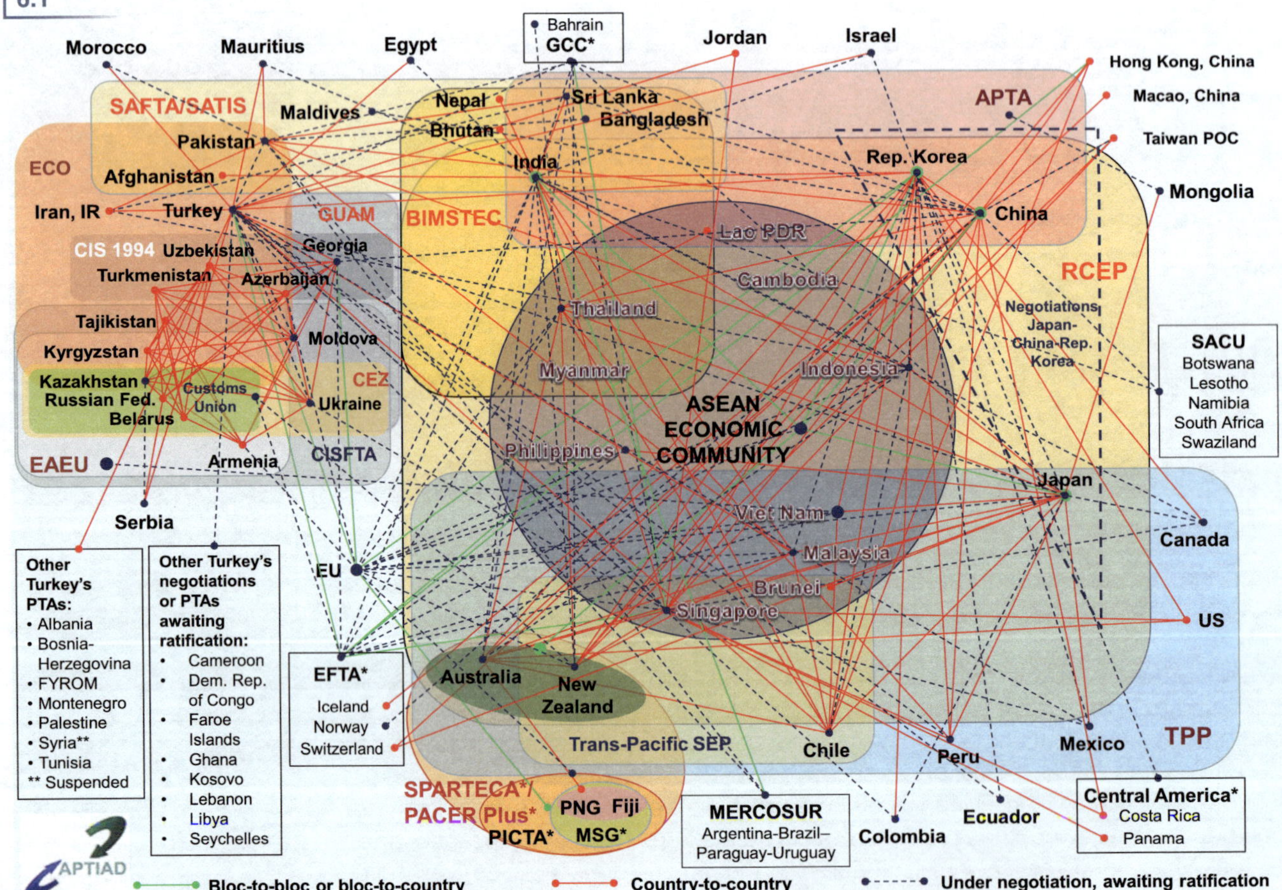

* Not all members shown / The following plurilateral PTAs are not represented: GSTP, D-8 PTA and PTN (in force) and TPS/OIC (under negotiation)

Source: APTIAD database 2015 and 2016, ESCAP.

of APTIR, the noodle bowl implies higher search costs for the best routes of supply/purchase, often depriving small and medium-sized enterprises of full or any benefits from preferential trade. Despite many analysts pointing to this undesirable and damaging impact from the multiplication of various PTAs among the same partners, not much action has been taken towards streamlining, consolidating and rationalizing PTAs (see the annex to this chapter on a few cases in the region). A formation of mega-regional trade deals may, in principle, enable the economies to consolidate existing PTAs, as some of them may be made redundant after the conclusion of a wider and deeper deal. This, of course, is neither a necessary nor automatic result from introducing new mega-regionals, as it depends on the qualitative difference between the new and old agreements and their liberalization depth. However, if consolidation were to occur, it would streamline trade processes and allow for the reduction of trade costs, a crucial step towards participation in global and regional value chains or production networks.

B. TRENDS IN PREFERENTIAL TRADE AGREEMENTS: SELECTED FEATURES AND STYLIZED FACTS

1. Agreements already negotiated

As found by ESCAP (2015), there was a short-lived pause of about two years prior to 2015 when the economies in the Asia-Pacific region slowed their initiatives on PTAs. However, in 2015, there was again an increase in the number of PTAs signed and enacted in the region. Nine new bilateral PTAs as well as one Custom and Economic Union – the Eurasian Economic Union (EAEU) – were put into force during that period. Most of the bilateral PTAs were between economies within the Asia-Pacific region – Australia-China, Australia-Japan, Republic of Korea-China, Republic of Korea-New Zealand, Republic of Korea-Viet Nam, Turkey-Malaysia and Turkey-Islamic Republic of Iran. Furthermore, two PTAs were signed – one bilateral free trade agreement (FTA) (Singapore-Turkey) and one country-bloc FTA (Viet Nam-EAEU). Between January 2016 and July 2016, two agreements came into force – the Japan-Mongolia Economic Partnership Agreement (EPA) and the Republic of Korea-Colombia FTA. Three other agreements were signed – the Trans-Pacific Partnership (TPP), the Georgia-EFTA FTA and the Philippines-EFTA FTA (increasing the number of agreements EFTA has signed with economies in the Asia-Pacific region to 11).

"In 2015, 10 more PTAs were signed and/ or enacted by Asia-Pacific economies."

PTAs in the Asia-Pacific region are getting more complex in nature (see section D), and/or involve a larger number of partners with different development levels and views on the role of trade, so it may take longer to negotiate and ratify such agreements. For example, the two mega-regional agreements – Regional Comprehensive Economic Partnership (RCEP) and TPP – involving exclusively or mostly partners from Asia and the Pacific; both facing difficulties in this regard. The completion of RCEP negotiations, first round of which was held in May 2013, has already been postponed twice. The TPP, which was signed in February 2016, faces a long ratification process at best.

"PTAs, mainly bilateral and among developing economies, are increasingly being signed with economies outside the Asia-Pacific region."

Developing economies in the Asia-Pacific region continue to pursue more and more PTAs with other developing economies, providing a dynamic force for South-South trade and cooperation. A total of 72% of PTAs enacted by Asia-Pacific economies comprise only parties that are developing economies.[6] However, as figure 6.2 shows, the number of PTAs among developing economies is growing at a diminishing rate. Between 2011 and 2015 the Asia-Pacific economies put into force an average of eight trade agreements per year (6.6 bilateral agreements) compared with an average of 9.2 (7 bilateral agreements) during 2006-2010.

Until the early 1990s, most of PTAs were signed among the economies within their own subregion;[8] however, the focus then shifted to the other economies of the region as well as outside Asia and the Pacific. At present, Asia-Pacific economies have 87 PTAs (51%) with partners outside the region. The trend in signing PTAs with partners outside the region (figure 6.3) reflects the efforts by policymakers to seek additional access to non-traditional export markets, especially in the context of low trade growth in past five years.

Until 1992, there were only nine PTAs in force in the Asia-Pacific region, most of which were partial scope plurilateral agreements. Some of them were only within the region, such as the Asia-Pacific Trade Agreement (APTA) and the South Pacific Regional Trade and Economic Cooperation Agreement (SPARTECA), while

Figure 6.2 **Cumulative number of PTAs (notified and non-notified to WTO) put into force by Asia-Pacific economies, by level of development of parties, 1971-July 2016**

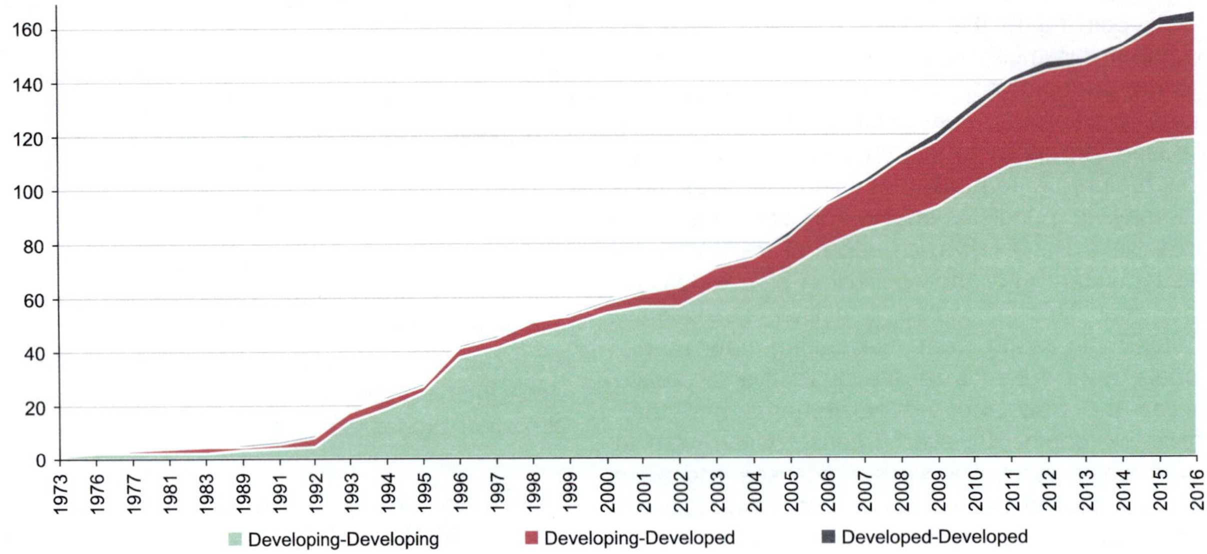

Source: ESCAP calculation based on data from APTIAD.

Figure 6.3 **Cumulative number of PTAs (notified and non-notified to WTO) put into force by Asia-Pacific economies, by geographical region of parties, 1971-July 2016**

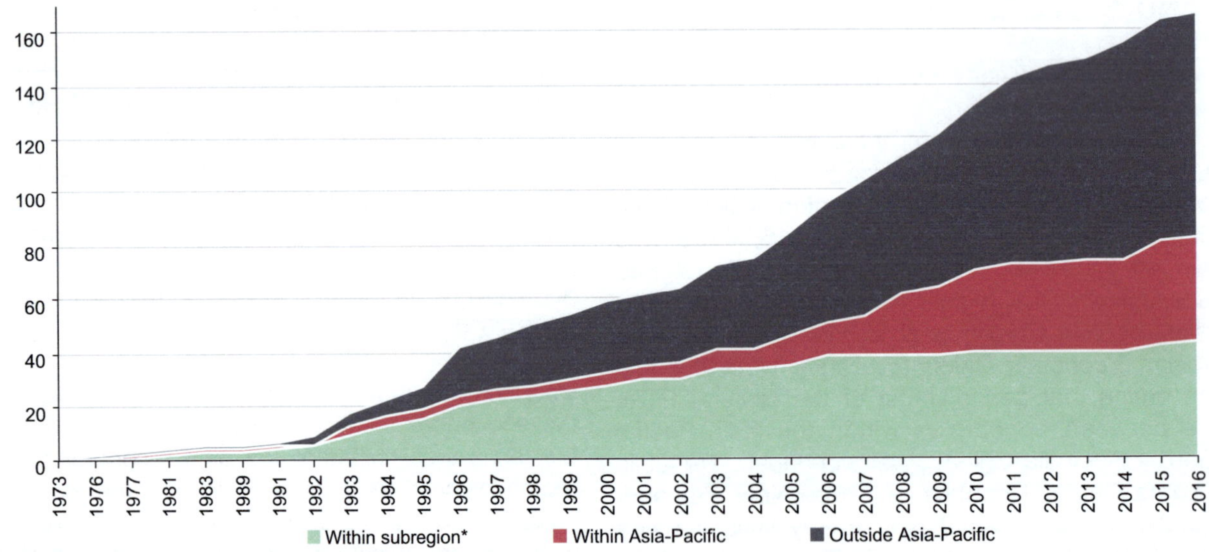

Source: ESCAP calculation based on APTIAD data.

* Asia-Pacific members of ESCAP are grouped into five subregions – East and North-East Asia (ENEA), North and Central Asia (NCA), South-East Asia (SEA), South and South-West Asia (SSWA) and the Pacific.

others also covered economies outside the region, e.g. the Protocol on Trade Negotiations (PTN), and the Global System of Trade Preferences (GSTP) among larger number of developing countries. The proliferation of bilateral deals began to dominate after 1992, covering only trade in merchandise goods. As of July 2016, 137 of the existing 169 agreements (81%) were bilateral (figure 6.4), of which 68 were with members from outside the region.[9] Despite the recent pursuance of plurilateral agreements (such as RCEP, TPP and EAEU) and country-bloc agreements – such as between Asia-Pacific economies and the European Union, the Gulf Coordination Council (GCC) and EAEU – there is no evidence that a bilateral approach might be abandoned in the near future.

In terms of types of agreement, 87.6% of all PTAs in force in the Asia-Pacific region comprise free

Figure 6.4 **Breakdown of trade agreements, by type and number of partners**

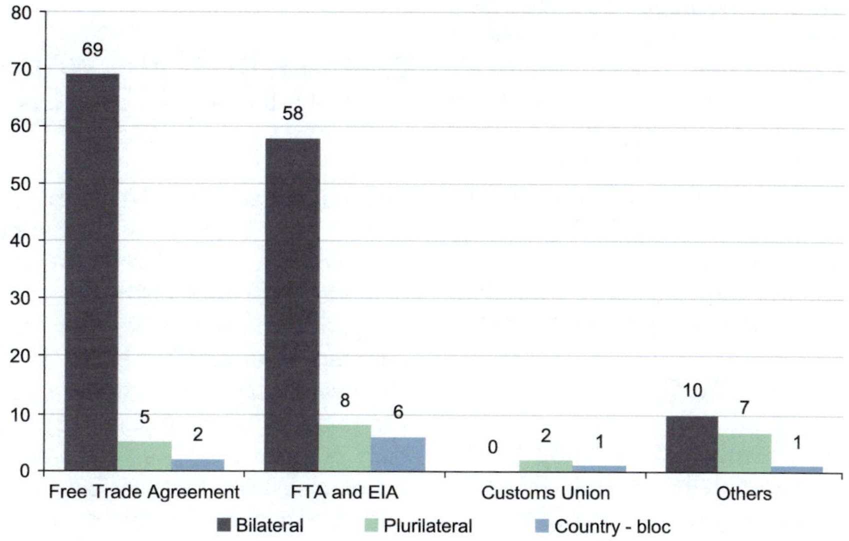

Source: ESCAP calculation based on APTIAD data.

trade agreements (FTAs), and combined FTAs and Economic Integration Agreements (FTAs and EIAs). On the other hand, 10.6% of PTAs (18 agreements) are partial scope agreements (PSAs)[10] and only 1.8% (three PTAs) are classified as Customs Unions (CU). One CU, the EAEU, includes also elements of services liberalization and thus is also classified as an EIA. Figure 6.4 also shows a breakdown of these agreements (PSAs appear as "Others").

There has also been a shift in terms of which areas of liberalization these agreements are addressing. In 2000, the share of PTAs covering both goods and services (also known as "FTA and EIA") was only 3%. In 2016 this share has grown to 43%. The increasing number of agreements covering both goods and services shows the recognition by Governments of the growing importance of services in international trade. Indeed, many trade agreements that initially only covered trade in goods have been expanded to include liberalization commitments in trade in services – for example, the FTAs between ASEAN and its dialogue partners, the SAARC Agreement on Trade in Services (SATIS), Pacific Island Countries Trade Agreement (PICTA) Trade in Services Protocol, and the APTA Framework Agreements on the Promotion and Liberalization of Trade in Services. However, many of these agreements are still under negotiation or waiting for negotiation to start.

The degree of market integration as well as the disciplines covered is determined by the willingness of economies to undertake deeper and more ambitious forms of integration, thus providing a good indicator of the level of political support for regional economic integration. In the Asia-Pacific region as well as at the global level CUs are rare and represent only 6.7% of the "physical agreements" notified to WTO.[11] Although common markets are an even more comprehensive form of integration as they provide full movement of all factors among the members, they are rare in this region. EAEU and the ASEAN Economic Community are two examples of economic integration processes in the Asia-Pacific region within which the members are working towards the consolidation of common markets.

2. Agreements under negotiation

Of the agreements currently being negotiated by Asia-Pacific economies, the majority are bilateral (42) followed by country-bloc (26). Moreover, 74% of PTAs being negotiated are with economies or blocs outside the Asia-Pacific region. As of July 2016, the Asia-Pacific economies involved in further negotiations were: Turkey (15), India (14), the Republic of Korea (9), China (8) and Japan (8). With regard to trade partners, the European Union and EFTA rank first with 11 and 6 processes of negotiation, respectively, with Asia-Pacific economies. GCC also ranked first in negotiations between the bloc and Australia, China, India, Japan, the Republic of Korea, Pakistan and Turkey; however, negotiations with this bloc were suspended when the GCC Council decided to review its trade agreement policy. In 2014, the GCC Council approved the resumption of trade negotiations; however, only the negotiations between China and GCC were formally resumed in March 2016. As in the case of negotiations with GCC, there are many other negotiations that have been suspended either because of overlapping with other negotiation processes (bilateral or plurilateral) or for technical or political reasons (e.g. Singapore-Canada, Armenia-European Union, Thailand-EFTA, Turkey-Libya, Belarus-Kazakhstan-Russian Federation-New Zealand, Belarus-Kazakhstan-Russian Federation-EFTA, Japan-Republic of Korea, and ASEAN-EU.

3. Status of notifications to WTO

The WTO members are required to notify to the WTO Secretariat of the details of their PTAs in force as well as to make an early announcement of any new negotiations or newly-signed PTAs. In this regard, all PTAs that are in force, pending ratification or under negotiation should have been notified to WTO. However, of the 169 PTAs currently in force, 32 have not been notified. Most of these non-notified PTAs are FTAs (only goods) and PSAs.

> *"More transparency is needed, especially with regard to participation in negotiations."*

In the case of the 12 PTAs signed and pending ratification, only 2 have had an early announcement. The situation is also critical with regard to the 78 PTAs under negotiation. Only 19 have had an early announcement. The exact reason for the low rate of providing early announcements is not known. One possibility could be a lack of awareness of the procedure. Another possibility could be the flexible wording of the provisions of the WTO Transparency Mechanism: "For participation in new negotiations aimed at the conclusion of a PTA, WTO members shall endeavour to so inform". Similarly, for newly-signed agreements, the Mechanism requires Members to convey information on the newly-signed PTAs when it is publicly available. However, the flexibility in the way these provisions were drafted does not preclude WTO members from fulfilling their transparency obligations.

Similarly, even though there is an obligation to notify changes affecting the implementation of a PTA, including once an agreement is terminated, further transparency of this aspect is needed, as discussed below.[12] It is only through greater transparency on the status of PTAs that economies can gain a clearer picture of the current status of PTAs (and the "noodle bowl" their proliferation creates) as well as assess and discuss their systemic implications for a multilateral trading system and regional economic integration.

C. SHARE OF TRADE WITH PREFERENTIAL TRADE AGREEEMENT PARTNERS VERSUS UTILIZATION OF PREFERENCES

The trade data on PTA partners are based on the overall trade between those partners as most of the economies in the region do not record or publish data on preferential trade utilization. Therefore, this indicates a higher value and share than the actual trade under preferential terms. The extent to which economies in the Asia-Pacific region trade with their PTA partners varies considerably (figure 6.5). However, despite the high number of PTAs, on average the Asia-Pacific economies exported only 33% of their global exports and imported only 44% of global imports from their PTA partners during 2012-2014.[13]

Comparing the shares of trade with PTA partners, in certain economies the import and export shares are not symmetric. For example, 90% and 75% of imports by Nauru and Niue, respectively, come from PTA partners (other economies from the Pacific subregion), while their share of exports to PTA partners accounted for only 34% and 19%, respectively. Similarly, in the case of Cambodia and Viet Nam, 90% and 79%, respectively, of their imports were from PTA partners, while only 24% and 41%, respectively, of their exports were to their PTA partners. Other economies with a high difference between their import and export shares with PTA partners included Bangladesh, Turkmenistan, Azerbaijan and Sri Lanka.

ESCAP (2015 and preceding years)[14] made a case for the usefulness of preferential utilization data to carry out a complete analysis of impacts from having PTAs. Some developed economies provide publicly available and updated statistics on preferential trade, which allows analysis of the level of utilization of PTAs. For example, based on statistics from the Interactive Tariff and Trade and Data Web of the United States International Trade Commission, it is possible to calculate the rate of utilization of PTAs of the United States with Australia, the Republic of Korea and Singapore. In 2015, 46% of total American imports from Australia, 23% of imports from the Republic of Korea, and only 8% from Singapore entered with preferences under their respective FTA with the United States. It is important to note that since the entry into force of these agreements, the utilization rates – despite being low – have been moving upward.

Figure 6.5 Share of trade with PTA partners (percentage, average for 2012-2014)

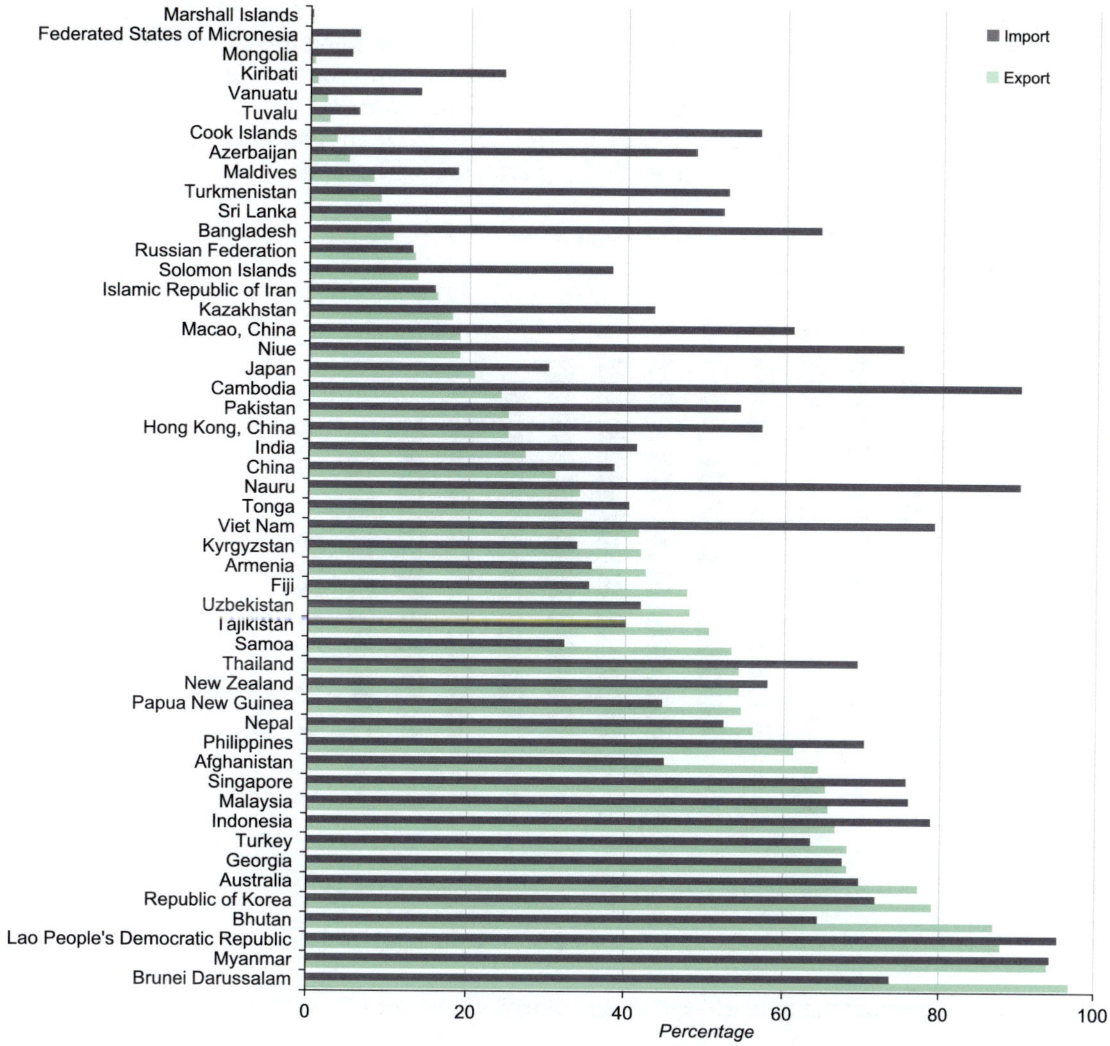

Source: ESCAP calculation based on United Nations COMTRADE data from WITS and APTIAD databases, accessed in August 2016.

Likewise, the statistical office of the European Union (Eurostat) also provides statistics at a disaggregated level. Based on those statistics, 78% of total European Union imports from Turkey in 2015 were covered under preferences within the Association Agreement (CU) between Turkey and the European Union (of which 98% were duty-free). European Union imports from other PTA partners, such as EPA partners Papua New Guinea and Fiji, also showed high utilization of preferences. Of the total European Union imports from Papua New Guinea and Fiji 72% and 77%, respectively, were imported using negotiated preferences. In contrast, only 42% and 39%, respectively, of total European Union imports from the Republic of Korea and Georgia relied on preferential access (of which 89% and almost 100%, respectively, were duty-free). Eurostat data also allow the calculation of imports eligible for preferential access but instead are using Most-Favoured Nation (MFN) regime. For example, while only 1% of the European Union's imports from Papua New Guinea that are eligible for preferential treatment were imported at the MFN duty rate, 17% of the imports from Georgia that were eligible for preferences were conducted under MFN terms (of which 5% were MFN duty-free and the remainder under MFN tariffs).[15] Further studies will be needed to understand the reasons for this result; possible explanations could include zero or near-zero MFN duties, overly-complex rules of origin, traders not being properly informed of the preferential trade opportunities, and/or costs associated with complying with PTA provisions.

Only a few developing economies of the Asia-Pacific region do provide information related to their PTA utilization rates. For example, during the sixth WTO Trade Policy Review of Turkey, the Turkish authorities provided information about the percentage of imports in 2014 entering under the European Union-Turkey CU and its FTAs that were in force by 2014 – i.e. 98.7% of imports from the European bloc were preferential (of which 98% were industrial imports). With regard to Turkish FTA partners, this percentage varied widely from 2.8% (Montenegro) to 99.5% (Jordan) (figure 6.6).[16]

Similarly, the Ministry of Commerce of Thailand provides information on its exports under PTAs. As shown in figure 6.7, in 2014 the rate of utilization ranged between 2% and 78% among the t PTA partners of Thailand.

Figure 6.6 **Turkey's share of imports entering through PTAs, 2014**

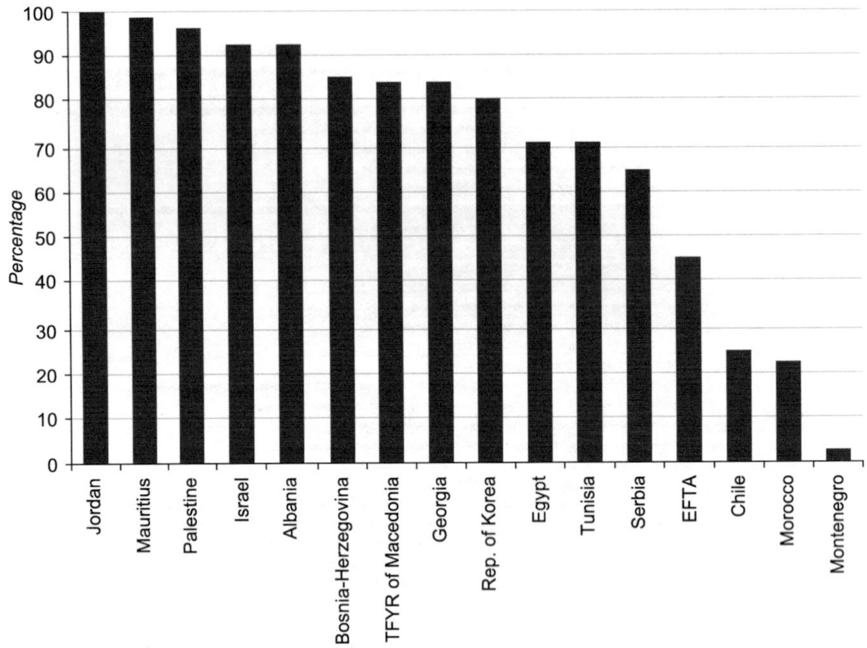

Source: WTO (2016c), Trade Policy Review – Report by the WTO Secretariat, 9 August 2016, WT/TPR/S/331/Rev.1.

Figure 6.7 **Thailand's preferential tariff utilization rate of exports under PTAs, 2014**

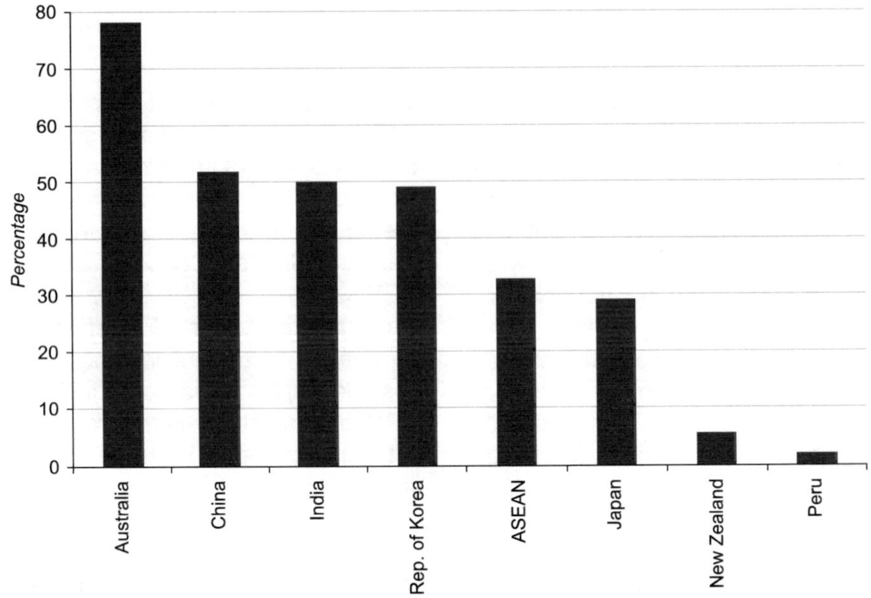

Source: ESCAP calculation based on United Nations COMTRADE data from WITS; and data provided by the Ministry of Commerce during Thailand's WTO Trade Policy Review (WTO, 2016d).

As already noted above, in the case of Turkey and Thailand the rate of utilization of trade agreements based on preferential data is different from the share of trade with PTA partners shown in figure 6.5. While the ESCAP calculation of Turkey's share of imports from PTA partners was 64%, in actuality only 41.8% of Turkey's total imports utilized existing preferences. Similarly, in the case of Thailand, the share of exports to PTA partners was 54% (figure 6.5) however; only 23% of Thailand's total exports enjoyed tariff preferences under PTAs.

The reasons why these differences between rate of utilization and share of trade exist are case-specific. The difference in preference utilization may be due to several causes. One is the fact that most PTAs exclude some products from tariff liberalization, so there cannot be any preferential trade of these products. The second reason could be linked to non-compliance with too-burdensome preferential rules of origin criteria (particularly if the margin of preference is low). Yet another reason arises from the duty-free treatment on an MFN basis that some countries provide for a large number of products; therefore, utilizing the PTA window does not make commercial sense due to the additional cost of compliance with PTA rules. For example, 24.6% of Turkey's tariff lines are already MFN duty-free. Likewise, many of the main PTA trading partners of Thailand, such as some ASEAN members (e.g. Singapore and Malaysia) and Australia already grant MFN duty-free treatment for 50% to 100% of their total tariff lines. Very often it is also simply a lack of knowledge about preferences being available on the part of traders, or the fact that most PTAs have a transition period of 10 years or more before tariff liberalization is fully implemented; therefore there is not much commercial benefit in the early years of implementation. Given that most PTAs in Asia and the Pacific are of recent vintage, it may be that many products have not been liberalized yet and thus there is no (more) trade on those tariff lines. If the latter are the reasons for low utilization, then utilization rates should increase when more trade agreements are fully implemented.

Box 6.1 **India-Sri Lanka bilateral FTA: Sri Lanka reaping the gains by the preferential margins**

Nearly 70% of Sri Lanka's exports go to India via the bilateral free trade agreement and benefits from the zero tariffs granted by India. Sri Lanka has been using FTA more than India (figure), also leading to the former recording a trade surplus under the deal with India in six of the 16 years since the Agreement came into force.

Figure. Trade flows under preferential tariffs of the Indo-Sri Lanka FTA (ISFTA)

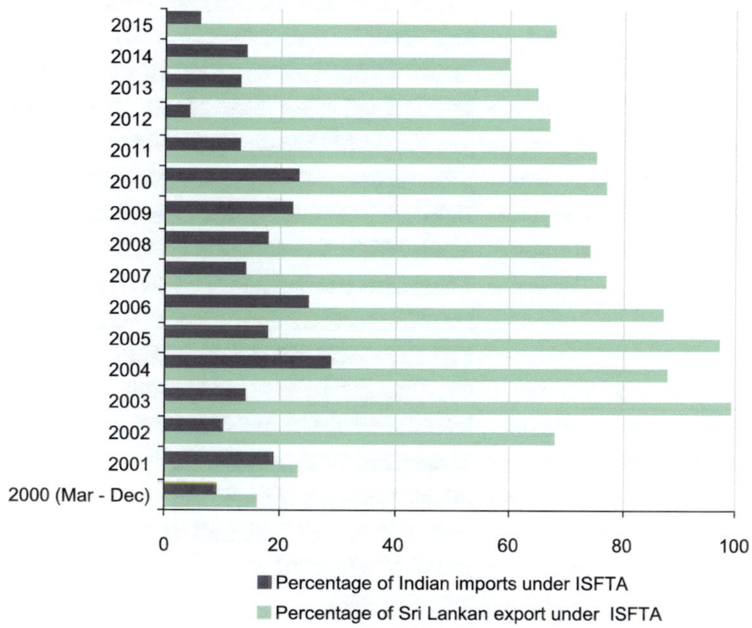

Source: Department of Commerce, Government of Sri Lanka. Contributed by Saman Kelegama, Executive Director, Institute of Policy Studies, Colombo.

In summary, the cases of Turkey and Thailand as well as Sri Lanka (Box 6.1) demonstrate how important it is for developing countries to start capturing preferential utilization rates. This will not only help policymakers to better evaluate the benefits of each PTA and improve the utilization; it will also help them in making more informed evidence-based policies while negotiating a new PTA or reviewing an existing PTA. Namely, audit of PTAs by using extent of utilization of preferences would indicate which agreements could be terminated without any loss for trade. Finally, information will also be useful for the private sector in seeking redress through trade defence mechanisms under PTAs.

D. WTO-PLUS AND WTO-BEYOND ISSUES

While many PTAs in the Asia-Pacific region mainly cover trade in goods (either as partial scope agreements or free trade agreements), more and more economies are becoming involved in agreements that allow liberalization in goods, services, or changing regulation in the intellectual property right (IPR) regime as well as many other areas that are currently not covered by WTO multilateral rules (such as competition, investment and government procurement, environment and labour). Even though the number of already signed agreements containing provisions constituting "next generation" trade agreements is still low (figure 6.8), their coverage in PTAs under negotiation are much higher. These trends are visible in the negotiation of mega-regional blocs (TPP and RCEP), the consolidation of EAEU and the negotiation of free trade agreements with developed economies within and outside the region (Australia, Japan, New Zealand, the European Union and EFTA).

> *"New PTAs are dealing with more WTO-plus and WTO-beyond issues."*

TPP appears to be one step ahead, even with regard to the other "next generation" trade agreements covering WTO-plus provisions or "WTO-beyond" areas. For example, in addition to provisions in IPRs, competition policy, government procurement, environment and labour, TPP incorporates new and

Figure 6.8 **Areas of liberalization pursued by Asia-Pacific PTAs**

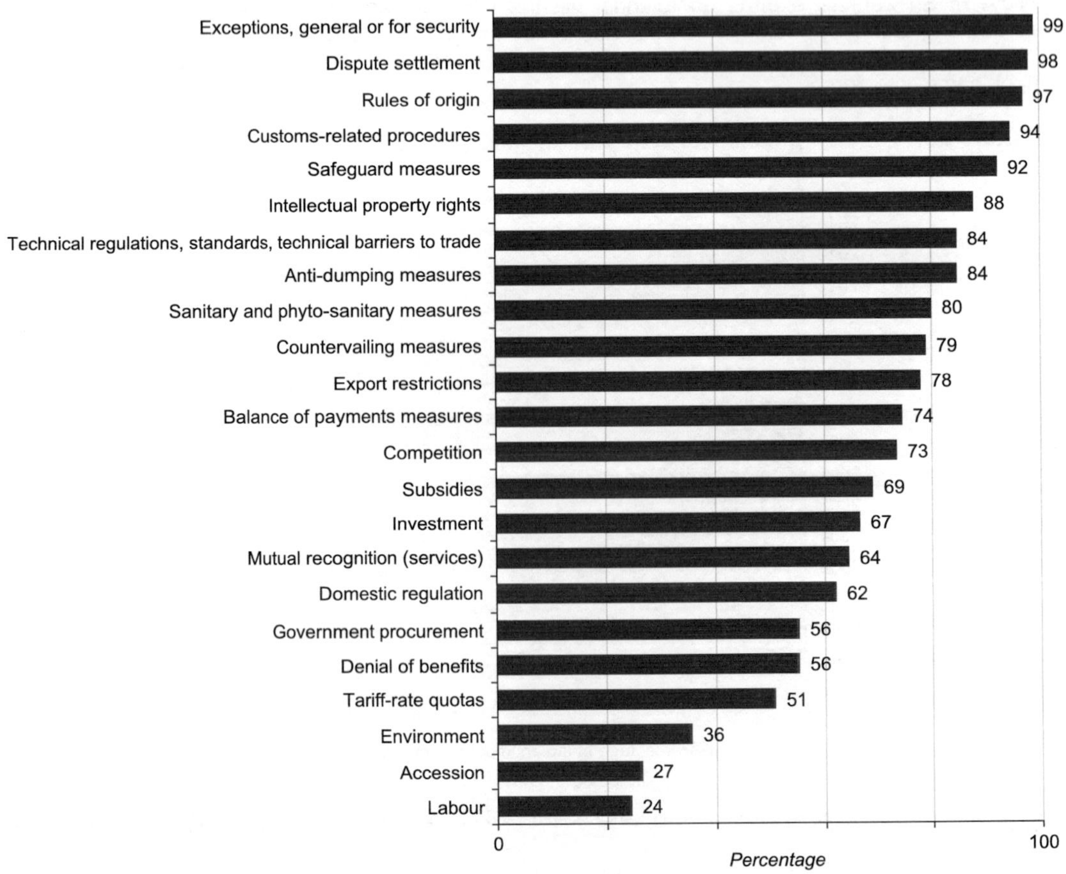

Source: World Trade Organization RTA-IS, accessed 1 August 2016

emerging trade issues and cross-cutting issues such as the Internet and the digital economy, the participation of state-owned enterprises in international trade and investment, the ability of small businesses to take advantage of trade agreements. As pointed out by ESCAP (2015), on the positive side, switching from bilateral agreements towards high-standard plurilateral agreements may help in resolving "noodle bowl" problems. However, on the negative side, these high-standard plurilateral agreements have the potential to undermine the existing WTO system and rules.

E. CONCLUSION

The negotiation of PTAs all around the world continues to grow amid the current global economic slowdown (and the consequent lower growth rate of trade), and the stagnation of multilateral trade negotiations. The Asia-Pacific region is now the major contributor to the build-up in the number of PTAs. In recent years, there have been new developments in Asia-Pacific regional economic integration. For example, more and more economies are becoming involved in agreements that not only allow liberalization in trade in goods, but also commitments in trade in services, and rule harmonization in many other areas, whether or not they are covered by WTO Agreements. The region lacks the effort to fulfil the obligations of transparency in WTO that are related to preferential trade agreements. There are several PTAs that should have been notified to WTO; however, this has not yet happened. Similarly, a number of agreements have been nullified and have become inoperative, yet have not been notified as such to WTO and thus continue to create doubt about their operations.

This chapter also comments on the absence of correlation between the number of PTAs, trade intensity among the partners in those agreements and actual utilization of preferences. While some economies have chosen rationally the partners with which to conclude trade agreements, and much of their trade is covered under such agreements, it is still not certain how much trade utilizes negotiated preferences. Data on preferential utilization rates is very scarce (typically available for trade of developed countries). By using the examples of Turkey, Thailand and Sri Lanka, it is argued that more efforts are needed to fully use existent PTAs. A strong argument is made for better statistics on utilization of preferences. This will not only help policymakers to better evaluate the benefits of each PTA; it will also help them to learn how to negotiate new PTAs that are more easily used by the private sector. Furthermore, an audit of PTAs by using the extent of utilization of preferences would indicate which agreements could be terminated without any loss of trade. Finally, information will also be useful for the private sector in seeking redress through trade defence mechanisms under PTAs.

Globally, but particularly in the Asia-Pacific region, there has been a lack of effort by economies to abolish or annul bilateral agreements between economies that have moved on and signed regional or plurilateral agreements among the same set of economies (ESCAP, 2015). The proliferation and overlapping of PTAs, a phenomenon called the "noodle-bowl", continues to impose challenges for, and additional burdens on firms, especially when data show that there is no correlation between the number of PTAs and the share of trade and its expansion under PTAs. To reduce that impact, several economies involved in mega-regional initiatives aimed at consolidating their multiple and overlapping network of PTAs. The most important efforts in the Asia-Pacific region that are underway are TPP, RCEP and EAEU. While each initiative has its own characteristics and challenges, all have the potential to reduce the complexity of PTA networks in the region. It is necessary that once a larger PTA with additional countries is signed, the bilateral PTAs and partial scope plurilaterals should be nullified. Such a phenomenon was seen in the past in the process of consolidation by the European Union, but never in Asia and the Pacific.

However, a recent effort was noted in the formation of the Free Trade Area between members of the Commonwealth of Independent States (CIS) where the economies in the North and Central Asia subregion decided to nullify some of their bilateral PTAs (see annex), which was a positive step towards simpler and more transparent regional economic integration, and which moves in the right direction towards the consolidation of PTAs; this is an action that ESCAP has been suggesting during recent years in its policy recommendations. Similarly, RCEP has the potential to reduce the complexities of the Asia-Pacific "noodle bowl" by integrating ATIGA, ASEAN+1 and other bilateral PTAs between RCEP members. At the same time, TPP can also supersede the existing bilateral PTAs between its members if enters into force. However, several other PTAs among the parties of the CIS-FTA and EAEU should also have been terminated as well, but such terminations have not yet been notified to WTO. These few examples clearly illustrate the need for Asia-Pacific economies to review all such PTAs and decide on their termination, as that will make it easier for traders to carry on their business in a more efficient way.

Endnotes

[1] The ESCAP secretariat monitors trends and developments in the area of preferential trade agreements in Asia and the Pacific through regular updates of the Asia-Pacific Trade and Investment Agreements Database (APTIAD). APTIAD provides information on the provisions of preferential trade agreements involving one or more economies from the Asia-Pacific region that have been signed, are in force or under negotiation. Available from artnet.unescap.org

[2] In line with much of the existing literature, this report also uses the term "preferential trade agreement" (PTA) as a generic term for any form of negotiated reciprocal preferential trade agreement between two or more economies. The WTO convention is to use "regional trade agreements" as the generic term encompassing both bilateral and multi-country (plurilateral) agreements. However, because of the specific characteristics of the economic integration process in Asia and the Pacific, which comprises five subregions that are all pursuing some form of "regional" liberalization, it was thought that using preferential trade agreement as a generic form would fit better. The key features of any generic term here is that it must describe a process that is both reciprocal and discriminatory in the context of not providing trade preferences for all WTO members; however, preferences that are provided are on a reciprocal basis.

[3] This count includes trade agreements put into force by the ESCAP member States and associate members excluding non-regional member States (France, the Netherlands, the United Kingdom and the United States).

[4] This number refers only to the so-called "physical" regional trade agreements reported by WTO as of 30 August 2016 (see website at http://rtais.wto.org/UI/publicsummarytable.aspx). Normally, WTO reports the number of trade agreements based on notification requirements, which means that if a trade agreement includes both goods and services, it will be counted as two notifications – one for goods and the other for services – even though it is physically one trade agreement. To prevent unnecessary inflation of the number of agreements, only the physical number of trade agreements is reported here, counting goods and services between the same partners as one.

[5] There is one agreement that was in force but has been suspended due to political reasons since December 2011 (Association Agreement establishing a Free Trade Area between Turkey and the Syrian Arab Republic).

[6] This is also due to the fact that in the Asia-Pacific region only Australia, Japan and New Zealand are developed countries.

[7] The numbers presented in figure 6.1 are based on the established WTO practice of self-classification by economies with regard to their development level. Following that practice, only three Asia-Pacific economies are "developed" (Australia, Japan and New Zealand) and the remainder are "developing", including the special category of least developed countries, despite the fact that a number of them have a high rate of GDP per capita and a not insignificant share in world trade.

[8] The detailed list of subregional composition of economies is available from www.unescap.org/sites/default/files/Economic%20and%20Social%20Survey%20of%20Asia%20and%20the%20Pacific%202014.pdf.

[9] There are 102 bilateral PTAs between developing economies, 31 between developing and developed economies and 4 between developed economies.

[10] The most recent partial scope agreement is the Turkey-Islamic Republic of Iran Preferential Trade Agreement, signed in January 2014 and entered into force on 1 January 2015. Under this agreement, Turkey has granted concessions to the Islamic Republic of Iran on approximately 140 agricultural products while the Islamic Republic of Iran has granted concessions to Turkey on approximately 125 industrial products.

[11] The number of CUs does not take into account enlargements and accessions. It covers "customs unions" only and "customs unions and economic integration agreements".

[12] One can argue that this is covered by paragraph 14 of the Transparency Mechanism, which requires members to notify changes affecting the implementation of a regional trade agreement (RTA) or the operation of an already implemented RTA. It can be easily argued that the termination of an RTA would fall into the category of "changes in the operation of an RTA".

[13] This average includes American Samoa, French Polynesia, Guam, New Caledonia, Northern Mariana Islands, Palau and Timor-Leste, which have no PTA in force and, therefore, no share of trade with PTA partners.

[14] These are ESCAP 2014, 2013, 2012a, 2012b, 2011, 2010 and 2009.

[15] Further explanation is due here. The cited percentages of "imports eligible for preferences" represent different things and should not be summed up. For example, in the case of Georgia, the 39% refers to the share of imports that actually entered under a preferential rate (zero or non-zero) out of total imports. Seventeen per cent represents the share of imports eligible for preferential treatment but which instead use the MFN regime, out of

total imports eligible for the preferential rate. We thank Jo-Ann Crawford for pointing out the need to explain this further.

16 Again, this finding begs further explanation, which is outside the scope of this chapter. It is not clear whether the tariff lines associated with the MFN zero duties (e.g. 24.6% in this case) enter into the calculation of preferential utilization rates (because they would appear as zero rates, both in RTA and MFN regimes but of course no preferences will be granted in this case). It is probable that goods entering under MFN duty-free treatment are also considered as preferential trade, especially if the agreements contain a provision specifying that the Parties apply the lesser duty, resulting from a comparison between the preferential rate and the existing MFN rate, to originating goods traded between them under FTA. However, further investigation would be needed to confirm this presumption. Another problematic issue with regard to preference utilization by Turkey (and other countries) is related to the coverage of agriculture in FTAs, which is typically low; Turkey's FTAs are no exception. Therefore, the average utilization would obscure an implicit bias towards industrial products. Indeed, in the WTO Trade Policy Report for Turkey (WTO, 2016c, table 3.4, page 56), it is shown that the average tariff under MFN and FTAs for agricultural goods was around 50%, and that barely 15% of tariff lines were duty-free treatment not only under MFN but also FTAs. Therefore, much of the trade between Turkey and its preferential partners is only in industrial products, given the exclusion of agriculture in FTAs and prohibitive tariff rates. We are grateful to Jo-Ann Crawford for pointing out this asymmetry.

17 This calculation differs from the one provided in the WTO *Trade Policy Review of Thailand - Report by the Secretariat* (WT/TPR/S/326/Rev.1, 10 February 2016) because the rate of utilization is calculated using total exports to the PTA partner, instead of exports of eligible goods (WTO, 2016d).

REFERENCES

Economic and Social Commission for Asia and the Pacific (2009). *Asia-Pacific Trade and Investment Report 2009: Trade-led Recovery and Beyond.* Sales No. E.09.II.F.19. Available from www.unescap.org/resources/asia-pacific-trade-and-investment-report-2009-trade-led-recovery-and-beyond

_____ (2010). *Asia-Pacific Trade and Investment Report 2010: Recent Trends and Developments.* ST/ESCAP/2590. Bangkok. Available from www.unescap.org/resources/asia-pacific-trade-and-investment-report-2010-recent-trends-and-developments.

_____ (2011). *Asia-Pacific Trade and Investment Report 2011: Post-crisis Trade and Investment Opportunities.* Sales No. E.11.II.F.8. Available from www.unescap.org/resources/asia-pacific-trade-and-investment-report-2011-post-crisis-trade-and-investment.

_____ (2012a). *Asia-Pacific Trade and Pacific Report 2011: Update March 2012.* Bangkok. Available from www.unescap.org/tid/ti_report2011/download/Asia-Pacific-Trade-and-Investment-Report-2011-Update-March-2012.pdf.

_____ (2012b). *Asia-Pacific Trade and Investment Report 2012: Recent Trends and Developments.* ST/ESCAP/2650. Bangkok. Available from www.unescap.org/resources/asia-pacific-trade-and-investment-report-2012-recent-trends-and-developments

_____ (2013). *Asia-Pacific Trade and Investment Report 2013: Turning the Tide – Towards Inclusive Trade and Investment.* Sales No. E.14.II.F.2. Bangkok. Available from www.unescap.org/resources/asia-pacific-trade-and-investment-report-2013-turning-tide-towards-inclusive-trade-and .

_____ (2014). *Asia-Pacific Trade and Investment Report 2014: Recent Trends and Developments.* Bangkok. Available from www.unescap.org/resources/asia-pacific-trade-and-investment-report-2014-recent-trends-and-developments

_____ (2015). *Asia-Pacific Trade and Investment Report 2015: Supporting Participation in Value Chains.* Sales No. E.15. II.F.15. Available from www.unescap.org/resources/asia-pacific-trade-and-investment-report-2015-supporting-participation-value-chains.

World Bank (2016). *Global Economic Prospects, January 2016: Spillovers amid Weak Growth.* Washington, D.C. Available from https://openknowledge.worldbank.org/handle/10986/23435.

World Trade Organization (2006). Transparency mechanism for regional trade agreements: decision of 16 December 2006. 18 December. WT/L/671. Available from http://ptadb.wto.org/docs/pta_transparency_rta_en.pdf.

_____ (2011). *World Trade Report 2011 – The WTO and Preferential Trade Agreements: From Co-existence to Coherence.* Geneva. Available from https://www.wto.org/english/res_e/publications_e/wtr11_e.htm .

_____ (2016a). Trade growth to remain subdued in 2016 as uncertainties weigh on global demand. Press Release, PRESS/768, 7 April. Available from https://www.wto.org/english/news_e/pres16_e/pr768_e.htm.

_____ (2016b). Notification by the Russian Federation. Committee on Regional Trade Agreements. 1 April. WT/REG/GEN/N/8.

_____ (2016c). Trade Policy Review – Report by the Secretariat: Turkey. Revision. 9 August. WT/TPR/S/331/Rev.1.

_____ (2016d). Trade Policy Review – Report by the Secretariat: Thailand. Revision. 10 February. WT/TPR/S/326/Rev.1.

WEB PAGES

Eurasian Economic Union. Available from www.eaeunion.org/?lang=en.

China, State Council. Available from http://english.gov.cn/beltAndRoad/.

ONLINE DATABASES

Economic and Social Commission for Asia and the Pacific. Asia-Pacific Trade and Investment Trade Agreements Database. Available from http://artnet.unescap.org/databases.html#second.

Eurostat. Available from http://ec.europa.eu/eurostat/web/international-trade/data/database?p_p_id=NavTreeportletprod_WAR_NavTreeportletprod_INSTANCE_yMiooQ47vf0e&p_p_lifecycle=0&p_p_state=normal&p_p_mode=view&p_p_col_id=column-2&p_p_col_count=1 .

United Nations Statistics Division, Department of Economic and Social Affairs. United Nations COMTRADE database. Available from www.comtrade.un.org.

United States International Trade Commission. Interactive Tariff and Trade and DataWeb. Available from http://dataweb.usitc.gov.

World Trade Organization. Regional Trade Agreements Information System (RTA-IS). Available from http://rtais.wto.org/.

World Bank. World Integrated Trade Solution (WITS). Available from http://wits.worldbank.org/

ANNEX

TOWARDS CONSOLIDATION OF PREFERENTIAL TRADE AGREEMENTS

ESCAP has highlighted the complexity associated with the "noodle bowl" phenomenon where countries sign many different agreements with the same group of countries. Globally, and but particularly in the Asia-Pacific region, there has been a lack of effort by economies to abolish or annul bilateral agreements between economies that have moved on and signed regional or plurilateral agreements among the same set of economies (ESCAP, 2015). ESCAP has also proposed that when a larger PTA with more countries is signed, the existing bilateral PTAs and partial scope plurilateral should be nullified. Such a phenomenon was seen in the past in the process of European Union consolidation, but never in the Asia-Pacific region. However, such an approach has recently been seen in the formation of the most recent plurilateral agreements in the North and Central Asia subregion.

In October 2011, eight members of CIS[a] signed a new treaty, the CIS-Free Trade Area 2011. The FTA began entry into force from September 2012 for those CIS members that ratified it.[b] This treaty replaced the CIS Agreement 1994 among the Parties that signed the CIS-FTA 2011. Therefore, the CIS Agreement 1994 became ineffective for all its Parties except Azerbaijan, Georgia, Turkmenistan and Uzbekistan. The termination of the CIS Agreement 1994 for the Parties of CIS-FTA 2011 was notified by the Russian Federation to WTO in 2013. The CIS-FTA 2011 also stipulated that the Parties would take measures to terminate existing bilateral treaties and, as such, replace many bilateral PTAs between the Parties. However, as of July 2016, the Russian Federation had notified WTO of the termination of its bilateral free trade agreements with Armenia, Belarus, Kazakhstan, Kyrgyzstan, Moldova and Ukraine (although the bilateral agreements were terminated between 2012 and 2013, the notification was made in March 2016).

On the other hand, the treaty that created EAEU absorbed the earlier CU and single economic space. As a consequence, among other agreements, the Eurasian Economic Community was terminated as of 1 January 2015, according to a Decision of the Interstate Council of the EAEC. However, the termination of EAEC has not been notified to WTO.

Based on available official information, seven PTAs have been removed from APTIAD (table).

PTAs that have been removed from APTIAD due to termination

Agreement	Members	Year of entry into force	Year of termination
FTA Russian Federation-Armenia	Russian Federation, Armenia	1993	2012
FTA Russian Federation- Belarus	Russian Federation, Belarus	1993	2012
FTA Russian Federation-Kazakhstan	Russian Federation, Kazakhstan	1993	2012
FTA Russian Federation-Kyrgyzstan	Russian Federation, Kyrgyzstan	1993	2013
FTA Russian Federation- Moldova	Russian Federation, Moldova	1993	2012
FTA Russian Federation- Ukraine	Russian Federation, Ukraine	1994	2012
Eurasian Economic Community (EAEC)	Belarus, Kazakhstan, Kyrgyzstan, Russian Federation, Tajikistan	2000	2014

Sources: WTO (2016b), Notification by the Russian Federation, WTO Document WT/REG/GEN/N/8, 1 April and Decision of Interstate Council of EAEC No. 652 "On termination of the functioning of the EAEC" (10 October 2014) available from www.evrazes.com/news/.

The previous examples prove that there is no rationale for failing to terminate agreements that have been surpassed by more advanced versions.[c] The enactments of the Treaty on a Free Trade Area between members of CIS (in force since 2012) and EAEU (in force since 2015), accompanied by the termination of former bilateral and plurilateral agreements, were positive steps towards a simpler and more transparent regional economic integration. This was a move in the right direction towards the consolidation of PTAs, which ESCAP has been suggesting over the years in its policy recommendations. However, there are several other PTAs among the Parties of CIS-FTA and EAEU that should have also been terminated, but these terminations have not yet been notified to WTO.[d]

The effort to cancel superseded agreements must be accompanied by an effort to notify WTO in a timely manner. In fact, apart from Turkey and the Russian Federation (and its preferential trading partners), Asia-Pacific economies have not notified terminated agreements, even though several agreements may be candidates for termination (e.g. the Lao People's Democratic Republic-Thailand PSA, superseded by the ASEAN Economic Community agreements, and the Afghanistan-India PSA, superseded by SAFTA). In any case, these few examples clearly illustrate the need for Asia-Pacific economies to review overlapping PTAs and decide on their termination, which will make it easy for traders to carry on their business more efficiently.

Similarly, RCEP has the potential to reduce the complexities of the Asia-Pacific "noodle bowl" by integrating the ASEAN Trade in Goods Agreement (ATIGA), ASEAN+1 and other bilateral PTAs between RCEP members. At the same time, TPP can also supersede the existing bilateral PTAs between its members once it enters in force.

a Armenia, Belarus, Kazakhstan, Kyrgyzstan, Moldova, the Russian Federation, Tajikistan and Ukraine.

b Dates of entry into force: 20 September 2012 for the Russian Federation, Belarus and Ukraine; 17 October 2012 for Armenia; 8 December 2012 for Kazakhstan; 9 December 2012 for the Republic of Moldova; and 13 December 2013 for Kyrgyz Republic.

c Australia and New Zealand did so when they reached a new agreement in 1982 and placed their previous agreement, signed in 1965, in the "inactive" category.

d For example, the WTO-notified bilateral FTAs of Armenia-Kazakhstan, Armenia-Kyrgyzstan, Armenia-Moldova, Armenia-Ukraine, Kazakhstan-Ukraine, Kazakhstan-Kyrgyzstan, Kyrgyzstan-Moldova and Kyrgyzstan-Ukraine.

CHAPTER

7

INTERNATIONAL TRADE IN A DIGITAL AGE

Digital technology is shaping the future of global trade and investment. One aspect of the adoption of digital technology by global exporters and importers is the purchase and sale of goods and services online, which is part of what is broadly understood as "e-commerce". The use of automated data exchange systems, cloud computing, big data and open source operating systems can help businesses run international supply chain management more efficiently. However, the use of digital technology in trade activities can, in fact, go beyond online buying/selling; in this chapter, the term "digital trade" refers to the use of digital technologies to facilitate businesses without limiting it to just online sales or purchases.

The impact of digital technology on global trade has attracted public attention worldwide with the discussions mainly focused on online sales. The rising importance of digital trade was already noted by international organizations in the late 1990s. For example, in 1999, UNCTAD stated that "electronic commerce has the potential to be a major engine for trade and development on the global scale" (UNCTAD, 1999, p. 1). WTO work in the same period stated that "the value of electronic commerce has catapulted from virtually zero to a predicted $300 billion in the 10 years up to the turn of the century" (WTO, 1998, p. 1). A decade later, OECD (2012) indicated that more than 95% of all companies in OECD countries use Internet in doing their business. According to the most recent estimates made by UNCTAD (2016a), "e-commerce includes both business-to-business (B2B) and business-to-consumer (B2C), valued respectively at around $19.9 trillion and $2.2 trillion each...This trade is mostly domestic, but is becoming more and more international."

Despite worldwide recognition of its importance, there are no official statistics on e-commerce or digital trade. Without proper valuation, there is also an absence of systematic discussion that can lend to evidence-based policy formulation in digital trade issues. Existing studies, mainly based on private data sources, are difficult to generalize because the data are often not comparable across countries, and are subject to variation in definitions and collection methods. Relative to the OECD countries, the dearth of data and analysis on digital trade issues is especially evident in developing countries. Without an internationally comparable measurement of digital trade, key questions for proper policy design and regulation remain unanswered. For example, "how large is cross-border e-commerce in comparison with domestic e-commerce?", "which sectors are involved in digital trade?", "how is the economy performing under these modern business models?", or "what does a digital value chain look like?"

Using the official statistics available, this chapter aims to contribute towards closing the knowledge gap by highlighting major trends and policy implications within cross-border digital trade. In doing so, it also focuses on a factual exploration of digital trade at the global and Asia-Pacific levels.

The chapter comprises four sections. Section A provides an overview of how digital technology has affected global trade. Section B highlights issues related to quantitative assessment and proposes an analytical framework that can be used to estimate relevant indicators for digital trade. Section C applies the framework with international statistics in order to provide a preliminary assessment of digital trade at the global and Asia-Pacific levels. Assuming that digital trade is becoming the mainstream of global trade in the future, section D suggests some recommendations for building supportive environment for the digital age of global trade. Although main policy implications are considered, recommending comprehensive policy actions is beyond the scope of the chapter.

A. BACKGROUND OF DIGITALIZATION OF TRADE

Underlying the rapid growth in digital trade is the revolution in computer and software technology, telecommunications technology and the expansion of Internet access. Since the mid-2000s, Internet access has greatly increased globally. According to the United States International Trade Commission (2013), while only 5.9% of the world's population had Internet access in 2000, the number had grown to an estimated 34.3% by 2012. Internet access has expanded greatly, both in developed and developing economies. For example, the Internet penetration rate, which is measured by the share of Internet users in total population, more than doubled from 37.3% in Japan and 33.8% in the United States of America to 79.5% and 78.1%, respectively, during 2000 to 2012 (USITC, 2013). However, it is in emerging economies, such as Brazil, China and India, where Internet penetration has rocketed from 2.9%, 1.8%, 0.5%, respectively, to 45.6%, 40.1% and 11.4% (USITC, 2013).

According to the International Telecommunications Union (2013), 2.3 billion people have access to the Internet and this figure is expected to grow to 5 billion by 2020. For Asia and the Pacific, the growth of ICT connectivity over the past decade has been leading the world average. A report prepared by ESCAP (2016a), reveals that more than 52.3% of the global fixed broadband subscribers are in the Asia-Pacific region; however, this impressive number is mainly driven by China and a few countries in East and North-East Asia (ESCAP, 2016).[1] Online connectivity has been greatly improved as a result of the increase in mobile telephones and social media activity, and the deployment of national and international fibre-optic networks (UNCTAD, 2015). As Internet accessibility expands, trade transactions are moving from physical interactions between sellers and buyers, to cyberspace – with the marketplace being based on online activities without requiring direct interactions.

For example, the virtual marketplace has proliferated in forms of websites and through the use of social media such as eBay and Craigslist. In this process, the widespread lowering cost of mobile phones and tablets has been an important means for digital trade, especially in developing countries (UNCTAD, 2015).

According to OECD (2012), the number of mobile phone subscriptions worldwide has more than doubled since 2005 and tripled in non-OECD countries. According to Ahmed and Andolas (2015, p. 1), mobile devices "will account for four out of five broadband connections by 2016". The latest statistics, released in June 2016 by ITU, indicate that the global mobile-broadband penetration rate was 49.4% while the penetration rate of fixed broadband was only 11.9%. The expansion of mobile broadband, in particular, is reducing the digital gap for developing economies whose access to fixed-broadband (8.2%) is much more limited than access to mobile broadband (40.9%). Therefore, it is not surprising that a survey by Fedrikkson (2013) found that 90% of online consumers in Latin America use smartphones to do online shopping. In China, "almost half of all online shopping is carried out on smartphones" (Wilson, 2016). Similarly, the survey by USITC (2013, p. 12) showed that "portability and wireless broadband, particularly when accessed via tablets, were key drivers of the increase in United States demand for digital content".

While the development of ICT hardware and infrastructure contributed greatly to the expansion of digital trade in the past decade, new ways of using technology and the information it generates, including big data, social networking and cloud computing, has increasingly become an important element of digital trade. Social networks, such as Facebook and Twitter, have become a standard means of communication between businesses and consumers.

B. TOWARDS THE QUANTITATIVE ASSESSMENT OF DIGITAL TRADE

1. Problems in measuring digital trade

Apart from the comprehensive quantitative analysis of digital trade in the United States by USITC (2013), there are few studies for other markets. The reasons behind this void in quantitative analysis are linked to limited data on digital trade or even e-commerce specifically. As noted by UNCTAD (2015, p. 12), "only a few countries – mainly developed ones – compile data on e-commerce revenue." The work on ICT for development done in partnership between UNCTAD and ITU suggest core indicators of digital trade; however, the indicators that measure the readiness of countries to engage in digital trade do not lend themselves well to measuring the value of such transactions. The problem is compounded when trying to separate domestic and cross-border digital trade. Without official statistics, previous studies have generally been based on private data sources, followed varying methodologies, and have limited geographical coverage (mainly OECD countries).

In trying to measure e-commerce, UNCTAD (2015) categorizes e-commerce into four types based on electronic relationships between governments, enterprises and consumers: (a) B2B (business-to-business); (b) B2C (business-to-consumer); (c) B2G (business-to-government); and C2C (consumer-to-consumer). Among these categories, B2B – which is the digital trade between businesses, such as between a wholesaler to a retailer – is dominant (UNCTAD, 2015; Asian Development Bank, 2015). An estimate of worldwide B2B e-commerce amounted to $19.9 trillion in 2015 and for global B2C about $2.2 trillion (UNCTAD, 2016a), while estimates for the e-commerce of the other categories are not available. The Asian Development Bank estimated that B2B transactions accounted for 90% of total e-commerce transaction value in Asia (ADB, 2015).

However, these estimates are based on limited data and depend very much on the method of measurement. Despite accounting for a smaller share in total digital trade globally, the previous studies used estimates based on B2C e-commerce statistics (such as online shopping) to discuss trends and developments in digital trade due to the fact that data on B2C are relatively more available. Overall, it is estimated that B2C e-commerce is growing faster than B2B, and with Asia and the Pacific seemingly growing faster than the rest of the world (UNCTAD, 2016b). Figure 7.1 shows the values of the B2C e-commerce index provided by UNCTAD for selected Asia-Pacific countries. It is important to note that indices such as this one measure e-commerce readiness from the capability or infrastructure perspective, and not actual trade flows. Even so, information is useful especially for countries aiming at strengthening their e-commerce enabling infrastructure.

Despite those efforts, there is still no official definition of e-commerce, which makes it difficult to do a cross-country analysis on digital trade (box 7.1). Instead, there are various working definitions of e-commerce, which may result in different value and growth rate estimates. For example, WTO (1998, p. 1) defined

Figure 7.1 UNCTAD B2C E-commerce Index, 2016

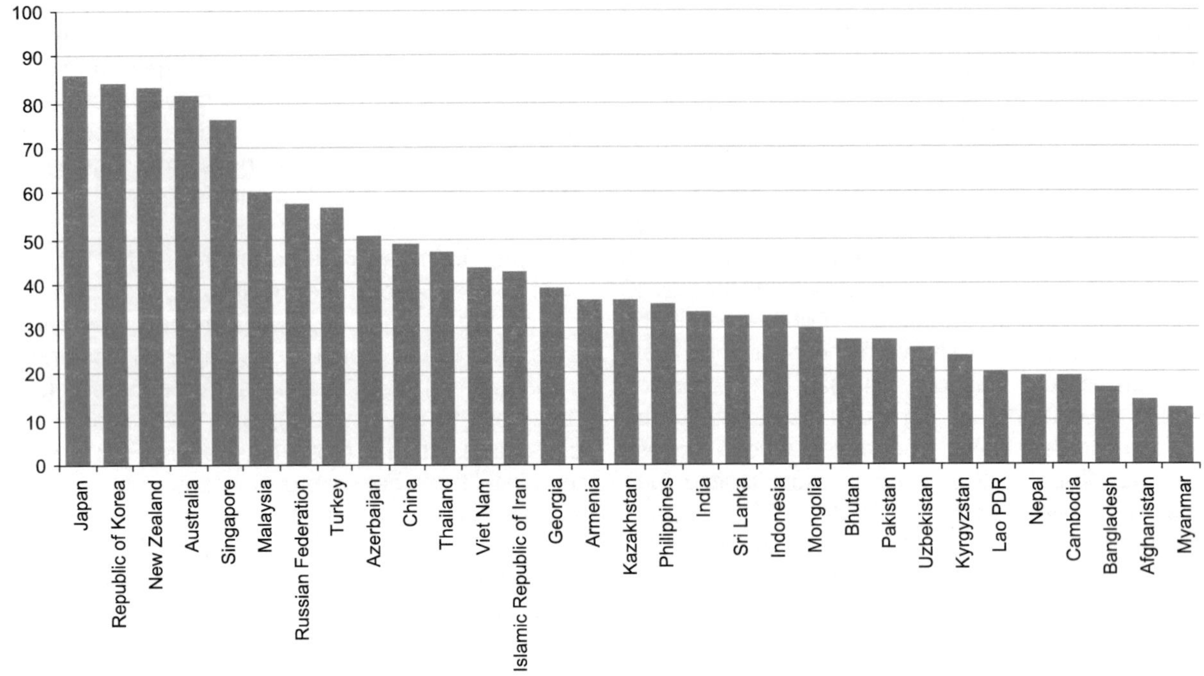

Source: UNCTAD (2016b).

e-commerce as "the production, advertising, sale and distribution of products via telecommunication networks". OECD (2013) defined e-commerce as "the sale or purchase of goods or services, conducted over computer networks specifically designed for the purpose of receiving or placing of order. The goods or services are ordered by those methods, but the payment and the ultimate delivery of the goods or services do not have to be conducted online". UNCTAD (2015, p. 3) defined e-commerce as "purchases and sales conducted over computer networks, using multiple formats and devices, including the web and electronic data interchange, using personal computers, laptops, tablets and mobile phones of varying levels of sophistication. E-commerce can involve physical goods as well as intangible (digital) products and services that can be delivered digitally".

Digital trade also has implications for the improvement of existing systems of international trade statistics. One aspect of this is the need for the improvement of trade statistics to catch up with the fundamental changes in trade. The growing digitalization of trade is blurring the boundary between trade in goods and trade in services. For example, the digital purchase and delivery of books, films or music have increasingly replaced physical transactions. In some manufacturing industries, 3-D printing is transforming the shipment of physical goods into the online transfer of a digital file that can be used to produce the good at its point of consumption. Digitization in trade has also turned part of non-tradeable services to become tradeable. For example, most of the medical and educational services were previously seen as difficult to trade across borders but today are almost a standard part of tradeables taking the form of Telehealth or online courses.

Current international trade statistics has not been able to track digital trade properly. The need for service trade statistics at the disaggregated level has become greater than ever. For example, trade in products that can be digitized is increasingly shifting from trade in physical products such as DVD books or films to trade in services such as in the subcategory of personal and recreational services. In addition, conducting digital trade depends on inputs from computer and information services, telecommunications services, and professional services such as web design, data engineers, IT professionals etc. Unfortunately, tracking trade in services is highly limited due to the lack of comprehensive data. For example, unlike statistics on trade in goods, there are still no official statistics providing bilateral trade in services. Data on international trade in services is available for broad categories under the sixth edition of the IMF Balance of Payments and International Investment Position Manual (BPM6) from the WTO database.[2] However,

Box 7.1 The definition and scope of digital trade used by some organizations

Without a common definition, the discussions and measurements of digital trade or e-commerce are fragmented and the approaches followed in previous studies vary. Overall, the scope and definitions of digital trade vary across countries and organizations. The narrowest definition is defining digital trade as trade in digitized products, while a broader definition of digital trade seems to be the use of digital technologies (ICTs) to conduct business. The definition and scope of the term "digital trade" or "e-commerce" used by some organizations is summarized below:

- **World Trade Organization** – In WTO the term "electronic commerce" has generally been employed rather than "digital trade". The WTO Work Programme on e-Commerce was launched in 1998. Under this programme the term "electronic commerce" is understood to mean "the production, distribution, marketing, sale or delivery of goods and services by electronic means" (WTO, 2016). Despite the efforts to date, WTO members have, so far, failed to agree on a new multilateral regime for digital trade or electronic commerce; WTO does not report separate trade statistics in this area. However, WTO members have agreed to continue the practice of not imposing customs duties on electronic transmissions for the time being. In addition, the WTO Information Technology Agreement lowers tariffs on ICT goods, and was renegotiated in 2015 to expand and update product coverage; however, given the constant pace of new product creation in the sector, the agreement is likely to necessitate further updating in future. Likewise, digital services are only partially covered in the specific General Agreement on Trade in Services (GATS) commitments by WTO members because the "positive list" approach requires active national commitments with regard to newly developed services (Weber, 2010).
- **Organisation for Economic Co-operation and Development** – An OECD (2013) study discussed some of the issues related to measuring the Internet economy in general, within which cross-border digital trade would be a subcategory. It noted that most existing industrial classification systems were too broad to identify relevant digital trade-related activities and that new composite approaches might be needed to gain a good understanding of the rapidly evolving digital economy.
- **United Nations Conference on Trade and Development** – UNCTAD (2015) defines e-commerce as purchases and sales conducted over computer networks. To UNCTAD, e-commerce can involve physical goods as well as intangible (digital) products and services that can be delivered digitally.
- **United States International Trade Commission** – USITC (2013) has adopted a relatively narrow definition of digital trade as the delivery of products and services over either fixed-line or wireless digital networks. It excludes commerce in most physical products, such as goods ordered online and physical goods that have a digital counterpart such as books and software, music and films sold on CDs or DVDs.
- **European Union** – The European Union has set a target of creating a "digital single market". This is defined operationally as "an area where individuals and businesses can seamlessly access and exercise online activities under conditions of fair competition, irrespective of their nationality or place of residence" (European Commission, 2016). This initiative goes beyond reforms to improve the environment for digital trade; it embraces increasing competition in the telecoms sectors, and improvements to data protections and privacy provisions.
- **McKinsey Global Institute** – McKinsey (2014) studies have used the volume of cross-border data flows as a primary measure of trends in digital trade. This broad measure encompasses the direct exchange of digital goods, and digitally enabled exchanges of services or labour. However, it also captures a huge range of cross-border data flows that would not normally be considered as "trade", such as personal communications. Other technical shortcomings include the likely overestimation of traffic as Internet hubs route data across multiple borders to connect two endpoints (Lund and Manyika, 2016).

Source: ESCAP compilation from various sources.

comparability of service trade data across countries is limited, especially when going into the level of service subcategory. Measurement problems surrounding service trade statistics include the differences between countries in terms of data collection methodology and the level of data disaggregation.

2. Suggested analytical framework

The analysis in this chapter is based on the concept proposed by the Markle Foundation (2005) in a report on *WTO, e-commerce and information technologies: from the Uruguay Round through the*

Doha Development Agenda, prepared for the United Nations ICT Task Force. The report, which gives an overview and discusses how WTO members can apply the WTO rules-based trading system to promote the development of the physical, human and legal infrastructure for e-commerce, suggests that discussions on policy issues in digital trade should consider four groups:

(a) Group 1 – Digital-infrastructure goods, i.e. IT goods providing hardware to conduct digital trade. Examples include computers, network devices, mobile phones, etc. that are the part of physical infrastructure needed to conduct digital trade. The Markle Foundation (2005) suggests that products under the Information Technology Agreement (ITA) can be a representation of this group;

(b) Group 2 – Digital-infrastructure services, i.e. services providing virtual infrastructure for conducting digital trade. According to the Markle Foundation (2005), these include basic and value-added telecommunications services, and computer and related services;

(c) Group 3 Digitized products – "Content" products, such as software, books, music, films and games that can be traded in a physical form on a carrier medium such as video tape or CDs, but are now traded electronically via the Internet and which may then fall into the services category, such as personal cultural and recreational services.[3]

(d) Group 4 – Electronically enabled service, which cover services that have adopted digital technologies to sell e-services. This is a large category because most services nowadays have adopted digital technologies and are selling e-services to varying degrees.[4]

The data analysis in this chapter follows the framework shown in figure 7.2. The first part of the quantitative analysis is looking at the digital intensity of exports at the global and Asia-Pacific levels. As there is no direct measure of this intensity, this chapter uses the share of services that are digital infrastructure (computer and related services, and telecommunication services) embedded in exports of a country as a proxy.[5] These services are highly relevant to digital technology and digital trade. For example, the emergence of Internet telephone and other Internet services such as e-mail, video conferencing etc., in particular, have enhanced and accelerated the developments of digital trade. Voice-over Internet Protocol (VoIP) has generated a surge in global cross-border telephone calls. Cross-border computer-to-computer Skype-calling has generated a torrent of cross-border data flows. People and companies are using digital and mobile connections to share ideas, collaborate and make social connections. These platforms range from e-commerce sites, including Amazon, Alibaba and Airbnb, to the G-Cloud of the Government of the United Kingdom, which provide electronic channels of distribution to small businesses providers of goods and service.

This analysis relies on an input-output approach to the classification of the analytical framework (figure 7.2). The data source is the OECD-WTO Trade in Value-Added (TiVA) database (October 2015 version).[6] Where relevant, international statistics on trade in services and goods have been used. Data on international trade in services are from the WTO database under the sixth edition of the IMF Balance of Payments and International Investment Position Manual (BPM6).[7] Data on trade in goods are based on HS classifications from the United Nations COMTRADE database which are available from the World Bank World Integrated Trade Solution (WITS) platform.

Figure 7.2 **Analytical framework**

C. PRELIMINARY ESTIMATES OF ELECTRONIC CONTENT IN EXPORTS BY ASIA AND THE PACIFIC

1. Digital technology used by Asia-Pacific exporters

Measured by the share of telecommunications[8] and computer-related services embedded in total exports there is a rise in digital intensity in total exports at the global and Asia-Pacific levels. The value added by telecommunications and computer-related services in world exports grew by 8.8% annually from 1995 to 2011.[9] The growth rate is higher than the growth of world gross exports of 7.6% during the same period, causing the share of value-added by telecommunications and computer-related services in total export value to increase from 2.7% in 1995 to 3.3% in 2011. Similar to the global trend, the share of value added by telecommunications and computer-related services in total exports of Asia and the Pacific economies increased from 2.1% in 1995 to 2.6% in 2011.[10] The smaller share in the Asia-Pacific region's exports compared with world exports, which may also be related to the lack of ICT infrastructure in the region as pointed out in ESCAP (2016b). It indicates that the region still has a great deal of latent potential for expanding the use of digital technology. Although developing Asia-Pacific economies are still considered to be latecomers to digital trade, they are catching up rapidly. The value of telecommunications and computer-related services rooted in total exports by the Asia-Pacific region grew by 11.1% annually from 1995 to 2011, while that of non-Asia-Pacific exporters was only 7.9%. Specifically, the use of computer technology by exporters in the Asia-Pacific region grew quickly at 14.6% per year, while the growth rate was only 11.1% for exports by the rest of the world.

2. Trade enabled by digital technology

The advancement of Internet and computer technologies has directly transformed the patterns of trade in goods that can be digitized. Goods that can be digitized are essentially software and media products, including films, various types of printed materials, video games and various types of recorded information on carrier media.[11] Cross-border merchandise trade in products that can be digitized was equivalent to 0.3% of world merchandise trade in 2014. Exports of printed books accounted for nearly half of this number (figure 7.3). Based on merchandise trade data, exports by Asia-Pacific economies account for about 30% of world exports of products that can be digitized. China dominates the region's exports of games and printed books, while Singapore leads the region's exports of software and sound media. The major Asia-Pacific exporter of films is Japan, followed by the Republic of Korea.

However, part of the declining merchandise trade value of goods that can be digitized after the peak in 2008 was replaced by the potential growth of trade in their digital counterparts. Digital downloads of these products (films, sound media, software etc.) may be classified as part of trade in services,

Figure 7.3 World exports of goods that can be digitized, 1996-2014

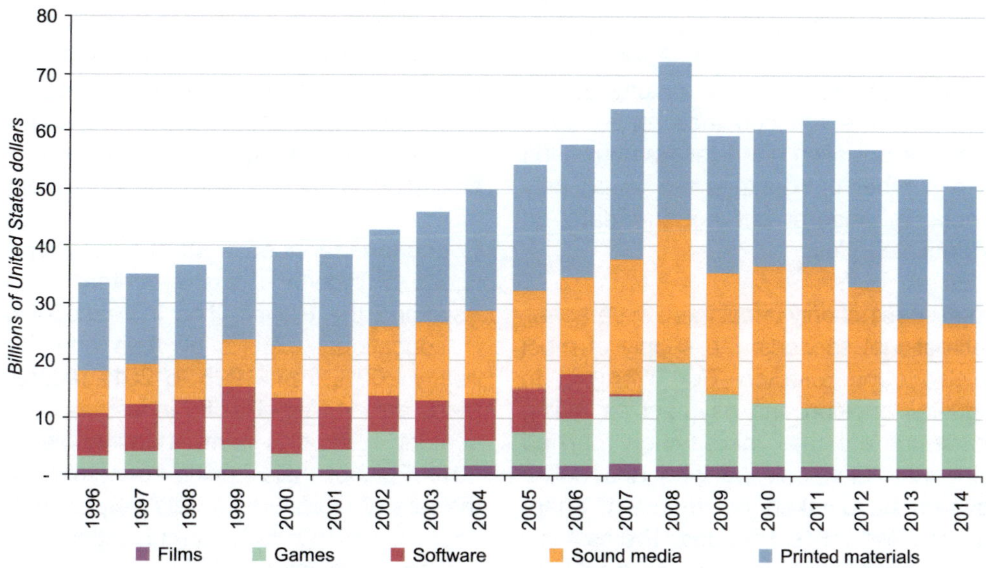

Source: ESCAP calculation using data from United Nations COMTRADE downloaded from WITS, accessed August 2016.

such as under the personal and recreational service subcategory. The change in trade classification has led to the interpretation of merchandise trade data for those products to potentially be misleading. For example, software trade has not been reported under merchandise trade for many countries since 2006. In addition, switching towards digital downloads may be a factor in explaining why merchandise exports of films by Japan were three times larger than the export of the same item from the United States (considering its strong motion picture industry) in 2014.

Using statistics on trade in services shows that the value of world exports of personal and recreational services increased steadily from $25 billion to $40 billion between 2006 and 2015. This suggests that the underestimation of trade in products that can be digitized is far beyond 50% of the value based on the merchandise statistics above.

Yet analysis using trade statistics for services is not fully possible due to complicated issues in recording those transactions. For example, an intuitive way of thinking about digital trade in books, films or music tends to be in terms of transactions that an individual might make in purchasing an e-book, film or sound recording from an online store or in subscribing to a service that provides on-demand access to a catalogue of printed materials, films or music. However, those types of transactions may not be registered as cross-border transactions due to the geographically-specific intellectual property rights protection of the content. There will only be the exchange of money from a firm in the importing country to a firm in the exporting country for the right to sell content that is protected by intellectual property laws in a given geographical area, but not the value of the e-product delivered to consumers in the importing countries. Furthermore, services trade statistics appear to be patchy across countries. For example, some countries report trade in computer-related information and telecommunication services while a number of countries still report only business services in general but not the data on those service subcategories.

Digital technology does not only affect trade in personal, cultural and recreational services; the supply of most services has also been affected. For example, in the tourism industry, booking and payment for airline tickets, hotels, tours etc. are increasingly carried out over the Internet. Electronic banking and online insurance provision have taken an important share of the financial and insurance services. Professional services, such as accounting, legal or medical, are increasingly based on Internet-based communications; news services transmitted by digital networks, together with Internet telephone, e-mail, voice mail etc., constitute a majority of the communication services provided. Furthermore, in the sectors where the supply of certain services across borders appear to be unfeasible, digital technology has allowed new forms of supply, such as Telehealth.[12] As the scope of Internet-enabled services is large, it then follows that cross-border trade in these sectors accounts for 88% or more of total world trade in commercial services. Digital technology is having an increasing impact on those services, but measuring it remains difficult. As explained above, the best that can be achieved is some estimation or approximation of the digital intensity of exports by using the proxy based on trade in value-added data. Therefore, any impact analysis is bound to be biased by having no exact data on the digital content in overall trade flows.

Trade in value-added data indicates that the growth of digital trade has a relatively stronger impact on service trade than merchandise trade. Measured by the use of computers and telecommunication services in export value addition, digital technology in general plays a larger role in the export of services than in the export of goods (figure 7.4). Among others, the sectors with high digital intensity include financial services (for example, Internet banking, although it is not possible to say how much of it is cross-border), telecommunication services, research and development and business services, and renting of machinery and equipment (car rental services etc.). In the case of exports of goods, the publishing industry – which involves digital trade of e-books, e-magazines, online newspapers etc. – has the highest degree of digital intensity. It is followed by relatively high-tech industries that use digital and telecommunication technologies to facilitate their operations and participation in global value chains (e.g. chemical products, computer equipment, and electrical machinery and transport machinery.

Education services lead the way in terms of the speed of growth of digital content in the exports by Asia and the Pacific. The increase of digital content in educational exports by Asia and the Pacific was nearly 200% from 1995 to 2011 (figure 7.5). Overall, there are 11 Asia-Pacific industries where the digital content in exports more than doubled from 1995 to 2011. For non-Asia-Pacific economies, it appears that the rate of digitization is relatively slower except in the case of printing, telecommunications and machinery-renting businesses.

Figure 7.4 Value added by digital infrastructure services to merchandise and service exports, by sector, 2011

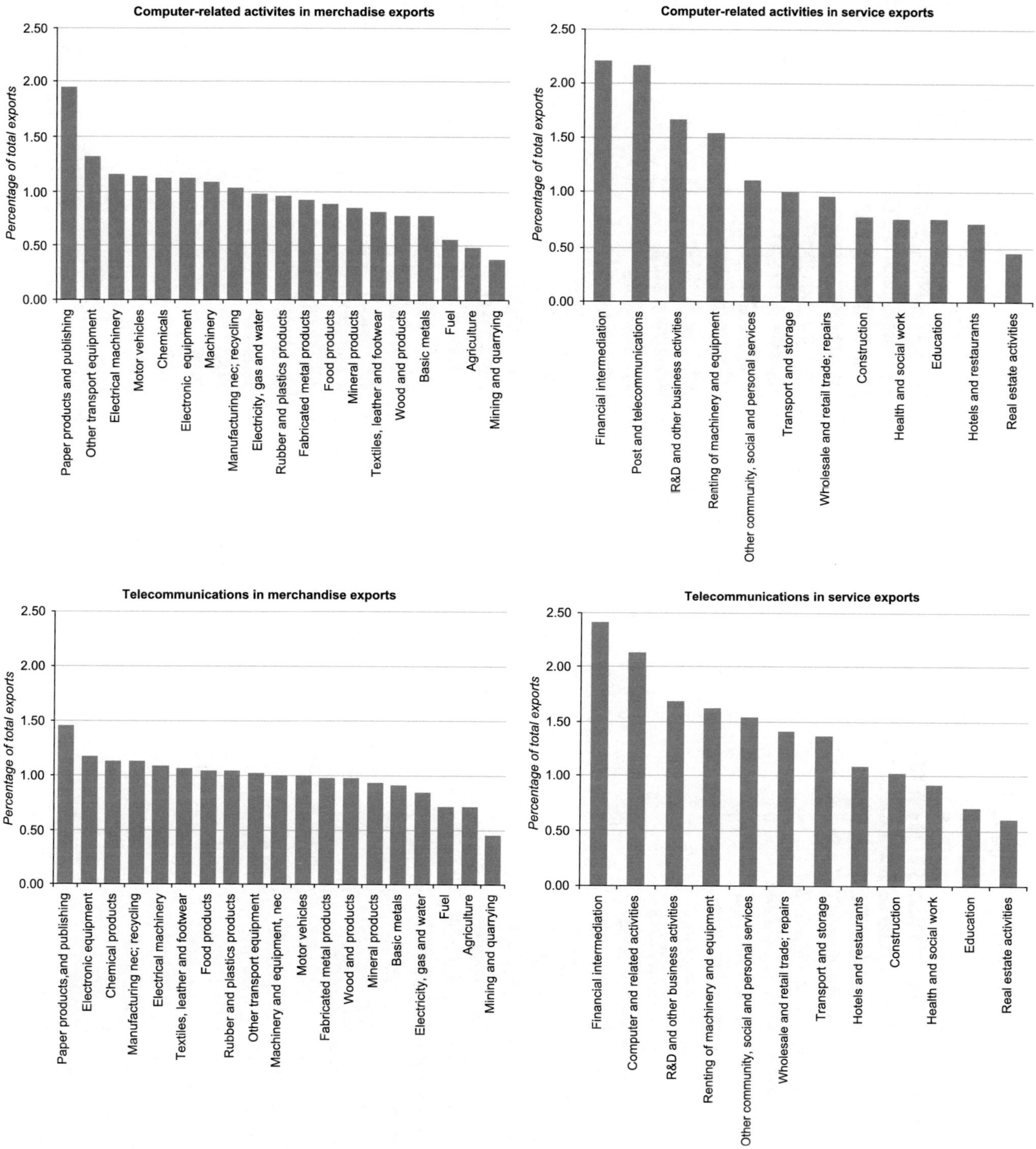

Source: ESCAP calculation using data from OECD-WTO TiVA, October 2015 version.

Figure 7.5 **Change in the share of digital content in exports, by sector, 1995 to 2011**

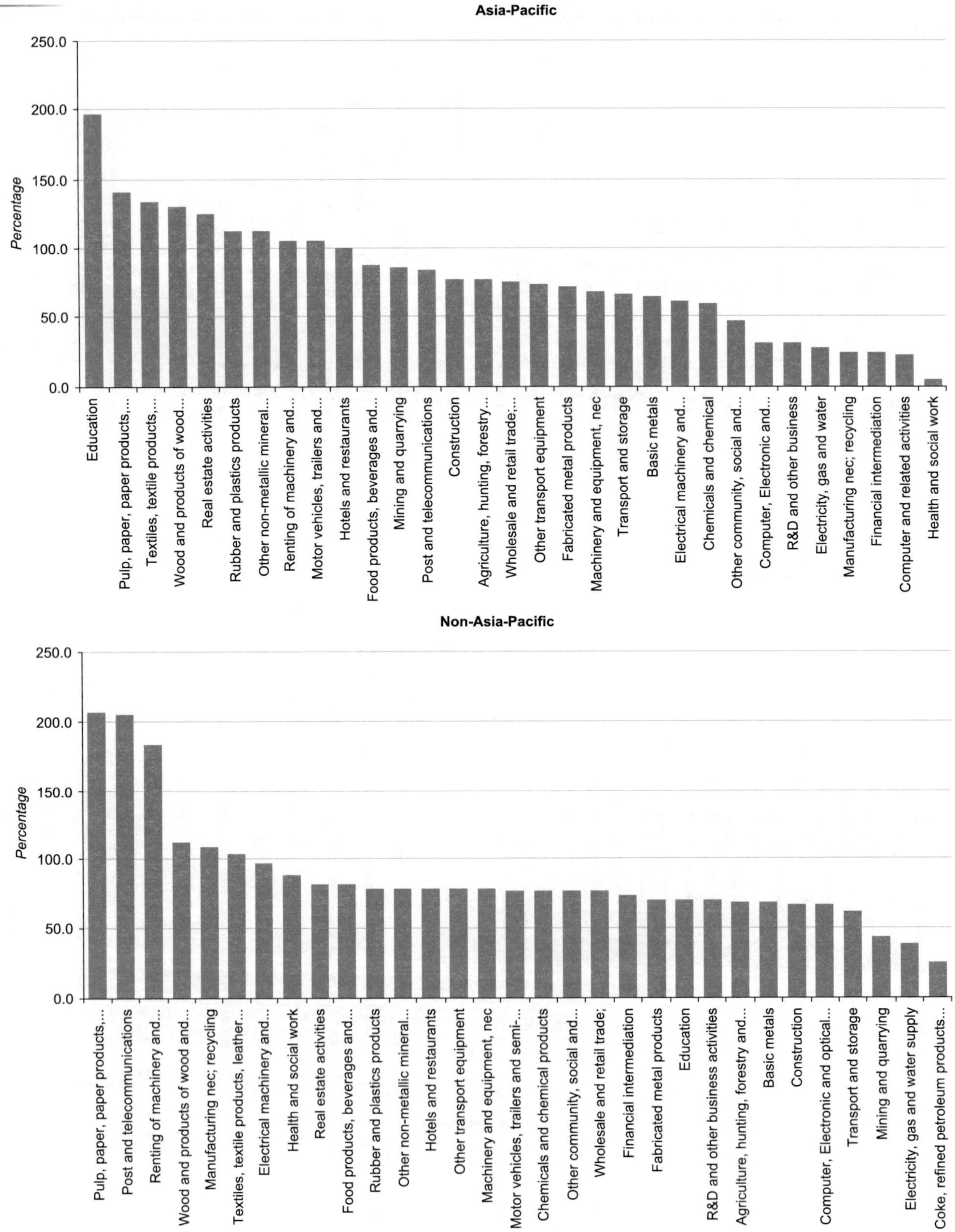

Source: ESCAP calculation using data from OECD-WTO TiVA, October 2015 version.

Note: Digital content in exports is proxied by the share of value-added by computer and related services.

3. Trade in infrastructure goods and services

The availability of digital infrastructure is important for the development of digital trade. Part of the investment in digital infrastructure is the import of infrastructure-related IT goods and services; however, the import intensity in each country differs, depending on various factors including domestic capacity to produce the digital infrastructure-related goods and services, and trade policy. Trade in value-added shows that the import share of digital infrastructure services in total exports globally increased from 14% in 1995 to 22% in 2011. In the case of Asia-Pacific exporters, the import share is higher than the world average. Since 1995, the share of imported telecommunication services has been 21% while the import intensity of computer and related services gradually increased from 23% in1995 to 25% in 2011. The growing significance of digital infrastructure-related imports implies that there is a need for an open trade environment for the sake of digital-trade development.

In addition, intraregional trade is growing together with the rising importance of digital trade, especially intraregional trade in computer and related services. From 1995 to 2011, intraregional imports of digital-infrastructure services grew faster than the imports from non-regional partners and domestic sourcing. As a result, the share of intraregional imports grew from 9% to 11% during those years (figure 7.6). In contrast, non-regional economies only source 2%-3% of the services from Asia and the Pacific.

While intraregional trade opportunity is growing, the major markets for digital-infrastructure services remain outside the region. At the global level, the United States is the largest user of computer technologies in terms of facilitating its exports, followed by Germany, the United Kingdom, France, Ireland and Italy (figure 7.7). China, the largest Asia-Pacific user of computer

Figure 7.6 Sources of computer-related services used in exports, Asia-Pacific and rest of the world, 1995 and 2011

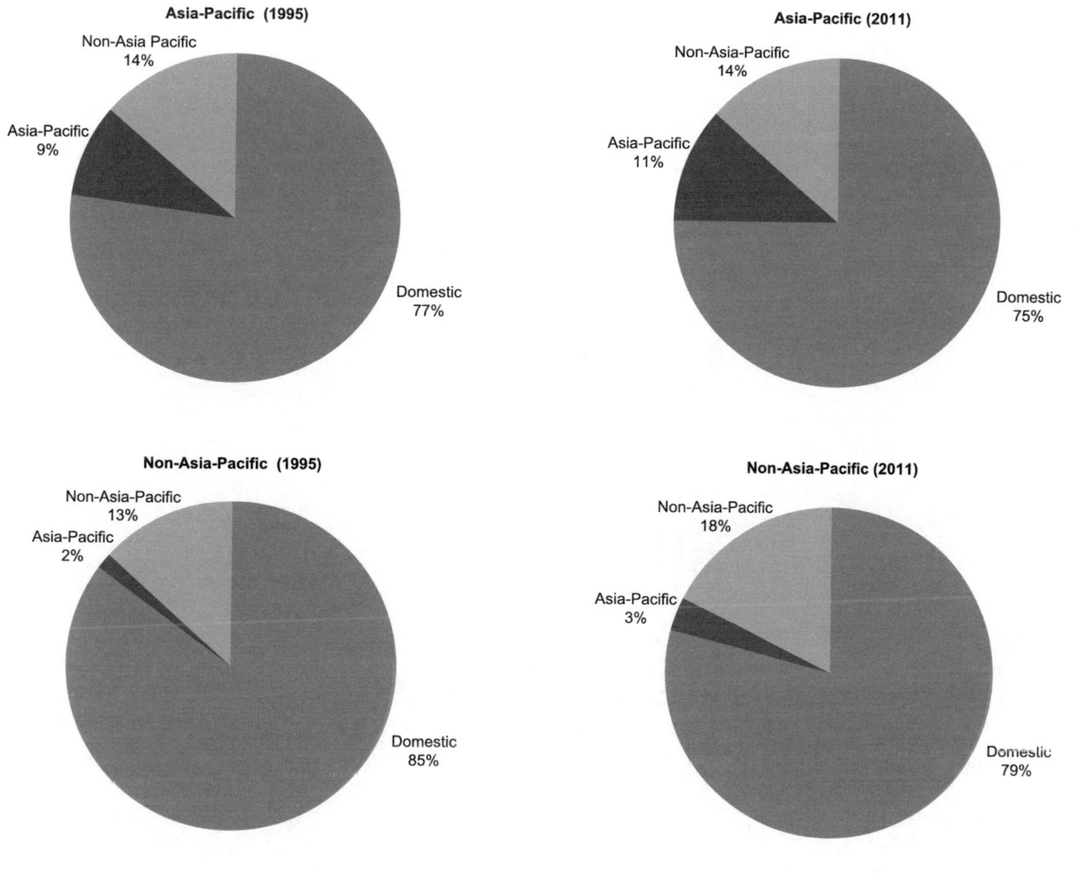

Source: ESCAP calculation using data from OECD-WTO TiVA, October 2015 version.

Figure 7.7 Important users of computer-related services for exports, by economy, 2011

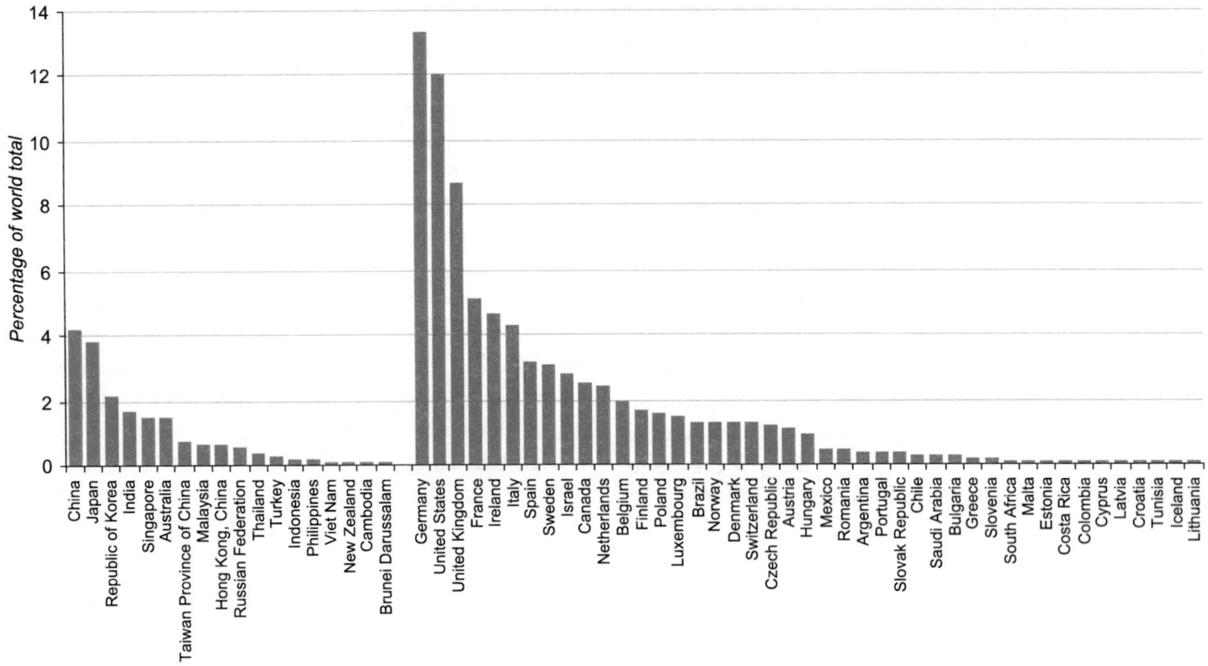

Source: ESCAP calculation using data from OECD-WTO TiVA, October 2015 version.

Figure 7.8 Important providers of computer-related services embedded in exports, by economy, 2011

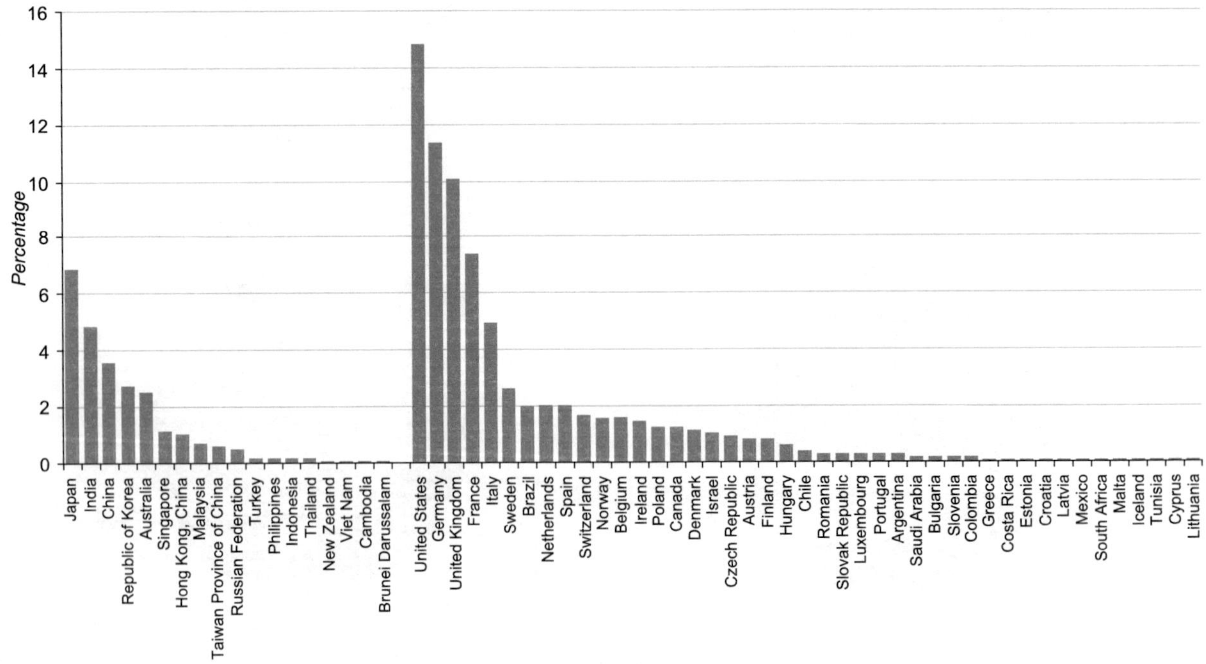

Source: ESCAP calculation using data from OECD-WTO TiVA, October 2015 version.

technologies in export processing, comes after Italy and is followed by Japan. The countries listed as the major users of computer technologies in their exports are also the major exporters of the computer-related services (figure 7.8). Thus, the figures indicate that an economy's competitiveness in digital-infrastructure services may be an important factor in export competiveness in the modern trade environment, where the Internet network has become an important platform of global trade.

For telecommunication services, the share of intraregional imports of telecommunications by Asia and the Pacific decreased from 8% in 1995 to 4% in 2011 (figure 7.9). On the one hand, this decreasing share of intraregional imports may indicate that Asia-Pacific economies still have limited capacity to compete with global service providers in telecommunications. On the other hand, the trend of digital technology has allowed consumers to order goods or services from suppliers operating outside the region, and thus cross-regional telecommunications is an important part of facilitating those cross-regional transactions.

However, the minimal share in overall telecommunication services of the Asia-Pacific region masks the distinct performance of China in comparison to other Asia-Pacific economies. In fact, China has caught up with the United States as an important user of telecommunication services to facilitate its export activities (figure 7.10). In addition, China has been the world number one in terms of indirectly exporting telecommunication services. This may indicate that the inputs from telecommunication services have contributed to the success story of China's exports during the past decade.

With regard to digital-infrastructure goods, based on the list of ITA products digital-infrastructure-related merchandise exports amounted to $1,600 billion in

Figure 7.9 **Sources of telecommunications services used in exports, Asia-Pacific and rest of the world, 1995 and 2011**

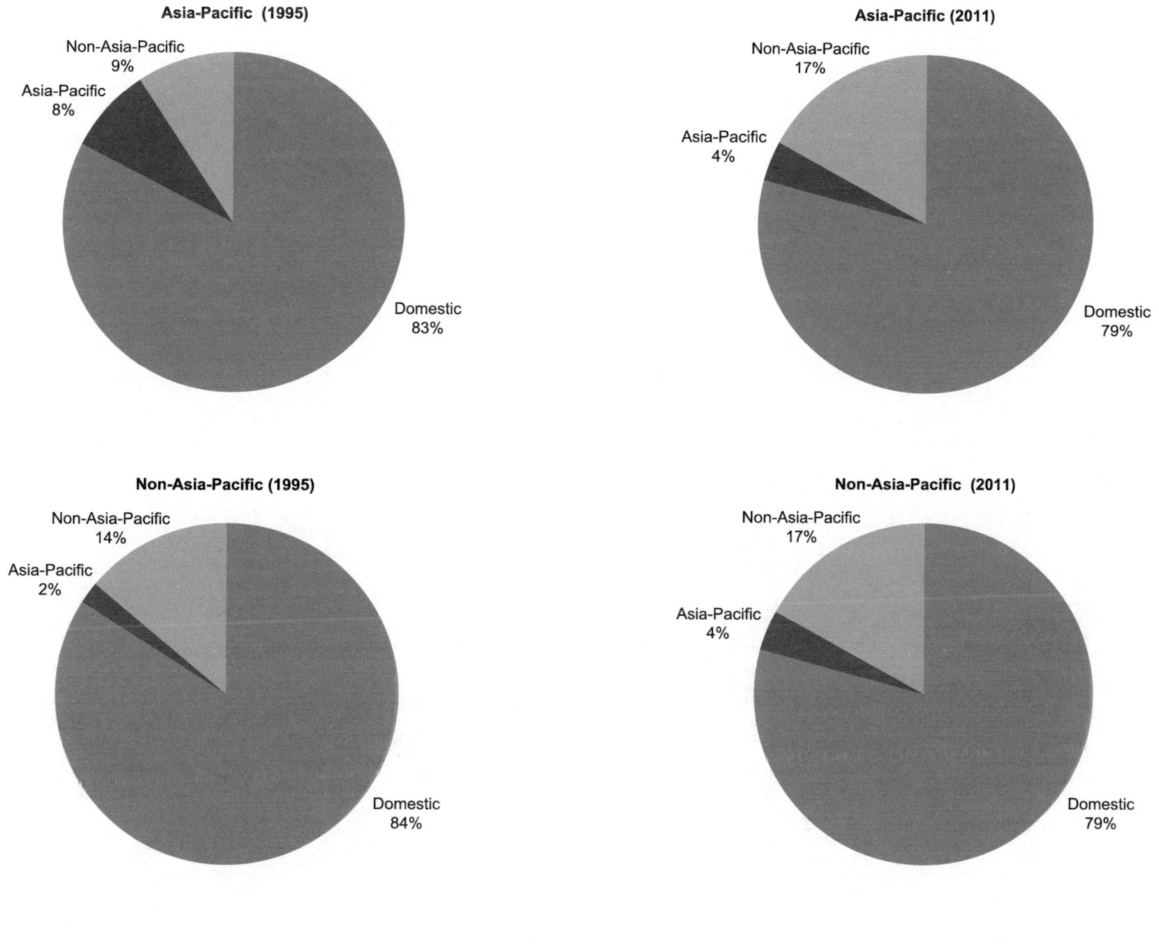

Source: ESCAP calculation using data from OECD-WTO TiVA, October 2015 version.

Figure 7.10 Important users of telecommunications for exports, by economy, 2011

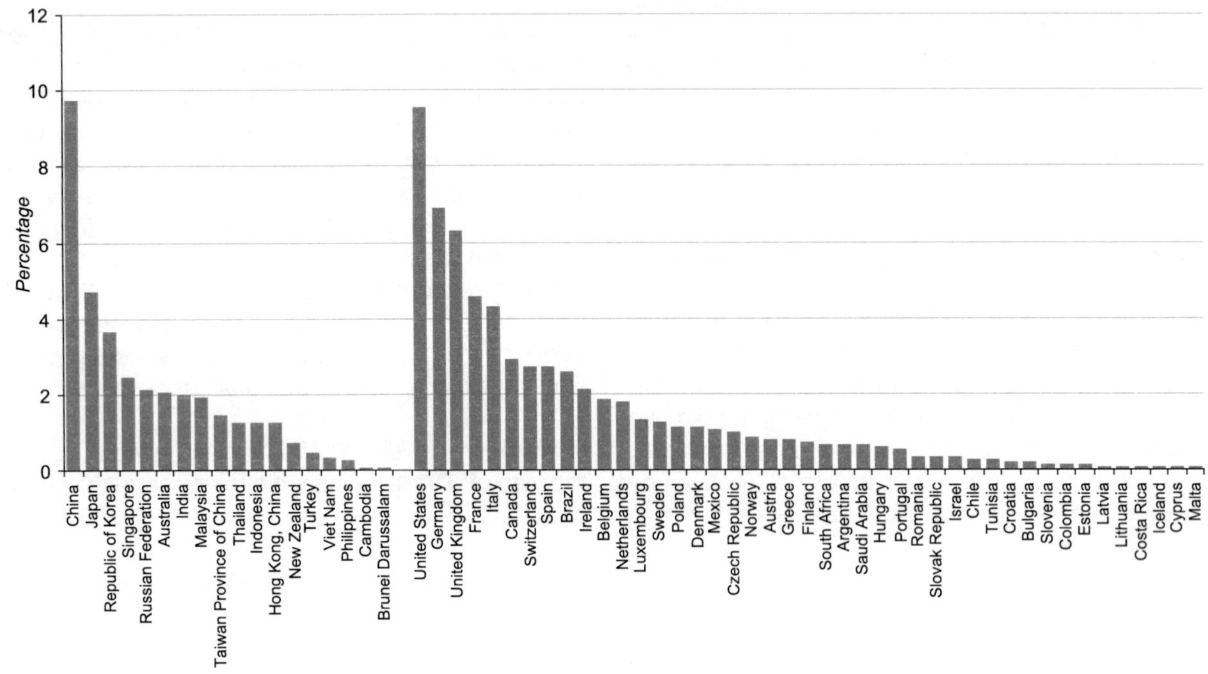

Source: ESCAP calculation using data from OECD-WTO TiVA, October 2015 version.

Figure 7.11 Important providers of telecommunications embedded in exports, by economy, 2011

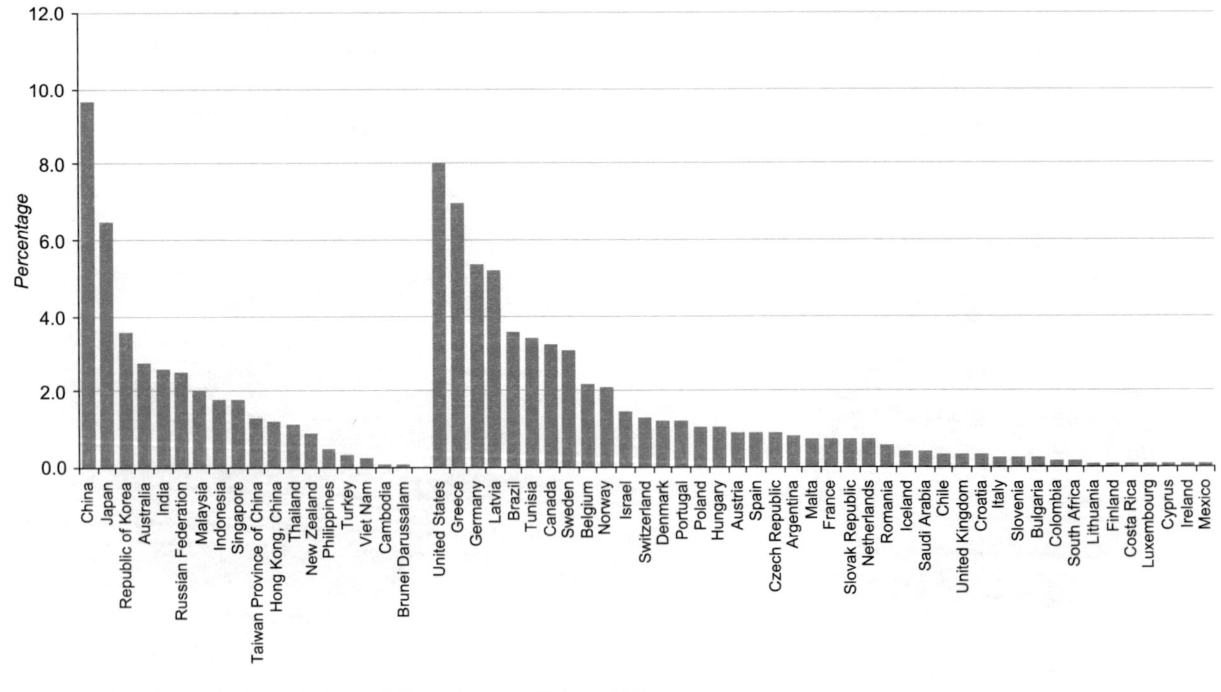

Source: ESCAP calculation using data from OECD-WTO TiVA, October 2015 version.

Figure 7.12 World exports of digital-infrastructure goods

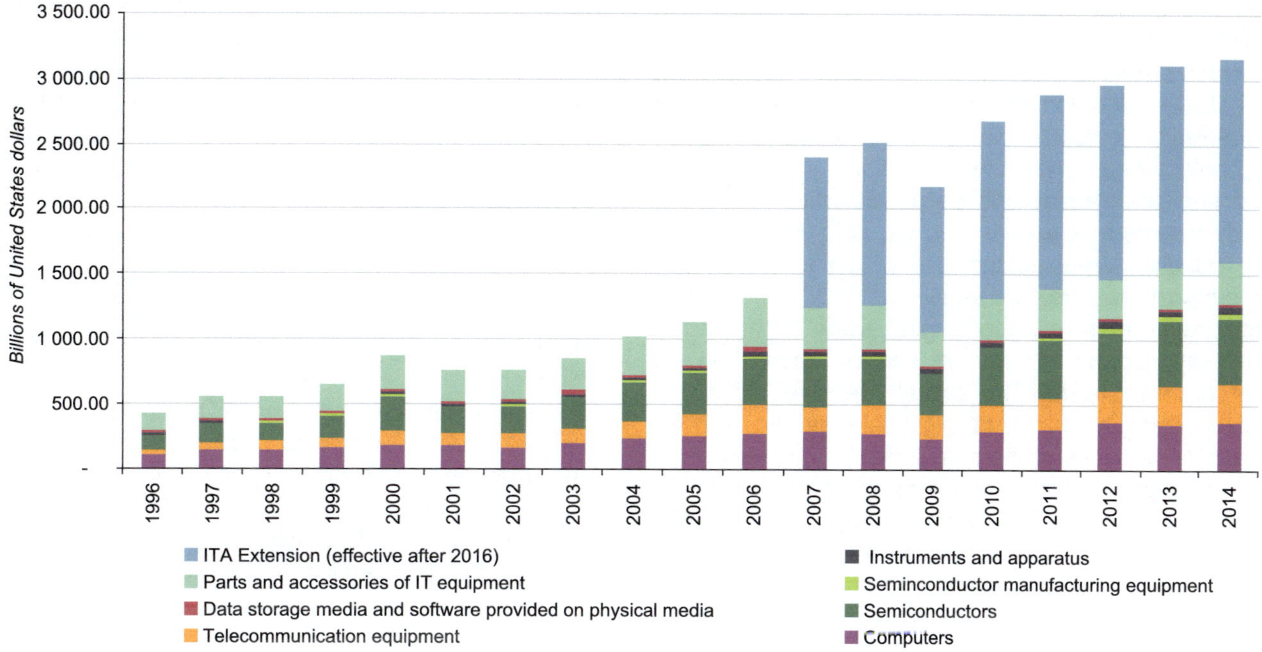

Source: ESCAP compilation, using data from United Nations COMTRADE, downloaded from WITS.
Note: Only product items that are identified in terms of HS are covered.

2014, which was equivalent to 9.2% of world exports. The extension of the ITA product list agreed upon in July 2016, covering the new generation of information technology equipment, will double the trade coverage of ITA (figure 7.12). Based on the share in 2014, the coverage of ITA will reach 18% of world merchandise exports if 201 new products of the ITA extension are included.

With the dominance of exports from China and East Asian economies, the Asia-Pacific region accounts for more than 64% of the world exports on the original ITA product list. The region represents slightly less for the new generation products, of which the technology is still new and owned by developed economies. However, the region is an important exporter, at least as a final assembler, with a share of 57.5% of world exports of products covered by the extension of ITA.

D. CONCLUSION

The growing digital intensity has caused fundamental changes in trade; as a result, there is the need for the improvement of trade statistics to catch up with this process. Official and market research on cross-border digital trade is starting to emerge; however, of particular concern with regard to measuring digital trade is the quality, methodology and transparency differences that inhibit cross-country benchmarking. The case studies tend to overstate the perception of B2C e-commerce, which in fact is not a good representation of cross-border digital trade in goods and services whereas B2B e-commerce is likely to be much more significant. Although cross-border data flows have been seen as an attractive proxy, they suffer from the same issues as any web-based indicators – the fact that not all data transfers are the result of digital trade. In addition, a number of other technical issues and regulations complicate comparability and ability to map the flows of data with regard to sources and destinations of international trade goods and services.

As discussed in this chapter, requirements for analyses of digital trade issues need a combination of data on trade in services, input-output linkages and merchandise statistics at the most detailed level that is comparable across countries. Without a unified definition, proper conceptual framework and systematic data collections, key questions concerning policy design and regulation remain inadequately answered.

Using the available official statistics, this chapter is aimed at contributing to closing the knowledge gap by suggesting proxies and a conceptual framework that can be indicative for highlighting major trends related to cross-border digital trade. The chapter focuses on a factual exploration of digital trade at the global and Asia-Pacific levels. In considering the use of digital technology and services in international trade in goods and services transactions as an attractive proxy, the study reveals that exporters in the Asia-Pacific region are rapidly increasing the use of digital technology to support their export activities, both directly and indirectly. The growth of digital trade is having a relatively stronger impact on service trade than on merchandise trade. The digital-intensive industries are relatively high-tech or high value-added. Digital-intensive services sectors include financial services (for example, Internet banking), telecommunication services, R&D and business services, and the renting of machinery and equipment (car rental services etc.). In the case of manufacturing, the publishing industry, chemical products, computer equipment, and electrical machinery and transport machinery are among the sectors with high digital intensity.

The availability of digital infrastructure is important to the development of digital trade. Imports of telecommunications and computer equipment play an important role in digital trade, especially that of Asia and the Pacific. This has opened intraregional trade opportunities as intraregional sourcing for those digital infrastructure products has been growing in recent years. However, the export opportunities are mainly clustered in large economies, especially China, Japan, India and the Republic of Korea.

The trends and developments discussed can shed light on a broader policy framework. The digitalization of international trade brings about a greater need for an open trade environment and international cooperation. Non-discriminatory principles and international harmonization of rules and regulation are essential. The concept of an open environment is not new; however, what is added is the fact that "openness" in the world of digital trade does not only mean free flows of goods or services, but also the need for the free flow of data across national borders. In addition, the growing importance of digital trade brings to the fore a greater need for international cooperation, as a supportive environment for digital trade is more dependent on multilaterally agreed policies than on unilateral ones.

Endnotes

1 The report indicates that more than half of the broadband subscriptions in the Asia-Pacific region were registered in China, while broadband access is still largely unavailable and unaffordable in one third of the countries in the rest of the Asia-Pacific region, especially in least developed countries, landlocked developing countries and small island developing States.

2 As per BPM6 definitions, telecommunication services encompass the broadcasting or transmission of sound, images, data or other information by telephone, telex, telegram, radio and television cable transmission, radio and television satellite, electronic mail, facsimile and so forth, including business network services, teleconferencing and support services. Computer-related services comprise hardware- and software-related services and data-processing services. (Data at the country and world levels, available from http://stat.wto.org/StatisticalProgram/WSDBStatProgramSeries.aspx?Language=E&subtopic=bp;bc).

3 Hellerstein (2002), Makoni, Tsikirayi and Mandizha (2013), Ruffle (2001), Schuknecht and Pérez-Esteve (1999), and Teltscher (2001) identify products that can be digitized in a relatively consistent manner. The analysis detailed in this chapter used a combined list of electronically-enabled goods as shown in annex 7.1.

4 Annex 7.2 provides the lists of electronically-enabled services based on BPM6.

5 Although IT goods are part of the e-commerce infrastructure, this study does not include the value-added by IT goods in total exports as part of the e-commerce intensity. This is because most exporters use computers and electronics equipment in everyday business even if digital trade is not involved.

6 The database contains useful estimates on the value of inputs used in producing exports globally that can be broken down into 62 economies (61 economies and an aggregate for the rest of the world). These 61 economies cover nearly 95% of world trade. The annual coverage includes 1995, 2000, 2005, 2008, 2009, 2010 and 2011. Of the 61 economies, 18 are located in Asia and the Pacific (Australia; Brunei Darussalam; Cambodia; China; India; Indonesia; Japan; Republic of Korea; Malaysia; New Zealand; Philippines; Russian Federation; Singapore; Thailand; Turkey; Viet Nam; Hong Kong, China; and Taiwan Province of China). As these 18 economies accounted for 97% of merchandise exports and imports by Asia-Pacific economies they are taken as a representative sample of the Asia-Pacific region. Data are available at the country level for 34 industries

classified under 2 digit-ISIC Revision 3, including 19 merchandise sectors (agriculture, mining, food products, textiles and apparel, wood, paper and publishing, fuel, chemicals, rubber and plastic, non-metallic minerals, basic metals, fabricated metals, machinery, computers and electronics, electrical machinery, motor vehicles, transport equipment, other manufactures and utilities) and 16 service sectors (construction, wholesale and retail, hotels and restaurants, transport and storage, post and telecommunications, finance and insurance, real estate activities, renting machinery and equipment, computer-related activities, research and development, other business services, public administrative services, education, health and social work, personal services and private household services). In the analysis of e-commerce services in this chapter, the focus is on digital trade in commercial services. Therefore, the results represented in this chapter do not include public administration services.

[7] As per BPM6 definitions, telecommunication services encompass the broadcasting or transmission of sound, images, data or other information by telephone, telex, telegram, radio and television cable transmission, radio and television satellite, electronic mail, facsimile and so forth, including business network services, teleconferencing, and support services. Computer-related services consist of hardware- and software-related services and data-processing services (Data at the country and world levels, available from http://stat.wto.org/StatisticalProgram/WSDBStatProgramSeries.aspx?Language=E&subtopic=bp;bc).

[8] Telecommunication services are the main carrier used for digital trade. The current version of OECD-WTO TiVA lists post and telecommunications as one industry. While it is not possible to separate them, this study assumes that telecommunication trends dominate. In addition, ADB (2015) indicated that postal service was important for conducting e-commerce, especially for B2C.

[9] The number is based on compound annual growth rates.

[10] The October 2015 version of the OECD-WTO TiVA database contains data for 17 regional members of ESCAP, including: Australia; Brunei Darussalam; Cambodia; China; India; Indonesia; Japan; the Republic of Korea; Malaysia; New Zealand; the Philippines; the Russian Federation; Singapore; Thailand; Turkey; Viet Nam; and Hong Kong, China. The database also includes Taiwan Province of China, which is not a member of ESCAP. These economies, including Taiwan Province of China, accounted for more than 97% of merchandise exports and imports by the Asia-Pacific region. Therefore, they are taken as a representative sample of Asia and the Pacific.

[11] Newer items entering trade on an increasingly systematic basis, such as software, have been progressively included in the categorization list under a number of previously existing codes, in particular under recorder media (HS 8524).

[12] For more information, see UNCTAD-WHO, 1998.

REFERENCES

Asian Development Bank (2015). *Aid for Trade in Asia and the Pacific: Thinking forward about Trade Costs and the Digital Economy.* Manila. Available from https://www.adb.org/sites/default/files/publication/167344/aft-report-2015.pdf

Ahmed, U., and G. Andolas (2015). Addressing barriers to digital trade. E15 initiative. Geneva: International Centre for Trade and Sustainable Development and World Economic Forum. Available from http://e15initiative.org/wp-content/uploads/2015/09/E15-Digital-Economy-Ahmed-and-Aldonas-FINAL-2.pdf

Bernier, I. (2012). Local content requirements for film, radio, and television as a means of protecting cultural diversity: theory and reality. Available from www.diversite-culturelle.qc.ca/fileadmin/documents/pdf/update031112section1.pdf.

Cimino-Isaacs, C., and J. Zilinsky (2016). Local content requirements: backdoor protectionism spreading under the radar. Trade and Investment Policy Watch, 22 July. Washington D.C.: Peterson Institute for International Economics. Available from https://piie.com/blogs/trade-investment-policy-watch/local-content-requirements-backdoor-protectionism-spreading

Economic and Social Commission for Asia and the Pacific (2016a). State of ICT in Asia and the Pacific 2016: uncovering the widening broadband divide. Technical Paper by the Information and Communications Technology and Disaster Risk Reduction Division. Bangkok: ESCAP. Available from www.unescap.org/resources/state-ict-asia-and-pacific-2016-uncovering-widening-broadband-divide.

_____ (2016b). *Harnessing Science, Technology and Innovation for Inclusive and Sustainable Development in Asia and the Pacific.* Sales No. E.16.II.F.12.

European Commission (2016). Digital Single Market website. Available from https://ec.europa.eu/digital-single-market/en/digital-single-market.

Fredriksson, T. (2013). E-commerce and development: key trends and issues. Presentation at the Workshop on E-Commerce, Development and SMEs, WTO, Geneva, 8-9 April. Available from https://www.wto.org/english/tratop_e/devel_e/wkshop_apr13_e/fredriksson_ecommerce_e.pdf .

Hellerstein, W. (2002). Electronic commerce and the challenge for tax administration. Paper prepared for the Seminar on Revenue Implications of E-Commerce for Development, Geneva, 22 April. World Trade Organization, Committee on Trade and Development, Geneva.

International Chamber of Commerce (2015). Global baseline *de minimis* value thresholds: policy statement. February. Paris.

International Telecommunications Union (2013). *Measuring the Information Society Report.* Geneva. Available from www.itu.int/en/ITU-D/Statistics/Pages/publications/mis2013.aspx .

Lund, S., and J. Manyika (2016). How digital trade is transforming globalisation. E15 Initiative. Geneva: International Centre for Trade and Sustainable Development and World Economic Forum.

Makoni, E., C.M. Tsikirayi and E. Mandizha (2013). To charge or not to charge customs excise duty on digitized products: an assessment of the Zimbabwe Revenue Authority (ZIMRA) potential revenue losses through duty exemption on digitized goods. *International Journal of Education and Research*, vol. 1, No. 8.

McKinsey Global Institute (2014). *Global Flows in a Digital Age: How Trade, Finance, People, and Data Connect the World Economy.* Brussels, San Francisco and Shanghai: McKinsey and Company.

Markle Foundation (2005). WTO, e-commerce and information technologies: from the Uruguay Round to Doha Development Agenda – a report for the United Nations ICT Taskforce. New York. Available from https://www.wto.org/english/tratop_e/serv_e/sym_april05_e/wunschvincent_e.pdf

National Association of Citizens Advice Bureaux (2015). *Personal Data Empowerment: Time for a Fairer Data Deal?* London. Available from http://bit.ly/1XtrIBG

Organisation for Economic Co-operation and Development (2013). OECD Glossary of Statistical Terms. Paris. Available from https://stats.oecd.org/glossary/

_____ (2012). *OECD Internet Economy Outlook 2012.* Paris. Available from www.oecd.org/sti/ieconomy/oecd-internet-economy-outlook-2012-9789264086463-en.htm

Ruffle, D. (2001). Cross-border electronic commerce and international trade statistics. STD/NA/ITS (2001)1. Statistics Directorate. Paris: OECD. Available from www.oecd.org/std/its/2536014.pdf .

Schuknecht, L., and R. Pérez-Esteve (1999). A quantitative assessment of electronic commerce. Staff Working Paper ERAD-99-01. Geneva: World Trade Organization.

Teltscher, S. (2001). The impact of electronic goods trading on customs revenue. Paper prepared for the 14th Bled Electronic Commerce Conference, Bled, Slovenia,25-26 June. Available from https://domino.fov.uni-mb.si/proceedings.nsf/0/d7267a8c1b1a8799c1256e9f003130d5/$FILE/34_Telscher.pdf

United Nations Conference on Trade and Development (1999). Can electric commerce be an engine for global growth? Electric commerce and the integration of developing countries and countries with economies in transition in international trade – Note by the UNCTAD secretariat. Trade and Development Board, 1 June. TD/B/COM.3/23. Available from http://unctad.org/en/Docs/c3d23.pdf .

_____ (2015). *Information Economy Report: Unlocking the Potential of E-commerce for Developing Countries.* Sales No. E.15.II.D.1. Available from http://unctad.org/en/PublicationsLibrary/ier2015_en.pdf .

_____ (2016a). New initiative to help developing countries grasp $22 trillion e-commerce opportunity. UNCTAD News, 19 July. Geneva. Available from http://unctad.org/en/pages/newsdetails.aspx?OriginalVersionID=1281

_____ (2016b). *UNCTAD B2C E-commerce Index 2016.* UNCTAD Technical Notes on ICT for Development, No. 7. Geneva. Available from http://unctad.org/en/PublicationsLibrary/tn_unctad_ict4d07_en.pdf .

_____ (2016c). *Data Protection Regulations and International Data Flows: Implications for Trade and Development.* Geneva. Available from http://unctad.org/en/PublicationsLibrary/dtlstict2016d1_en.pdf.

UNCTAD-WHO (1998). International trade in health services: a development perspective. Geneva. UNCTAD/ITCD/TSB/5 – WHO/TFHE/98.1. Available from http://apps.who.int/iris/bitstream/10665/63939/2/UNCTAD_ITCD_TSB_5_PartI.pdf

United States International Trade Commission (2013). *Digital Trade in the U.S. and Global Economies, Part 1.* USITC Publication 4415. Washington D.C. Available from https://www.usitc.gov/publications/332/pub4415.pdf .

United States, Office of the United States Trade Representative (2016). Fact sheet: key barriers to digital trade. March. Washington, D.C.

Van der Marel, E. (2015). Disentangling the flows of data: inside or outside the multinational company? ECIPE Occasional Paper 07/2015. Brussels: European Centre for International Political Economy. Available from http://ecipe.org/app/uploads/2015/07/ECIPE-Data-Flows-final.pdf.

Weber, R. (2010). Digital trade in WTO law – taking stock and looking ahead. *Asian Journal of WTO & International Health Law and Policy*, vol. 5, No. 1, pp. 1-24, March.

Wilson, K. (2016). Smartphones drive e-commerce explosion. *China Daily Asia*, 10 June.

World Trade Organization (1998). *Electronic Commerce and the Role of WTO.* WTO Special Studies, No.2. Geneva. Available from https://www.wto.org/english/res_e/publications_e/special_studies2_e.htm.

_____ (2016) Electronic Commerce website. Geneva. Available from https://www.wto.org/english/tratop_e/ecom_e/ecom_e.htm.

ONLINE DATABASES

OECD-WTO Trade in Value-added (TivA) Database, October 2015. Available from https://stats.oecd.org/index.aspx?queryid=66237

United Nations Statistics Division, Department of Economic and Social Affairs. United Nations COMTRADE database. Available from www.comtrade.un.org.

World Bank. World Integrated Trade Solution (WITS). Available from http://wits.worldbank.org/ .

World Trade Organization. International Services Trade Statistics. Available from http://stat.wto.org/StatisticalProgram/WSDBStatProgramSeries.aspx?Language=E&subtopic=bp;bc.

ANNEXES

Annex 7.1. List of goods that can be digitized

HS code (1996)	Description
	Film (recorded)
3705	Photographic films
3706	Cinematographic films
	Printed matter-Books
4901	Newspapers
4902	Children's books
4903	Music
4904	Maps, atlases
4905	Plans (architectural, engineering, industrial, commercial)
4906	Postcards
4909	Calendars
4910	Commercial catalogues, pictures, designs
	Sound and media
852410	Records
852432	CDs
852439	CDs
852451	Tapes
852452	Tapes
852453	Tapes
852460	Cards
852499	Other (recorded disks)
	Software
852431	
852440	Software
852491	
	Games
950410	Video games

Source: Makoni, Tsikirayi and Mandizha (2013).

Annex 7.2. List of electronically-enabled services and product examples

Commercial services	Example of e-technology used	Example of e-products
Transport	Transport management systems Electronic data interchange Tracking technologies.	
Travel	Online-reservation and payment for hotels, car rental, tours	
Insurance services		Online insurance services
Financial services		Electronic banking services
Telecommunication services	Voice-over-the-Internet Protocol (VoIP) has generated a surge in global cross-border telephone calls.	Skype calling
Computer services		Customized software Remote data processing Web-site design Web-site hosting and maintenance IT/e-commerce solutions
Information services		On-line database services Social medias Cloud computing services
Other business services: • Wholesales and retails • Professional services	Online search and shopping platform (B2C, B2B, B2G) Online customer services	Online legal advice and documentation, and e-taxation services e-Accounting services Online engineering services Tele-health services
Personal, cultural and recreational services: • Audio-visual and related services • Education services		Digital transmission of books, games, films, music, Web-TV Online-training courses

Source: Compilation by ESCAP based on Ruffle (2001) and USITC (2013).

READERSHIP SURVEY

Asia-Pacific Trade and Investment Report 2016

The Trade, Investment and Innovation Division of ESCAP is undertaking an evaluation of the above publication with a view to improving its quality and usefulness. We would appreciate it if you could complete this questionnaire and return it to us, at the address printed below.

QUESTIONNAIRE

Rating for quality and usefulness (please circle)	*Excellent*	*Very good*	*Good*	*Poor*
1. How useful is this publication for your work?				
• Provision of information	4	3	2	1
• Clarification of issues	4	3	2	1
• Findings	4	3	2	1
• Policy suggestions	4	3	2	1
• Overall usefulness	4	3	2	1
2. Please indicate your assessment of the quality of this publication with respect to:				
• Presentation/format	4	3	2	1
• Readability	4	3	2	1
• Coverage of subject matter	4	3	2	1
• Timeliness of information	4	3	2	1
• Overall quality	4	3	2	1

3. Please give examples of how this publication has contributed to your work:

....

....

....

....

4. Your background information, please:

Name: ....

Title/position: ....

Institution: ....

Office address: ....

Tel: .... Fax: ....

Email: ....

Please return this questionnaire to:

Director
Trade, Investment and Innovation Division
ESCAP
United Nations Building
Rajadamnern Nok Avenue
Bangkok 10200
THAILAND
Fax: (66 2) 288 1027, 288 3066
e-mail: escap-tiid@un.org

Thank you for your cooperation.